Lewis H. Morgan on Iroquois Material Culture

Lewis H. Morgan. Photograph probably taken about 1850. (Courtesy of Department of Rare Books and Special Collections, University of Rochester Library.)

Lewis H. Morgan on
Iroquois Material Culture

Elisabeth Tooker

. . . . .
. . .
.

The University of Arizona Press · Tucson and London

The University of Arizona Press
Copyright © 1994
The Arizona Board of Regents
All rights reserved

99 98 97 96 95 94   6 5 4 3 2 1

Library of Congress Cataloging-in-Publication Data

Tooker, Elisabeth.
    Lewis H. Morgan on Iroquois material culture / Elisabeth Tooker.
      p.   cm.
    Includes bibliographical references and index.
    ISBN 0-8165-1347-3 (alk. paper). —
    ISBN 0-8165-1462-3 (pbk. : alk. paper)
    1. Iroquois Indians—Material culture.   2. Morgan, Lewis Henry,
1818–1881.   3. Morgan, Lewis Henry, 1818–1881—Ethnological
collections.   I. Title.
E99.I7T66   1994   94-12164
973'.04975—dc20   CIP

British Library Cataloguing-in-Publication Data
A catalogue record for this book is available from the British Library.

This publication has been supported by grant no. RP-21531-92 from the
National Endowment for the Humanities.

CONTENTS

ILLUSTRATIONS

Frontispiece. Lewis H. Morgan

Figures in Part 1, Chapters 1–6

Figures in Third Regents Report, Chapter 8

Figures in Fifth Regents Report, Chapter 8

Figure in Appendix 2

PREFACE

Without question, one of the most remarkable of all anthropologists was Lewis H. Morgan.[1] Born in 1818 on a farm in upstate New York, he moved about the time of his twenty-sixth birthday to Rochester, where he remained until his death in 1881. In almost four decades between 1844 and 1881, he not only amassed a small fortune and served two terms in the state legislature—one as assemblyman and one as senator—but also published several books that have become classics in the discipline. Of these, the most famous is *Ancient Society* (1877), a study of social evolution, which continues to influence anthropological work in some quarters, especially Marxist anthropology through Frederick Engels's summary of it in *The Origin of the Family, Private Property and the State*. Morgan's *Systems of Consanguinity and Affinity of the Human Family* (1871), published six years earlier, established that most esoteric of all anthropological studies: kinship. And his still-earlier *League of the Ho-dé-no-sau-nee, or Iroquois* (1851), the first true ethnography, remains the best single study of these noted Indian peoples.

Not so well known is Morgan's research on Iroquois material culture, what is perhaps the most comprehensive study of this important aspect of Iroquois life, and one that Morgan had undertaken in the belief that these objects "speak a language, which is silent, but yet more eloquent than the written page."[2] The reasons are several. The collection of articles he made for the state of New York was largely destroyed in the disastrous Capitol fire of 1911. Although Morgan incorporated material, both descriptive and illustrative, from one of his reports in *League of the Iroquois*, the reports themselves have not been reprinted.

It is my intent in this volume to correct this neglect. Reprinted here are Morgan's reports to the regents of the University of the State of New York on the collections he made for the state—what are essentially monographic studies of Iroquois material culture. Also included are Morgan's hitherto-unpublished descriptions of the objects in this collection recorded in his field notes (now in the Morgan Papers, Department of Rare Books and Special Collections, University of Rochester Library), an account of how he came to make the collection, and description of such archaeological work as he did. His archaeological research never consumed Morgan as did ethnography. What he accomplished, however, equals in quality, if not quantity, the survey work of others, notably that of Ephraim George Squier, who incorporated some of it into his own.

Morgan brought to the study of Iroquois material culture the same kind of vision, the industry and insight that he did to his other, better-known researches. Just as he did not collect isolated ethnographic facts—as did so many of his contemporaries—he also did not purchase objects for their aesthetic excellence or historical associations. Little of what he collected was notable for having once belonged to some famous Indian. He sought to save from oblivion the memorials of Iroquois artistic and inventive genius not by merely choosing a few fine pieces, but by obtaining examples of all the various types of Iroquois manufactures. He did not collect objects of obviously Western origin, and consequently the materials he sent to the state do not represent all objects then in use among the Iroquois. (In many respects, Iroquois life at the time resembled that of neighboring whites.) Nonetheless, the collection's comprehensiveness within the limits Morgan set for himself and his concern with providing ethnographic context is still a model as well as an important source of information on Iroquois culture.

Morgan provided no classification of these objects. Perhaps because he regarded each type of object (moccasin, ladle, snowshoe, etc.) as a "species," he merely described them in no particular order in his Regents reports and listed them in no particular order on the separate inventory lists of articles sent, also published in the Regents reports. The fact, however, that Morgan sent to the state in several lots more than 500 objects representing more than 125 species makes necessary some kind of classification, if only to provide the basis for an index to the descriptions and illustrations in the Regents reports and field notes. The index itself, Synopsis of Ethnographic Articles Sent to the State in chapter 6, also includes information on the number of objects Morgan sent and when.

Although Morgan's last Regents report was not published until 1852, it was written early in 1851, just before his *League of the Iroquois* appeared in print. Together they represent a summing up of the field studies Morgan had begun in 1844, researches that had included studies of Iroquois socio-political organization, religion, and geography (place names and trails) as well as material culture. In none of his publications on the Iroquois did Morgan give more than passing mention of how he obtained the data he had. He made only casual reference to how he came to take up the study of Iroquois society and culture, to his visits to several Iroquois reservations over a six-year period, to his experiences on those reservations, to the individuals with whom he talked, to what he observed, or to how these encounters affected his feelings and thinking. In fact, Morgan included so little mention of his field methods in his writings on the Iroquois that many have mistakenly presumed he was recording only "memory culture"—although, like later ethnographers, Morgan learned information crucial to his understanding through "participant-observation."

Something of Morgan's field methods as well as other information relating to his scientific interests is to be found in his papers at the University of Rochester. Late in life, Morgan added a library to the Morgan house (the house itself was owned by his wife). In this room he kept his books and collections, which he subsequently bequeathed to the University of Rochester. He also kept there various papers that were transferred, perhaps inadvertently, with his books and collections to the university. Those papers included few having to do with his personal life, his law practice, his business interests, or his political activities. Most had to do with his scientific work, including those ethnographic and archaeological studies he made that are the subject of this volume.

The collection Morgan made for the state was intended for future study. He undoubtedly envisioned that others would personally inspect the objects, and apparently for this reason did not include the kind of information now considered de rigueur in catalogue descriptions: dimensions, details of workmanship, materials, and the like. His descriptions of the articles furnished were largely limited to information that would not be familiar to most and that could not be gained from only looking at the objects themselves.

Morgan also envisioned that the collection he made would form the nucleus of a larger collection. This did occur, and a number of objects of

Iroquois manufacture were added to the state's collection, especially in the closing decade of the nineteenth century and the first decade of the twentieth.

The potential that the state museum's Iroquois collection represented was largely destroyed by a 1911 fire that burned the section of the Capitol building where much of the collection was on exhibit. Only 10–15 percent of the artifacts that Morgan had collected some sixty years previously survived. The massive devastation made even the calculation of what was lost difficult to ascertain, given inadequate records and limited personnel.

This still remains a question. Some of the objects collected by Morgan are easily identified as such from the illustrations in the Regents reports, from the catalogue numbers on the objects (when the labels survived), or by other means. A number, however, are not. Although identification of all those objects in the Morgan collection that survived the Capitol fire has been the goal of the staff of the museum and others interested in the collection, identification remains incomplete. For this reason, no mention of surviving objects is made in this volume's synopsis of articles in chapter 6, nor are photographs included here.

Those objects that still survive—in the collections of the New York State Museum, in Morgan's personal collection bequeathed to the University of Rochester (now in the Rochester Museum and Science Center), and in a smaller collection sent to the Royal Danish (now National) Museum in Copenhagen through Morgan's offices—are currently being studied by William C. Sturtevant and Sally McLendon. Detailed descriptions of artifacts are to be included in a planned volume on these three collections.

Somewhat similarly, only material in the Lewis Henry Morgan Papers, Department of Rare Books and Special Collections, University of Rochester Library, that relates to Morgan's study of material culture—both Iroquois ethnographic and New York State archaeological—is here considered. Another volume on Morgan's study of Iroquois sociopolitical organization and religion is planned.

Morgan attempted to give the Seneca name for each object he collected, including it in the lists of objects he sent to the state and in his reports. In preparing this volume, it seemed advisable to include modern transcriptions of these Seneca words, and Marianne Mithun generously provided these transcriptions and glosses—no small task given Morgan's lack of linguistic talent and knowledge. These were subsequently checked in draft by Wallace Chafe.

I am also particularly indebted to Karl Kabelac and the late Alma Creek for much help in my study of the Morgan Papers in the University of Rochester Library, and also to Elizabeth Carroll-Horrocks and other members of the staff of the American Philosophical Society Library. Additionally, I have had the benefit of William C. Sturtevant's and Sally McLendon's advice and knowledge of the Morgan collections.

The Department of Rare Books and Special Collections, University of Rochester Library, has kindly granted permission to publish materials in its collection, as have the Cornell University Library and the William L. Clements Library, University of Michigan. The Academy of Natural Sciences in Philadelphia loaned the rare books containing Morgan's Regents reports.

Muriel Kirkpatrick drew the map of New York State and took the (uncredited) photographs. They were printed by Paul Reckner.

EDITORIAL METHOD

Citations to the Regents Reports

"Regents reports" here refers to the first five annual "Reports of the Regents of the University (of the State of New York) on the Condition of the State Cabinet of Natural History" (the title of this series was later changed to "Annual Reports of the New York State Museum"). Each of these Regents reports contains a letter, "Report to the Legislature of the State of New York," from the regents, lists of articles acquired that year for the cabinet, and accompanying papers. The lists of articles Morgan sent to the state cabinet, those he donated in 1848 and 1849, and those he purchased in 1849 and 1850, as published in the Regents reports, are here reprinted in appendix 1. His three accompanying papers or "reports" on the articles sent are reprinted in chapter 8. The Academy of Natural Sciences in Philadelphia was kind enough to loan the rare books containing these documents and allow reproduction.

As the running heads of these Regents reports indicate, they are also New York State Legislature documents:

1. 1847 Senate document, no. 72
2. 1848 Senate document, no. 20
3. 1849 Senate document, no. 75
   ["Revised Edition" printed by order of the Assembly]
4. 1850 Senate document, no. 30
5. 1851 Assembly document, no. 122

The full citations to Morgan's reports in these Regents reports are as follows.

In the second Regents report (also cited as 1848 report):
"To the Honorable the Board of Regents of the University of the State of New-York." In *Second Annual Report of the Regents of the University, on the Condition of the State Cabinet of Natural History, with Catalogue of the Same,* pp. 84–91. Albany: C. van Benthuysen, 1849.

In the third Regents report (also cited as 1849 report):
"Report to the Regents of the University, upon the Articles Furnished the Indian Collection: By L. H. Morgan, December 31, 1849." In *Third Annual Report of the Regents of the University, on the Condition of the State Cabinet of Natural History, and the Historical and Antiquarian Collection, Annexed Thereto,* pp. 65–97 [pp. 63–95 in the revised edition]. Albany: Weed, Parsons, 1850.

In the fifth Regents report (also cited as 1850 report):
"Report on the Fabrics, Inventions, Implements and Utensils of the Iroquois, Made to the Regents of the University, Jan. 22, 1851, by Lewis H. Morgan, Illustrative of the Collection Annexed to the State Cabinet of Natural History." In *Fifth Annual Report of the Regents of the University, on the Condition of the State Cabinet of Natural History, and the Historical and Antiquarian Collection Annexed Thereto,* pp. 67–117. Albany: Charles van Benthuysen, 1852. (The state legislature did not appropriate the money to publish this report until 1852. Hence, it appeared as an appendix to the fifth Regents report, not in the fourth Regents report as might be expected.)

Citations to Manuscript Materials

Abbreviated citations are also used below for some manuscript materials:

"Morgan Papers" refers to the Lewis Henry Morgan Papers in the Department of Rare Books and Special Collections, University of Rochester Library.

Manuscript Journals refers to the volumes in these papers bound and so titled by Morgan. There are six such volumes, the first two of which contain manuscripts published here.

Editorial Conventions

All manuscript materials published here have been edited in accordance with modern method: abbreviations (including the ampersand) have been written out, capitalization and punctuation standardized, and misspellings silently corrected. Material in brackets are my additions and emendations. A question mark in brackets—[?]—immediately after a word indicates an uncertain reading of Morgan's handwriting.

In Morgan's day the New-York Historical Society did not hyphenate New York. For this reason, it is not so hyphenated below except when reference is made to the present-day society or when an author so uses the hyphen.

Orthography Used in Transcription of Seneca Words

Modern transcriptions of Seneca words and glosses enclosed in brackets are those supplied by Marianne Mithun and Wallace Chafe, based in large part on Chafe's *Seneca Morphology and Dictionary* (1967) and *Handbook of the Seneca Language* (1963). The orthography is the same as that which was used in those two works, with the following differences:

Tooker	Chafe 1963	Chafe 1967
ę	ɛ	ɛ (nasalized vowel)
ǫ	o	o (nasalized vowel)
æ	ä	æ (low front vowel)
'	ʔ	ʔ (glottal stop)

The Seneca vowels, as written here, are:

a, æ, e, ę, i, o, ǫ

The Seneca consonants, as written here, are:

h, j, k, n, s, t, w, y, and '

It should be noted that the consonants "k" and "t" are pronounced "g" and "d" respectively before a vowel, as well as before "w" and "y." The colon indicates vowel length, and the acute accent indicates an accented, or high-pitched, vowel.

Morgan's Orthography

Morgan indicated the following spelling conventions:

ä as in arm (here written "a")
ă as in at (here written "æ")
a as in ale (here written "e")

Morgan's spellings, however, are inconsistent, and he did not always spell a Seneca word the same way each time he wrote it. He often did not hear the nasalization of the vowels "ę" and "ǫ," and wrote them in various ways. Furthermore, in his handwriting, "u" and "n" often look the same; in a few cases what is printed here as "u" may in fact be "n."

I
· · · · ·
Morgan's Research

1
· · · · ·

Iroquois Material Culture in 1850

When "discovered" by Europeans, the Iroquois—as the Mohawk, Oneida, Onondaga, Cayuga, and Seneca tribes (or nations) are collectively known—lived in that region of the present New York State that stretches from the Mohawk River to the Genesee. Speaking related (but not mutually intelligible languages) and having similar cultures, the five tribes of the Iroquois had formed a confederacy or league. (The Tuscarora joined as the sixth member of the League of the Iroquois about 1722–23.) In the seventeenth and eighteenth centuries this confederacy so successfully pursued military, political, and economic interests of its members that the Iroquois held the balance of power in the region.

This changed at the end of the eighteenth century. New sachem or League chiefs continued to be "raised up"—as the Iroquois say—to replace those on the council of the League who had died or had been deposed, but the Iroquois no longer had the power and influence they earlier had. During the American Revolution, the Iroquois could not agree as to the course of action to be taken: whether to remain neutral, to side with the Americans, or to continue their old alliance with the British. These divisions, combined with the victory of the Americans, contributed to the dispersal of the Iroquois in succeeding decades. Some continued to live in New York State on lands they had reserved out of the land sales, and for this reason called "reservations." A number of others moved to Canada, and still others to the west. Although Morgan visited several of these reservations, most of his field work was done on the Tonawanda reservation—one of the three Seneca reservations in the state. There are undoubtedly a number of reasons he did so, one of which was the fact that Ely S. Parker, who became Morgan's interpreter and collaborator, was born and raised there.

By the mid-nineteenth century, the Tonawanda Senecas, like other Iroquois groups living in New York State, were an ethnic enclave. All spoke Seneca, but only a few were fluent in English, and for this reason, interpreters were a necessity when dealing with whites. Only a small percentage were Christians, and like Ely Parker's family, members of the Baptist church. Most adhered to the traditional Iroquois religion, keeping up the annual round of Thanksgiving festivals—Midwinter, Maple, Planting, Strawberry, Green Bean, Green Corn, and Harvest ceremonies. Most, too, followed the doctrines of Handsome Lake, the Seneca prophet who preached from 1799 until his death in 1815. The "central fire" of this religion was at Tonawanda, the place to which Iroquois from other reservations in New York and Canada came each fall to hear Jemmy Johnson recount the life and teachings of the prophet.[1]

A council consisting of a dozen chiefs governed the reservation, although "headmen" (heads of families) and "warriors" (other adult men) also signed memorials and other petitions.[2] The two leading chiefs were John Blacksmith—the only League chief at Tonawanda—and Jemmy Johnson. By this time, the League itself had lost much of its power and there was little for the council of League to discuss; it met infrequently, if at all. The Iroquois, surrounded as they were by whites and cut off from hunting—especially beaver trapping that had earlier sustained them in the fur trade—and from war, had few concerns that demanded the concerted action of all the tribes.

The matrilineal clan organization was still important, as were the matrilineal moieties into which they were grouped. Property was customarily inherited in the female line, the husband receiving nothing on the death of his wife.[3] The kind of kinship terminology that Morgan later reported in *Systems of Consanguinity and Affinity of the Human Family* was still in use.[4] The economy of the Tonawanda Senecas, however, closely resembled that of the surrounding whites. Of necessity, so also did many aspects of material culture.

These changes had begun in the sixteenth century. The Iroquois were located astride one of the two gateways to the West, a route that led up the

Mohawk River and across a short portage to the interior. They also had easy access to the other, the St. Lawrence River. Taking full advantage of this geographic position, they effectively controlled a significant part of the trade that so dominated economic affairs in the region—trade in Indian furs for European manufactured goods, especially guns, axes, knives, kettles, and other items of metal, cloth, beads, rum, and brandy.

Although after the American Revolution this kind of economy could not be sustained, the Iroquois might have remained undisturbed in their ancient territory after the Revolution except for the desire of Americans for their land. Earlier, following the victory of the English in the French and Indian War (Seven Years' War) and the transfer of Canada to England, the Crown had attempted to prevent white settlement of western land, decreeing that the region west of a line drawn along the crest of the Appalachians was Indian territory. When these lands became part of the United States by the Treaty of Paris that concluded the American Revolution, Americans were no longer constrained from settling them.

The Treaty of Paris, however, made no provision for the Indians. They were left to deal separately with the British and with Americans. A number of Iroquois chose to go to Canada, most of them to the large Grand River reserve there—land granted to them by the Crown. An approximately equal number, including most of the Senecas, elected to remain in the United States. Those who stayed were forced by necessity to sell much of their land.

In 1788 the Senecas sold the eastern part of their territory, that generally east of the Genesee River. In 1797, by the Treaty of Big Tree, they sold the remainder, the western part. They retained only those lands where their villages were then located: six small reservations along the Genesee, a large reservation at Buffalo Creek, and three smaller ones—Allegany, Cattaraugus, and Tonawanda—located respectively on the Allegheny River, Cattaraugus Creek, and Tonawanda Creek. In 1803 one of the Genesee reservations, Little Beard's village, was sold; and in 1826, the Seneca ceded the remainder of their lands along the Genesee, 60 percent of the Buffalo Creek reservation, and all but 12,800 acres of the Tonawanda reservation.

The annuities the Senecas received from the sale of these lands partly replaced the proceeds they had earlier received from the sale of furs, income that had allowed them to buy goods of white manufacture. Hunting for food—most importantly deer hunting—necessarily also declined, although the full effect was not immediately felt. As whites at the time well knew, when land was brought under cultivation, the animal population declined. The gradual settlement of what had been Seneca lands also brought with it a gradual restriction of localities in which to hunt, particularly in the first quarter of the nineteenth century.

The decrease in reliance on hunting could only be met by an increase in crop production. In the eighteenth century, and for at least a half dozen centuries before that, the Iroquois had depended not only on hunting and fishing but also on horticulture. Men cleared the fields where the women planted, cultivated, and harvested the principal crops of corn, beans, and squash—called by the Iroquois "the three sisters," as like sisters they were found together in the fields. Men also built the houses of the villages on land they cleared. In these houses the women stored the provisions they had grown and what the men brought back from their hunting, war, and trade expeditions into the woods beyond the clearings.

This changed at the end of the eighteenth century when the land base of the Iroquois was restricted to the limits of the reservation. No longer could the village move when the surrounding fields became exhausted. This, coupled with a need for increased production, made necessary the adoption of white agricultural practices, including dependence on plow rather than slash-and-burn agriculture.[5] The capital goods necessary for such farming came, in part, from the annuities.

These changes were gradual ones, and as in the case of the white population, not all Iroquois became successful farmers. By the mid-nineteenth century, however, the process was complete. For example, out of a total population of approximately 500 people (100 families) living on the Tonawanda reservation, thirty reportedly were farmers. They had perhaps 600 acres under cultivation: 200 in wheat, 170 in corn, and 100 in oats, as well as lesser amounts in barley, buckwheat, rye, peas, potatoes, turnips, and beans. The Tonawanda Senecas also raised livestock: more than 300 cattle; about the same number of hogs; 130 horses; about 90 milk cows; and 50 sheep. One hundred eighty acres of meadow were cut, and there were more than 1,200 fruit trees.[6]

From a longer historical perspective, these changes were a continuation of earlier ones. Although the data are scanty, such as do exist indicate that in the eighteenth century the large, bark-covered, multi-family longhouse characteristic of the seventeenth century became much smaller. Earlier, each dwelling had housed an average of ten families, some having many more, a few less. The length of the longhouse depended on the number of families occupying it; the larger ones were also used for council meetings. In the eighteenth century, the longhouses became shorter and the houses were more dispersed. Circumstances no longer required building the compact village surrounded with a palisade. Some Iroquois built log houses after the fashion of those made by whites, but the larger longhouse still served as a council house.

The fruit trees, pigs, and various cultivated foods, including potatoes, cucumbers, and watermelons, were introduced during the eighteenth century. The variety and importance of these introductions is most evident in the records of the 1779 Sullivan-Clinton expedition, whose members reported cutting down innumerable fruit trees, particularly apple trees, as well as destroying the villages and crops still standing in the fields.[7]

Earlier, in the seventeenth century, trade with whites had resulted in Iroquois substitution of metal objects of European manufacture for those made of stone and clay. Metal axes and knives, for example, quickly replaced stone ones. Copper kettles replaced clay pots. The Iroquois continued to make objects of wood and bark—bowls, dishes, spoons, ladles, and the like—but carving became easier with metal tools.[8] They still used the mortar and pestle to prepare corn. The gun largely, but not completely, replaced the bow and arrow. However, the war club, blowgun, and traps of wood continued to be made, as were canoes and snowshoes.

Cloth partly replaced skin in the manufacture of clothing. The blanket, for example, substituted for the skin robe. And some new articles of clothing, such as shirts and blouses, were introduced. However, the Iroquois continued to make moccasins and bags of skin. Glass beads largely, but not entirely, replaced quill work. Silver brooches, rings, and earrings were popular.

By the mid-nineteenth century, everyday Iroquois dress had become almost indistinguishable from that of whites.[9] The more distinctive Iroquois dress worn only on special occasions continued to mark the ethnic distinctiveness of the Iroquois. So also did religion and some recreational practices. Iroquois songs, accompanied often by rattles and drums, remained an important part of religious ritual and a frequent social activity. Iroquois games, some of which were also played in ceremonials, retained their popularity.

Some of the objects, then, that Morgan acquired for the state and the practices he recorded had their origin in precontact Iroquois culture; others were of European origin, transformed by Indian genius into distinctive Iroquois ones. Whatever their source, the artifacts provided by Morgan were representative of what he and the Parker family saw as still distinctive of Iroquois material culture and of Iroquois life generally.

2
· · · · ·

Lewis H. Morgan and the
Study of Material Culture

In early December of 1881, Lewis H. Morgan's last study, *Houses and House-Life of the American Aborigines,* was published. For several years Morgan's health had been slowly declining. By that December he was unconscious most of the time, so ill his wife could not make him realize that it was his book she wished him to see. Only near the very end did he feebly turn the pages and just as feebly murmur, "My book."[1] He died on the 17th.

Morgan had written *Houses and House-Life* at the urging of John Wesley Powell, director of the then newly formed Bureau of (American) Ethnology, who had promised publication as a volume in his geological survey series, *Contributions to North American Ethnology.* Powell's offer had afforded Morgan an opportunity to publish what—because of his proclivity to write longer books than could be reasonably contained within two covers—had been removed from the end of his two previous ones. Morgan had planned to include in his *Systems of Consanguinity and Affinity* a fourth part on North American Indian ethnology. This final section was to have contained four chapters: one on the physical geography of the continent; one on the migrations of Indian tribes; another on their domestic institutions—clan organization, naming practices, dance, and burial customs; and a final chapter on Indian architecture and agriculture.[2] The first three parts, however, proved rather lengthy. As published, *Systems* ran to 600 pages: 400 of text and 200 of tables. Morgan dropped his plan to include the fourth, and published what had been intended as the chapter on Indian migrations as a two-part, 100-page article in the *North American Review* in 1869–1870.

Morgan subsequently expanded a portion of the chapter on "domestic in-stitutions," those devoted to clan organization, in *Ancient Society*.

As originally planned, *Ancient Society* was to have had five parts. But like *Systems*, *Ancient Society* proved too long and the final section on architec-ture was omitted. As published, *Ancient Society* contained some 550 pages, 60 percent of which were devoted to the subject of clans. A summary of what was to have been the final part appeared in 1875 as "Architecture of the American Aborigines" in *Johnson's New Universal Cyclopaedia*. The chapter on Aztec houses formed the basis of "Montezuma's Dinner" pub-lished in 1876 in the *North American Review*, and the chapter on "Houses of the Mound Builders" was another article in the *North American Review* that same year.[3]

In the summer of 1878, the year after *Ancient Society* was published, Morgan made a trip to the Southwest.[4] A report on one of the ruins (now called Aztec) that he visited on the Animas River in New Mexico was pub-lished by the Peabody Museum in 1880, the year the Archaeological Insti-tute of America published his "A Study of the Houses of the American Aborigines." These reports, along with the articles published earlier, were incorporated into *Houses and House-Life*, what Morgan regarded as a re-vised version of what he had intended to be the final part of *Ancient Society*.

In *Houses and House-Life*, Morgan wove together more extensively than he had previously those several concerns that had dominated his anthropo-logical research: sociopolitical organization, material culture, and prehis-tory. Of these concerns, it is the results of his interest in sociopolitical or-ganization—his ethnographic study of Iroquois social organization and his comparative one of kinship systems—that are most familiar today. It is also an interest apparent in Morgan's organizational efforts on behalf of the secret society called the Grand Order of the Iroquois in the 1840s, of the group of Rochester intellectuals known as the Pundit Club he helped found in 1854, and of the American Association for the Advancement of Science in the 1870s. His success in such endeavors, however, was limited to organizations of like-minded men, "men of mind." He was a poor prac-tical politician. He served only one term in the state assembly, only one in the state senate, and received none of the foreign diplomatic appointments he sought. Those qualities that served him so well in his scholarly, scien-tific pursuits were those that ill-suited him for the life of a politician. As a contemporary wrote in 1861:[5]

Mr. Morgan is one of the most active and ambitious men in the [state] Legislature. The difficulty, however, with him is, that he lacks the ability to enable him successfully to gratify his ambition. His efforts are always consistent, there being seldom a question before the House on which he does not thoroughly ventilate himself; but the more he struggles the less progress he seems to make. He is like a person upon a boggy foundation, gradually descending with every struggle for a better footing; and he is now already so far within the filthy depths, that not even a pair of stilts could scarcely save him. Meanwhile, he is too independent ever to conciliate many very warm friends in his difficulties, and unless he very materially modifies his plan of operations he will never ascend high enough in the scale of honorable distinction to gratify the aspirations of either himself or his friends. Were he to follow the example of those of the same calibre as himself, by remaining quiet in the House, he would stand much better in the estimation of his associates; but his persistent determination to thrust himself forward on all occasions upon the deliberations of that body has rendered him completely ridiculous in the eyes of all.

Morgan's long interest in prehistory is not so familiar except as it was incorporated into *Ancient Society* as an interest in evolution. There Morgan proposed six periods or evolutionary stages following the period of "Lower Savagery." Each stage was marked by an invention: Middle Savagery by knowledge of fire; Upper Savagery by invention of the bow and arrow; Lower Barbarism by the invention of pottery; Middle Barbarism by domestication of animals in the Old World and by irrigation in the New; Upper Barbarism by iron smelting and use of iron tools; and Civilization by invention of phonetic writing.

That Morgan should have chosen to characterize each period by a technological advance is perhaps not unexpected. The evidence of social change brought on by new inventions was all about him. Born on a farm in central New York State in a region that only a few decades before had belonged to Indians, Morgan knew well the changes wrought by Western agricultural practices. When he was only six years old, the Erie Canal was completed, opening the way to industrial development in the towns along its length. One such town was Rochester, to which Morgan—just turned 26 and eager to make his fortune—moved and where he spent the remainder of his life.

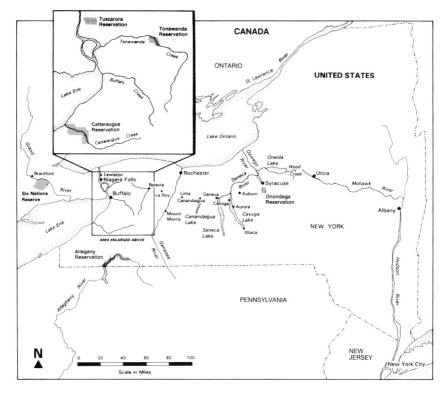

Figure 1. Map of New York State.

The wealth he acquired was from his investments in new railroads and iron mines.

For all its discussion of evolution, *Ancient Society* grew out of Morgan's earlier interest in ethnology: the mapping of the peoples of a region and through a comparison of their languages and customs to infer their past history. *Systems,* as Thomas R. Trautmann has recently and correctly observed, is such an ethnological study.[6] So also is Morgan's study of Indian migrations. This same concern with history is also evident in Morgan's archaeological investigations, among them his field study of the mounds of central New York State in the 1840s and the archaeological ruins in the Southwest in 1878.

Morgan came to believe—not unexpectedly given his fascination with social organization—that the archaeological remains in various parts of the continent held evidence of "the form of the family and the plan of domestic life." "Its growth," he added, "can be traced from the hut of the savage, through the communal houses of the barbarians, to the house of the single family of civilized nations, with all the successive links by which one extreme is connected with the other."[7]

Morgan, however, viewed these works not just as evidence of social conditions, but also as expression of the mind, and so as evidence of the mind. This view of the works of man is the same as that which underlies Morgan's *The American Beaver and His Works.* To Morgan, the beaver was "a mute, not a brute." The beaver's "works"—dams, lodges, burrows, canals, and trails—were to Morgan proof of the beaver's mental powers, just as were man's inventions and discoveries testimony of the "growth of intelligence," the evolution of man's mental powers through experience.

To Morgan, ever concerned with the mind and happiest in the company of men of mind, "ideas" were what mattered. For example, in *Ancient Society* he suggested that differences in form of government were evidence of the "growth of the idea of government"; differences in kinship systems, of the "growth of the idea of the family"; and differences in rules respecting ownership and inheritance, of the "growth of the idea of property."

Morgan had taken up the study of the beaver in favor of brook trout fishing.[8] Trout fishing, it may be presumed, afforded Morgan only the opportunity to collect trophies; collecting information on the works of the beaver, the opportunity of insight into the mind. In an article, "Mind or Instinct" published in 1843, twenty-five years before publication of his "beaver book" and a year before his first article on the Iroquois appeared, Morgan had argued that instinct was a fictitious non-principle. However, he had only anecdotal evidence in support of this contention. His visits to Michigan in connection with his business interests afforded him the opportunity to collect first-hand data on beaver behavior. How remarkable Morgan considered the beaver to be is evident not only in the book itself but also in the comment he wrote in his journal after first seeing a copy of *Systems:* "I shall never look it [*Systems*] over with as much pleasure as I have the Beaver Book."[9]

Morgan's concern with the "mind" and "ideas" was also the motivation behind the collection of artifacts of Iroquois manufacture that he made for the state of New York in 1849 and 1850. This collection contained few "trophies," articles notable for their association with famous persons, for extraordinary excellence of manufacture, or for rarity or uniqueness. What Morgan did attempt to gather was a representative collection of Iroquois artifacts then being made—to a considerable degree selected by the Indians themselves—supplying the Seneca word for each artifact, along with a description of its use as provided by the Iroquois.

The collection Morgan amassed for the state was by far the largest at the time from a single Indian group. Among other things, Morgan envisioned that it would serve as a model for collections from other Indian groups, which together would form a memorial of the whole Indian family. It may have become such. Morgan's collection in the state museum may have been more familiar to museum people in the nineteenth century than in the twentieth. Little of what was in the minds of those who made the collections that transformed the "cabinets of curiosity" into "museums" made its way into print, however, and consequently Morgan's influence on them cannot be ascertained.

More important, however, than any possible effect on museum collecting in the nineteenth century is what Morgan's work can teach us now. Genealogy, after all, only serves as a kind of charter, validation of what already is, not a guide for what might be. It is Morgan's vision, not merely his findings, that most attracts us today.

Morgan left no extended statement as to what he believed to be the greater goals of anthropology, its principal findings, or its proper course of research. Such began to appear in number only after his death when, as anthropology was beginning to become professionalized, the need arose for statements justifying it. In fact, there is evidence that Morgan did not feel qualified to expound on these matters. Turning down Andrew D. White's invitation to become a non-resident professor at Cornell, he remarked:

> At some future time we may make it a subject of conversation. It is a question I think whether our students as a class would wish for lectures upon minute Ethnology. They would probably accept a presentation of the general facts of European and Asiatic Ethnology, and perhaps a large dose of American; but I doubt whether they could tolerate much detail in either. I also doubt my ability to hold a class of students on either, as my knowledge is limited, and I have no experience whatever as a teacher. I shall be too occupied for two or three years to give it attention, even though I saw the way clear.[10]

We cannot know with any certainty how Morgan would have seen the place of the study of material culture in anthropology or the contribution such a study might make. What we do know is that he believed that the manufactures of a people were silent testimony of their genius, a genius that Morgan believed embraced not only "social condition" but also "inventive intellect" and "artisan capacity"—qualities of the mind. It is these qualities he invites us to consider as he, in turn, describes each "species" of article sent the state:

> The Iroquois moccasin "is true to nature in its adjustment to the foot, beautiful in its materials and finish, and durable as an article of apparel . . . . With the sanction of fashion, it would supersede among us a long list of similar inventions."
>
> The war club "was a heavy weapon . . . . In close combat it would prove a formidable weapon."
>
> "The sap tub is a very neat contrivance, and surpasses all articles of this description. Our farmers may safely borrow, in this one particular, and with profit substitute this Indian invention for the rough and wasteful trough of their own contrivance . . . . Aside from the natural fact that the sap would be quite at home in the bark tub, and its flavor preserved untainted, it is more durable and capacious than the wooden one, and more readily made."
>
> The snowshoe "is a very simple invention, but exactly adapted for its uses. A person familiar with the snow shoe can walk as rapidly upon the snow, as without it upon the ground."

It is this vision, Morgan's unabashed appreciation for the accomplishments of the mind, that still commands our attention.

3

· · · · ·

Morgan's Early Iroquois Work

In 1847, at the suggestion of Governor John Young, who had visited the historical and antiquarian museum in Hartford, the regents of the University of the State of New York decided to establish a similar collection as part of the State Cabinet of Natural History. In furtherance of this aim, the regents sent to citizens of the state a circular "asking their aid, in furnishing the relics of the ancient masters of the soil, and the monuments and remembrances of our colonial and revolutionary history."[1] Morgan replied to this request, sending in 1848 plans of five archaeological sites he had mapped, about four dozen archaeological and ethnographic objects he had earlier collected, names of others in the state who had similar collections that the state might be able to acquire, and a report on the articles he himself had sent. He also stressed to the regents the importance of the project they had undertaken, and offered to further it in what ways he could.

The previous year Morgan had published a series of articles on his ethnographic studies of the Iroquois in *The American Review*. These "Letters on the Iroquois" included a description of the Iroquois League, an account of the Seneca language, a brief account of Iroquois religion, and a description of Iroquois trails, tribal boundaries, and place names—much of which Morgan subsequently republished in his famed *League of the Iroquois*. He had not, however, included in these "Letters" such archaeological data as he had also obtained, and it may be for this reason that he particularly welcomed the request of the regents. Apparently he had no intention of pursuing these archaeological researches. In fact, at the time he received the request, he had no intention of pursuing any further research on the Iroquois and had turned his attention to the translation of Latin. The establishment of a historical and antiquarian collection as part of the state cabinet provided a place to deposit such specimens as he had, the number of which, he remarked, "is large enough to awaken a little curiosity, but too small to be of much importance by themselves."[2]

Morgan's initial interest in the Iroquois had been sparked after he graduated from Union College in 1840 and returned to Aurora, the village on Cayuga Lake where he had grown up. There he read law. He also joined a secret society called the Gordian Knot. This society, composed of young men of the village, was suffering—as such associations are so apt to—from lack of interest. Its members hoped to revive it by changing its organization, to "cut the knot," as they said, and to reform it as an "Indian society" modeled on the Iroquois confederacy.[3]

The village of Aurora had been settled by whites only fifty years before on land just purchased by the state from the Cayuga Indians. A few years later in 1792, Lewis's grandfather, Thomas, and his family (including Lewis's father, Jedediah) moved from Connecticut to a farm a few miles south of Aurora. Lewis was born there in 1818, the fourth son of Jedediah by his second wife.[4]

By this time the Cayuga Indians had long departed. They had sold their last remaining reservation land in 1807. But the evidence of their former occupation had not been erased. Some of the fruit trees they had planted still survived. (The Cayuga village at Aurora had been known as Peach Town from the large peach orchards there.) The archaeological evidence of their former villages also remained, including that of the principal village of the Cayugas, located only a few miles north of Aurora. And the early settlers still living had memories of the Indians who had once made the region their home. Morgan could scarcely be unaware of these, or of Fort Hill, an archaeological site in Auburn, which he mapped in 1841.[5]

By a kind of mystical connection with the land, many white Americans of the time viewed themselves as heirs of the Indian, destined to build a civilization on the continent that rested on ideas similar to those of the first inhabitants—but in keeping with a belief in progress, a civilization that was a superior embodiment of the ideals that the continent engendered. Such a notion fitted the nationalism of the day. The country had only recently established its independence from England, and its citizens, ever conscious of the uniqueness of the American experience and history, made the Indian its symbol.

The members of the reorganized "Indian Knot" were no exception. They saw their order, what they came to call the Grand Order of the Iroquois, as the "New Confederacy of the Iroquois," destined to replace the "dying" old Confederacy of the Iroquois. Based on Indian-American principles, it would shine, they believed, even more brilliantly than its predecessor.

Morgan expressed the inevitability of such a succession in "Vision of Kar-is-ta-gi-a, a Sachem of the Cayugas," delivered to the Aurora chapter of the Grand Order on June 7, 1844, and published a few months later in *The Knickerbocker,* a widely read magazine of the day. The "vision" Morgan describes is one he imagines Steeltrap (Karistagia) to have had about ninety years before. In it, Steeltrap sees Aurora as it was to become, witnessing in a grove there a ceremony of initiation of a "new Cayuga" by warriors "clad in the costume of the ancient Cayugas." Disturbed, Steeltrap consults the Cayuga "prophet," Copperhead (Delanoga), who informs him that the first part of his dream "foretells that the pale-faces will ere long people the land, and the Indian be compelled to wander from the home of his fathers." Copperhead says that the second part of the dream signifies that after the Indian has departed, the "Great Spirit" will guide him back "to inherit the land of his fathers." "A new and brighter day will dawn upon the Indian, and ever afterward will he roam these boundless forests in full security and independence."[6] Morgan did not need to tell his audience at Aurora that the initiation was a ceremony of the order, and the Indians whom the Great Spirit guided back were members of the order.

Little of the genius that so characterizes Morgan's work is evident in this fanciful piece. Its manifestations lie elsewhere: in the decision of the order to model its organization on that of the Iroquois League itself. Throughout the history of the United States, various organizations, some large, some small, have patterned their activities on Indian "principles"—what their members know or think they know of Indian custom. Few, if any, have sought with the intensity of the New Confederacy to learn the actual organization, and as new information was gained, to successively revise their constitutions. It is true that some of the Grand Order's constitutional revisions were of the sort so common in fledgling organizations—attempts to forestall flagging spirits. It is also true that the basic form of organization, despite these introductions, remained the familiar white one, and that the whole attempt was abandoned in favor of a structure more like that of established secret fraternities such as the Masons and Odd Fellows, after which the G.O.I.—as its members were fond of calling it—died.

To judge from the surviving records, it is also true that the order's principal attraction was the opportunity for fellowship among its members, engendered by meetings held in a grove or in the Masonic Lodge building (unused by the Masons in the wake of anti-Masonic agitation that followed the William Morgan incident). Initiation of new members was one of the high points of the meetings, as were dances performed in Indian costume. (Morgan himself believed full Indian costume essential to the maintenance of interest in the society.) But underneath these various appurtenances, including liberal use of Indian metaphor, there remained a genuine concern with the Iroquois. As the Constitution adopted on August 19, 1844, stated:[7]

> Believing that the institution of an Indian order, having for its object a literary and social confederation of the young men of our state; for the purpose of making such order the repository of all that remains to us of the Indians, their history, manners, and customs, their government, mythology, and literature; and for the further purpose of creating and encouraging a kinder feeling towards the red man, founded upon a truer knowledge of the virtues and blemishes of the Indian character; and finally to raise up an institution that shall eventually cast the broad shield of protection, and the mantle of its benevolence, over these declining races. . . .

One of the order's members was later to remark that Morgan was "the life and soul of the 'grand order.'"[8] As "Grand Sachem" for two years (1844–46), Morgan directed its activities, carrying on an extensive correspondence to strengthen it and further its purposes.[9] Undoubtedly before that time he also was the organization's guiding spirit. It was also Morgan who urged on the order research into Iroquois culture and history, doing much field work himself.

The beginning of this research may be fairly dated to the spring of 1844 when Morgan met a remarkable young Seneca Indian, Ely S. Parker, in an Albany bookstore.[10] Earlier Morgan had met the distinguished Onondaga chief Abram La Fort. Both La Fort and Joshua V. H. Clark, then researching his history of Onondaga County, were made honorary members of the order in January of that year.[11] Morgan may also have met Peter Wilson, a Cayuga Indian, then attending the medical college at Geneva. But it was Parker who provided Morgan an entree into Seneca society, who served as his interpreter and collaborator for the next six years, and to whom he dedicated *League of the Iroquois*—"the materials of which are the fruit of our joint researches." Parker, then a teenager of 16, was in Albany serving as interpreter to a delegation of Tonawanda Seneca chiefs headed by Jemmy Johnson (Sose-há-wä). Morgan took advantage of the opportunity; with Parker interpreting, he interviewed Johnson, "grandson"[12] of the Seneca prophet Handsome Lake and himself the religious leader of the Tonawanda Seneca, on the organization of the League. Morgan's interpretation of the information he received—as such initial data so often are—was flawed. Morgan apparently misunderstood some of what was told to him.[13]

Late that same year Morgan moved to Rochester, there beginning his practice of the law. He quickly organized a Rochester chapter of the order, and devoted considerable time that spring to planning the order's anniversary meeting to be held in August in Aurora. That meeting featured a poem by William H. C. Hosmer and an address by Henry R. Schoolcraft, then establishing himself as a leading authority on the Indian.[14] Two weeks after the meeting, Morgan began writing a paper summarizing what he knew of Iroquois culture and society, much of which he later noted was erroneous.[15]

What led Morgan to this conclusion was the information he obtained while on a weeklong field trip that fall to the Tonawanda Seneca Reservation, some forty miles west of Rochester. Morgan, two other members of the Rochester chapter of the order, one member of the Aurora chapter, and Ely Parker undertook the trip to witness the council held there, the first in some years, for the purpose of "raising up" League chiefs to fill vacancies occasioned by death. It was to prove a turning point in his research. A prominent rite in the ceremony for installation of chiefs, the Condolence ceremony, is the Roll Call of the Chiefs—the list of the fifty chiefs of the League. These fifty name-titles were then on the minds of participants, and Morgan obtained two lists, one from Abram La Fort and the other from Peter Wilson.[16] In an important sense, the Roll Call of the Chiefs is the key to the organization of the League, a fact that Morgan quickly recognized. Each of the fifty name-titles belongs to a particular clan in a particular tribe. To know the Roll Call of the Chiefs is not only to know the composition of the League council, but also the manner of their selection.

Morgan returned from Tonawanda, as he wrote Schoolcraft a few days later, his head "so crammed with matters pertaining to the Iroquois that I intend for my own relief to set down immediately and write a series of essays upon the government and institutions of the Iroquois for publication."[17] He did so, and a month later delivered a long paper on the subject to the Rochester chapter.[18]

Ten days later Morgan left Rochester on an extended trip. His birthday, November 21, found him in Geneva, where he visited the college and medical school. The following day he visited the locally well-known site of Kanadesaga, once the "capitol" of the eastern Senecas. In 1756, after the outbreak of the French and Indian War, Sir William Johnson had a stockade and two blockhouses built there[19]—the remains of which Morgan saw. The village had been destroyed in 1779 by members of the Sullivan Expedition.

Extract from Morgan's Journal[20]

On [November] 22 visited the old Indian settlement at Canasateago[21] about 2 miles northwest of Geneva. The old orchard is yet standing, the burial ground untouched, and much of the old fortification still visible and easily traced. The reason is that when the Indians departed, they deeded the land to Immer Crittenden, with a covenant that for one hundred years nothing should be disturbed.[22] Mr. Crittenden who died in 1826 aged 60, 8 months, 20 days to his praise, and his son after him have religiously observed this pledge, and as one consequence I was able to trace out this old blockhouse or picket enclosure from the direction of the trench which is deeply traced in the ground,[23] but which the plow and drag would have effaced if the sod had ever been turned. The following diagram will convey an idea of this old fortification.

Ground plan of the Indian picket enclosure at Canasateago situate on the banks of a creek 2 miles northwest of Geneva, and on the old trail going west from Onondaga to Canandaigua.

[*For sketch here in journal, see fig. 2.*]

From the old farmer whom I chanced to meet on my return or rather to ride down with in a lumber wagon, I learned that he had been in the country 53 years, and that when he came the stubs of the pickets were still standing as they had been left by General Sullivan in 1779 after his army had cut them down and burned them. Each picket was

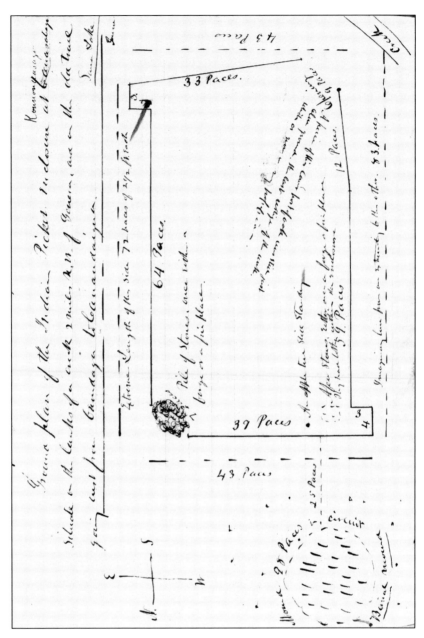

Figure 2. Morgan's sketch of Kanadesaga, November 22, 1845, in Manuscript Journals, *vol. 1, no. 10, Morgan Papers. (Courtesy of Department of Rare Books and Special Collections, University of Rochester Library.)*

about a foot square and 15 feet above the ground originally. The timber was squared out rudely—a deep trench dug as marked out in the ground plan above, and now as distinct as the lines on this paper; the timbers were then set in the ground side by side as you would set a single post, thus making a large enclosure, surrounded by a wooden wall about one foot thick. There was but one small piece or stub left, and that was at the door as marked on the diagram. This I broke off, and have preserved. It is oak and sufficiently sound to be preserved, and is perhaps the last positive fragment of an Indian fortification in New York. The orchard was also cut down by General Sullivan. It however grew up again from the roots and the trees have many of them two and three prongs. A very few that were girded survived. This orchard still covers three or four acres and was [?] to the northwest of the enclosure, but near it. One tree is standing within it, and consequently is older than the fortification itself. The trees are set out without any regularity. The mound a few paces north is considered an artificial elevation. The absence of all similar elevations in the fields adjacent supports the hypothesis, but as this mound which is but 100 paces or about 250 feet in circuit and not over 8 or 10 feet high, could receive but a few of the vast number who have been interred in this vicinity, and as we have no knowledge that the Indian ever raised mounds for this purpose, and finally as there is nothing in the mound itself unnatural or singular, the better opinion would be that the mound was a mere knoll, left by the hand of nature. The Indians for the past fifty years until quite recently have made annual visits to this Indian burial place, and former seat of government of the Seneca Indians. Even last year one solitary Indian was seen kneeling upon the mound, and apparently engaged in the performance of some religious ceremony. In the fields adjacent, bodies are frequently ploughed up and the kettle and other ornaments buried with the dead. One of these brass kettles which would hold about 2 quarts I purchased. It had been ploughed out about 5 years before; and as the Indians abandoned this settlement after its destruction by General Sullivan, it must have lain in the earth at least 60 years. The kettle is in a good state of preservation. The handle however, which is made of heavy wire, is much oxidated [oxidized].

General Sullivan in this destructive inroad cut down about 50 acres of corn, just in an eating condition or as they say in the milk. He also burned the Indian village, or the numerous wigwams which dotted the

forest here and there in great numbers,[24] for the Indians never have [?]
or built which might be called a village ever of wigwams. It would be
no difficult matter by the aid of old farmers to locate the old trail starting at Utica, thence to Onondaga, thence to the fording place of the
Cayuga, a little to the north of the bridge, thence past the foot of the
Geneva [Seneca] Lake and along the bank of this creek to the old
council house of [the] castle of Canasateago above described, thence
across the county to Canandaiga, and thence to Geneseo etc. etc.

At the time, the Tonawanda Senecas were engaged in a seemingly hope-
less fight to retain their reservation, which along with the Buffalo Creek
Reservation had been sold by a treaty signed in 1842. This treaty, com-
monly known as the Compromise Treaty of 1842, rescinded the patently
fraudulent one signed in 1838 (but not proclaimed until 1840) by which the
Senecas sold all four of their reservations in New York State.[25] Negotiated
with considerable aid from the Quakers, the Compromise Treaty left to
the Senecas the two reservations to which the Quakers had given economic assistance—the Allegany and Cattaraugus—and sold the two they
had not. The residents of the two reservations that had been sold were to
remove to the two that had not been sold or to land set aside for the Iroquois west of the Mississippi.

By the provisions of the Compromise Treaty of 1842, two arbitrators
were to assess the value of all Seneca reservation lands and improvements.
One arbitrator was to be appointed by the Secretary of War (at that time
the Department of War had responsibility for Indian affairs) and the other
appointed by the Ogden Land Company. The arbitrators were to determine what proportion of the reservations' value (taken to be $202,000–
$100,000 for the land and $102,000 for the improvements) was for land
and improvements of the two reservations sold, the Buffalo Creek and Tonawanda reservations. The arbitrators were also to determine the amount
to be paid to individuals for their improvements. Within one month of the
filing of the arbitrators' report, the unimproved lands were to be surrendered to the Ogden Land Company, and within two years, the improved
lands were to be surrendered.[26]

Few residents of the Buffalo Creek reservation protested the treaty, and
most moved, many to the Cattaraugus reservation. But virtually all of
the residents of the Tonawanda reservation dissented and refused to leave.

They maintained that the treaty was not binding on them because none of their chiefs had signed it and almost all of the Tonawanda Senecas were opposed to it. They were determined to remain on their reservation, and immediately after the treaty was signed, began efforts to get the provisions of the treaty that applied to them overturned, petitioning various government officials. When the two arbitrators arrived at Tonawanda in October of 1843 and again in December, they were led off the reservation to prevent them from making the appraisals. The arbitrators nonetheless filed a report based on what information they could obtain from local whites, estimating the improvements to be worth $15,018.36.

The refusal of the Tonawanda Senecas to have their improvements appraised left the matter at an impasse. The land company asked the United States government to enforce the treaty, but it said it had no legal power to do so as it was not a party to the treaty; the treaty was a covenant between the Indians and the purchasers. Meanwhile, whites had been moving onto those Tonawanda lands that the Ogden Land Company had sold on June 19, 1843, in Batavia, and the attempt to have the whites removed by warrant had failed.[27] By the end of 1846, the impasse had become a crisis. Under the stipulations of the treaty, the Indians were to remove by April 1, 1847, and no resolution was in sight. Appeals to the Quakers had fallen on deaf ears; the Quakers had been instrumental in negotiating the Compromise Treaty, and they urged the Tonawandas to accept it. The Tonawandas had little recourse but to turn to other whites for support. Here they were fortunate. Unlike the large Buffalo Creek reservation so near the growing city of Buffalo, the relatively small Tonawanda reservation was of little economic interest to neighboring whites. Also, by this time, the land company's dealings with white settlers had engendered much bad feeling. Its reputation was not enhanced by the fact that it would pay only about $1.50 an acre for Indian land worth about $10.00 an acre.[28] Not unexpectedly, then, many residents of the region supported the Tonawandas against the "great public wrong" about to be committed. As the Batavia newspaper expressed it:

> Men, women and children who have done us no injury; who are guilty of no violation of law, no disturbance of the public peace, who have conducted themselves in a manner at once orderly and unobtrusive are to be torn from their homes without the consent of a single individual among them, and to be driven away from an inheritance which has

been guaranteed to them by treaties, and to which they are attached by every consideration which can endear to men the place where they were born and have lived.[29]

The members of the order were equally outraged at the actions of the land company, and late in 1845, began discussing what they could do. Morgan wrote the Tonawanda Indians offering them the aid of the order, and at a council held January 1 and 2, 1846, the chiefs and warriors (i.e., adult men) agreed to accept this offer of assistance. Early that month the order printed petitions for distribution throughout the state for signatures. The order also decided to send Morgan to Washington that spring.[30]

On January 14, Morgan left Rochester for a trip up the Genesee. Why he did so is uncertain. The only record of the trip is contained in his notes on the archaeology of the area, although it seems likely that his primary purpose in making the trip was to collect signatures on the order's petitions in the Tonawandas' behalf.

Extract from Morgan's Journal [31]

Stayed over night with Mr. Pekham formerly of Scipio [in Cayuga County], a clever gentlemanly farmer. He showed me a stone [he] found on the surface of which could be traced a nude figure. It was evidently cut with some instrument. He lives upon the ridge road up to which the lake doubtless originally came. He said he cut a ditch through this ridge a few years since, and 17 feet below the surface found roots and stumps only partially decayed one tree entire which laid northwest and southeast [was] about one foot thick, the bark was perfect, but yielded readily to the touch. He also informed me that upon his farm arrowheads were ploughed up in great quantities. One of his young men saved a quart [probably of arrowheads], found on one field.

January 16. Took dinner with Charles Graves [?], a farmer of Chili, Monroe county.

In the matter of Indian curiosities he gave me a stone chisel of black marble which he had ploughed up on his farm, also five arrowheads of different sizes. He finds such things in abundance on his land. He also mentioned a large clay pipe which he had found some ten years since, but which he could not find. From his description it was like one now in my collection only larger.

While in the county of Onondaga [I] recently found at Jacks Reefs on the Seneca [River] a long stone resembling a pestle, also learned that arrowheads were found there. While in the south part of Tompkins [County] the last of December last, enquired of an old resident if he ever found any Indian curiosities upon his land, and he said not.

Monday, January 19. Stayed overnight with William Brown of Lima (Town), Livingston County and had a long conversation with him in relation to the Indian relics which he had ploughed up on his farm. He gave me a dog's head. This seems to have been manufactured as it is not as hard as stone. He says they ploughed up vessels made of the same material which will hold from one to four quarts, balls in great quantity and chisels, gorges and pestles of stone. The skeletons are all in a sitting posture, the gun resting over the left shoulder. Captain Frost[32] at Onondaga informed me recently that the Iroquois were never buried sitting; herein he must have been mistaken. Mr. Brown found three in a triangle, all in a sitting posture, with the feet crossed at the ankle and the hands upon the viscera, their heads were within two feet square. All ever taken out in this section were found in a sitting position.

In 1809 or 1810 Mr. Brown heard the following statement which he believes to be correct. A farmer on the road between Batavia and Lewiston, near the latter place had cut off the trees and finally commenced digging a cellar. He removed one tree between two and three feet through, and nearly under found a well stoned up, and on cleaning out the well found an anvil, some iron tools, and the nose of a bellows. The well was fixed up and used at once as of old. He could not give me any nearer clue to the matter, and the chief value of the discovery will be lost for the want of the means of proving it.

[*For sketch here in journal, see fig. 3.*]

January 21. Stayed over in Springwater, Livingston with Mr. Grover, a Cayuga classmate. He informed me of a fort or trench on a hill in the town of Livonia, on the road from Lima to Slab City or Hemlock Lake village [near the outlet of Hemlock Lake] about four miles south of Lima, and near Mungers.

[*For sketch here in journal, see fig. 4.*]

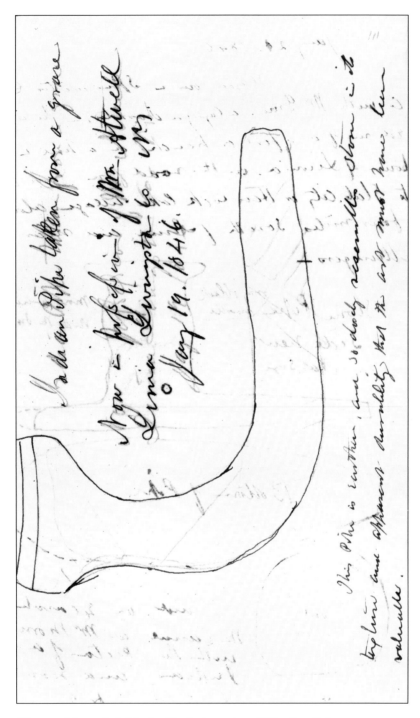

Figure 3. Morgan's sketch of a pipe in possession of Mr. Atwell, January 19, 1846, in Manuscript Journals, *vol. 1, no. 6, Morgan Papers. (Courtesy of the Department of Rare Books and Special Collections, University of Rochester Library.)*

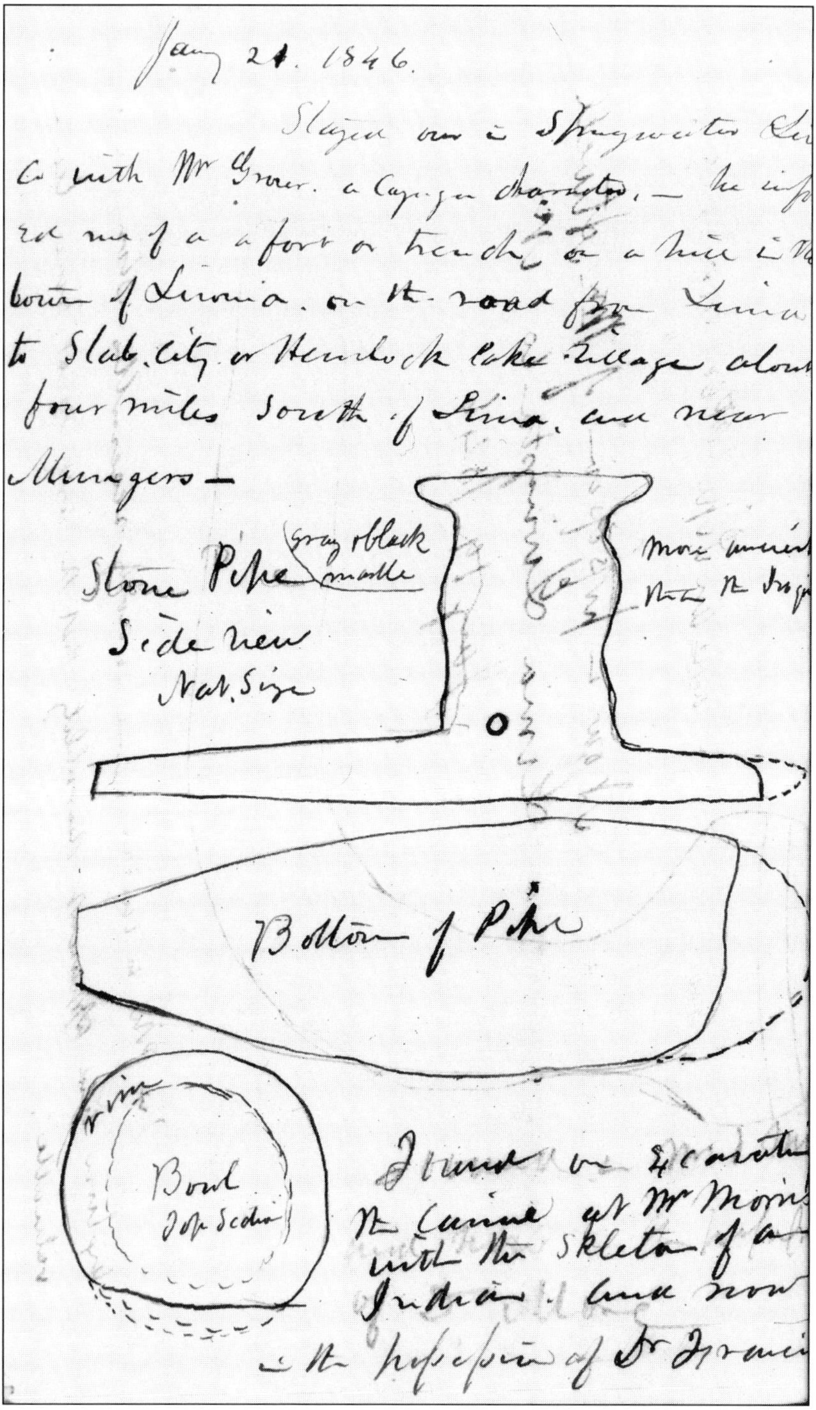

Figure 4. Morgan's sketch of a pipe in possession of Dr. Francis Moore, January 21, 1846, in Manuscript Journals, *vol. 1, no. 6, Morgan Papers. (Courtesy of the Department of Rare Books and Special Collections, University of Rochester Library.)*

Moore with whom I stayed January 22 resides between Dansville and Mt. Morris. He showed me a very perfect chisel, about 6 inches long, one side flat with the edges bevelled, the upper side horizontal [?], the other three planes being very accurately made.

January 23. Stayed at Thompson's [in] Piffardinia [northwest of Geneseo]. He showed me an unusually long arrowhead. Little Beard's town [a former Seneca settlement and reservation] was about three miles up the valley from this place, nearly opposite Cuylerville. There is now no trace of the town. The country down this valley is beautiful beyond all expression. The scenery is much like that upon our inland lakes strange to say.

January 24. Stayed in Lima. On my way home next day stopped at Mr. Sheldon's between Honeoye falls and Rush, about a mile from the latter place to make some inquiries. Found that there were two Indian burying grounds upon his farm, and the traces of an old fortification. Made an agreement to go out in the spring and dig up a grave (almost too outrageous) to see the position of the skeleton as all those interviewed in the valley of the Genesee and in Monroe County are in a sitting posture.

Mr. Wheeler of Honeoye Falls has some relics.

Morgan had no sooner returned to Rochester then he set out on another trip, this time to the Tonawanda and Buffalo Creek reservations. Apparently one purpose of the trip was to prepare petitions for the Buffalo Creek and the Tonawanda chiefs to sign and to otherwise advise them. He also talked with whites, finding that the residents of Batavia, the county seat, were opposed to removal of the Indians, but that the sentiment in Buffalo was against the Indians.

He gathered only a little archaeological information on this trip. Traveling on the Buffalo Road from Rochester to Batavia, he found no traces of former Indian occupation except arrowheads, an occasional stone chisel, and earthen pipe, but noted, "There are few or no streams on this route and away from rivers and creeks the Indian never locates." In Williamsville he learned from an old resident that he had found "a mound or heap of bones" (likely an ossuary) four miles up the creek that ran through the village, and that "pipes, earthen dishes, chisels, and tomahawks" were found in the vicinity. At Buffalo Creek he recorded the inscription on Red Jacket's tombstone and that on Mary Jemison's, but apparently no information on the earthwork within which the cemetery was located (see figs. 7 and 8). When Morgan returned to Tonawanda, Reuben Warren, son of the missionary in charge of the Baptist mission school, told him of a mound near Shelby and one on the east end of the Buffalo Creek reservation.[33]

A week after he returned to Rochester, Morgan set out again on another trip up the Genesee. His notes on this trip, like those of the previous month, contain information on the archaeology of the region.

Extract from Morgan's Journal[34]

February 19. Called upon Dr. Moore again. A very pleasant family. Gained no new information. Stayed overnight at Mt. Morris. A heavy snow during the night which blocked up the way. The week before had about two feet, and on the morning of the 20th a promise of as much more.

February 20. Left Mt. Morris, and reached at 8 P.M. Mr. Aaron Cartright's, two miles south of Le Roy, and about 12 from Mt. Morris. Snowed over one foot during the day, and we were obliged to walk nearly all the way. Stayed with Cartright overnight where I am now writing. In the Town of Covington, Wyoming County procured a chisel of Mr. Church, also a hexagonal stone, and received a promise from him that he would forward me a fine chisel in the spring.

At Pavillion, Genesee County saw a singular stone in the possession of Dr. Sprague resembling an ink stand, about 5 inches in diameter, much broken or rough, with a groove around the outside. The cavity must have been turned or worked out with some curious instrument. There is yet a mystery hanging over their stone manufacture. It was far more extensive and various than we are aware.

Had a confab with Rev. Mr. Smulter. He is somewhat odd in his views in relation to the Indian.

Mr. Cartwright gave me a singular stone implement resembling a chisel with a convex blade, evidently used for rounding out cavities, or as Mrs. Ewer (wife of Alfred Ewer of East Avon) suggested, an instrument for tapping trees.

The family spoke of Boning [?] Hill somewhere in Monroe County near Rush, or Churchville.

Mr. Ewer also informed me of a fort hill near his place in the Town of East Avon which I agreed to visit at the time I visited Mr. Sheldon (near Rush) as it is not more than three miles from the old fort on Sheldon's land.

Near South Le Roy there is a curious natural mound so much as to look rather artificial.

February 20 [sic]. On [the] way from Le Roy passed Fort Hill half way between Bergen Corners and Le Roy [see figs. 9, 11, 12]. It is a singular eminence, Allen's Creek on one side, and a deep gorge; on two others a deep projection having but a narrow neck connecting with the main land. Across this neck about 60 rods was a deep trench. When this country was first settled it was about two feet deep. Another trench met this at right angles, and [words unclear].

Mr. White, who lives in the stone house near[by], told me that 40 or 50 years since when the country was first settled, they found on this trench, or the breastwork the logs of wild cherry trees fallen, but not quite decayed and large oak trees three or four feet through growing directly upon them. In these trees they counted 300 and four hundred grains [rings], indicating as many years as he says. Removing the ages of the cherry and the oak and the lapse before the cherry began its growth, after the destruction of the place, and we shall have 500 to 900 years as the date of their last use. If the Satanas or Eries expelled by the Iroquois had any thing to do with this, the Iroquois would know of it.

They found in this hill many graves. The skeletons are all in a sitting position with their faces to the east, (I think he said) beside them they found pipes of various kinds with men's heads and animal heads figured on the bowls, the same as those I found at Lima. None of the skeletons were in a horizontal posture. They also found fragments of pots with them, but never found any metal of any kind. They find chisels of stone and arrowheads. Not far from Fort Hill, they have ploughed up Indians with tomahawks beside them etc. etc. These are undoubtedly Iroquois. The situation that would suit some Indian race would quite naturally another. They always lived upon creeks, as they had not the use of wells, which indicates great rudeness. The Jews used wells at an early day. They were however shepherds. The Greeks also.

The next night, after what he described as "a terrible tramp behind a cutter through the deep snow," Morgan stayed at Samuel Richmond's. Richmond's father-in-law, Nehemiah Woodworth, one of the first settlers in the Cayuga Lake region, was there, and Morgan had a long talk with him. Among other things, Woodworth told Morgan of some "forts" and Indian settlements.[35]

Extract from Morgan's Journal [36]

Mr. Woodworth mentioned the following forts: one near Tioga Point, between the Chemung and Susquehanna, nearest to the former, and about three miles from Tioga Point;[37] one in Hector, Tompkins County in pine woods, three or four miles southwest of Trumansburg, on a little elevation;[38] one in Chautauqua County, the lake Erie road passes through it, and the crossroad from Chautauqua lake to Lake Erie passes near it.[39] The fort was some three miles west of the crossing place.[40] This fort included about two acres, was square. The road passed through one gate, and out the other. The trench was about five feet deep. The fort at Hector had heavy timber growing upon the ridge. One other [fort] he had heard of northeast of Northville.[41]

· · · · ·

When Mr. Woodworth first settled in the county he saw where there had been an Indian village by the clearing etc. on the hill about 60 rods from Ithaca towards Owego. It was a little spot of about two acres between Six Mile Creek and the flat.

The Cayuga village, the main one was about a mile and a half northeast of Levanna, and about a mile from the lake. It was on the north side of Mud Creek at Crisses I should guess by his description. He said it was on the north side of the creek. There was no settlement at Union Springs. At the Indian Cove or Lockwood's or Utt's were a few houses. The Cayugas were very much scattered. They lived almost entirely by hunting and fishing. When they came in from hunting they frequently encamped at the Inlet, along the inlet. Sometimes there were 40 or 50 at a time or 10, or 12 wigwams or shanties, called Can-a-shoot. They would come in from the Chemung and Susquehanna, where among other things they hunted bears. They went in the fall, and came back in January. They would get [arrive] at the inlet at noon, in a deep snow, perhaps three feet, spread on skins on the snow, put the children upon it and then cover them with their blankets. They would then, women, young and old Indians, go to work to make a house. In the first place they would peel off basswood bark, and with it shovel away the snow.

The following is the ground plan.

[*For sketch here in journal, see fig. 5.*]

The first day or afternoon they would drive in seven stakes with boulders [?], or make the north half. They then put poles across and covered them with basswood bark which peeled as easily in winter as summer. Over the sides the bark was set slanting and the poles covered etc. The roof slanted to the north. The next day they made the other half, the roof slanting to the south, made just like the other, and covered in the same manner with bark. Over the floor they spread hemlock boughs, and upon them they spread their skins. The fire was in the center. In the half made the first day they found sufficient shelter, and one day was sufficient to make them a comfortable abode. The squaws as now did all the work and carried in these hunting expeditions all the baggage. They would sometimes stay in their bark houses for a month and then break up and depart on another expedition. The property, corn, or potatoes of the white settlers were never disturbed. The Indian never steals.

[*For sketch here in journal, see fig. 6.*]

After the main poles are set, a horizontal pole is wound around about a foot from the ground. Reeds are then set all around, and another pole is then wound around to hold them and so in repeated courses, the poles about two feet apart, until near the top which is left open for the smoke. The Cayugas were much on the lake in their canoes. The best kind was made of white birch bark, which must have been brought from north of lake Ontario.[42] This bark is thin, so thin that if you stepped off the ribs [of the canoe] you would go through. They were all sizes from 40 feet long, and large enough for 40 Indians to 8 feet and large enough for one. The birch bark canoes are not of one strip of bark but of many, formed upon the ribs, and sown together with the sinews of animals. They were very ingeniously made, so light that two men could carry one of the large [ones] for miles, and so frail that an inexperienced hand would turn one upside down in a minute. They had a stern of light wood, and a stern piece, to which the bark was shaped and fitted. The elm and hickory bark canoes were smaller and always made of one piece of bark. To make the bow, the bark was shaved and lapped etc.

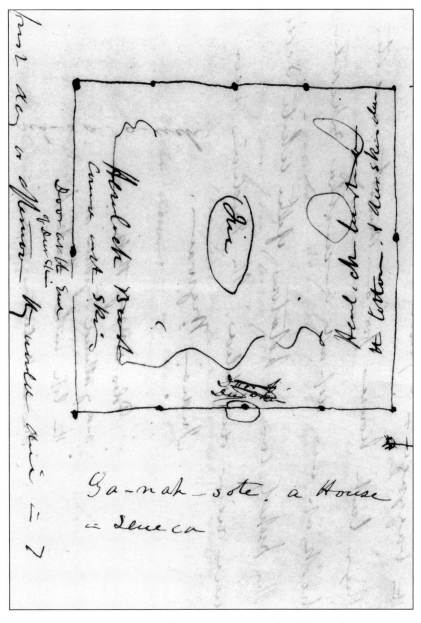

Figure 5. Morgan's sketch plan of a Cayuga house based on information from Nehemiah Woodworth, February 1846, in Manuscript Journals, *vol. 1, no. 7, Morgan Papers. (Courtesy of the Department of Rare Books and Special Collections,*

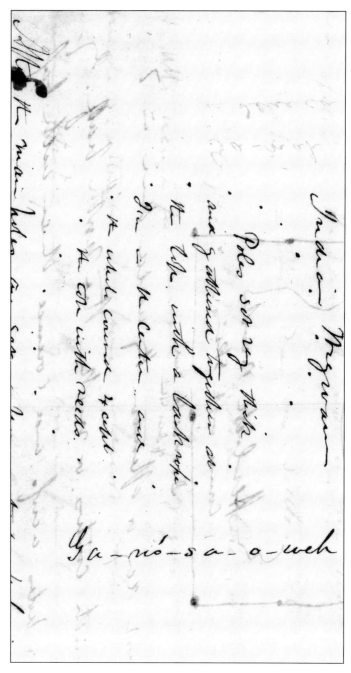

Figure 6. Morgan's sketch plan of the post arrangement in a Cayuga house based on information from Nehemiah Woodworth, February 1846, in Manuscript Journals, *vol. 1, no. 7, Morgan Papers. (Courtesy of the Department of Rare Books and Special Collections, University of Rochester Library.)*

One of these birch bark canoes left Kingston with 1800 weight of furs, and made across to Little Sodus Bay and of course was out of sight of land on the passage. The canoe was then carried to the Canandaigua Outlet, thence to Montezuma, thence up to Aurora, where it was sold to Colonel [Edward] Payne of Payne's Creek. The whole amount of 1800 pounds of fur was also brought to Aurora, and from thence was sent to Albany in a batteau. This canoe Mr. Woodworth had seen frequently. It was a fine canoe, and would hold 30 men. This happened about four years after he came to Ithaca and he settled at Ithaca the very year that Governor Clinton made a treaty with the Senecas at Geneva by which he bought all the land between the Seneca lake and the Genesee River. This will furnish the date of the transaction.[43] Colonel Payne[44] came in the year after he did and located his land. Captain [Roswell] Franklin and J[onathan] Richmond a year or two afterwards.

Early in March Morgan made another trip to the Tonawanda and Buffalo Creek reservations. His notes on this trip do not record the purpose of the trip, nor do they record any information on archaeological sites.

Of all those outraged at the actions of the Ogden Land Company, perhaps the most influential was John Martindale, a lawyer in Batavia who had been appointed district attorney of Genesee County in 1842. Under an act passed by the New York State legislature in 1821, Martindale had attempted to have the whites who had settled on the Tonawanda Reservation removed and had failed.[45] It was perhaps this failure that led the grand jury meeting in Batavia on February 24, 1846, to consider what might be done. The grand jury concluded that it could take no action. It did, however, unanimously recommend that a mass meeting be called for March 21 at the courthouse in Batavia. When it met that day, the meeting was so largely attended that it filled "every nook and corner" of the courtroom. A memorial and resolutions were drawn up and adopted by acclamation, and Morgan (who had spoken at the meeting but who was not an officer of the meeting nor a member of the committee that drew up the memorial, perhaps because he was not a resident of the county) was appointed to bear the proceedings of the meeting to the Senate in Washington.[46]

Morgan left Aurora on April 3 on this mission, stopping in New York City where he presented a paper to the New York Historical Society on the government and institutions of the Iroquois—a slightly revised version of the paper he had given to the Rochester chapter of the order on November 7.[47] What efforts Morgan made on behalf of the Tonawanda Senecas after he arrived in Washington are not known. His notes on the trip are silent on this subject.[48]

Neither Morgan's nor Parker's more-extensive lobbying efforts that spring and summer produced the desired results. On August 6, the Senate Committee on Indian Affairs postponed the matter until the next session. That month, on his way back from Washington, Parker stopped in Aurora to attend the annual meeting of all the chapters of the Grand Order of the Iroquois. Morgan had been collecting data on the trails, territories, and Indian place names, and at this meeting gave a paper on the subject. A new grand sachem of the order was elected, ending Morgan's two terms of that office.[49]

No longer grand sachem (leadership of the order had passed to another faction), Morgan decided to write up his materials for publication, and late in October went to Tonawanda on a ten-day visit to check his draft.[50] The revision was published as a series of "Letters on the Iroquois" in the February, March, and April issues of *The American Review*.

The next month, at the May meeting of the New York Historical Society, Morgan gave a long paper, "On the Territorial Limits, Geographical Names and Trails of the Iroquois."[51] Later that year he published a condensation of it as the concluding "Letters on the Iroquois" in *The American Review*.

Parker's efforts that year to get the United States Senate to resolve the Tonawanda question failed, and the Tonawanda Senecas then concentrated their efforts to winning their case in the courts. The issue was not resolved until 1857 when an agreement was reached in which the Tonawanda Senecas "bought back" their reservation. Morgan took no part in the long, drawn-out legal contest that made that resolution possible.

4

. . . . .

Archaeology of the State

Some six decades before Morgan began his study, interest had increased in the archaeological remains to be found on the continent. The reasons were several. As a consequence of English victory in the French and Indian War, England gained the lands east of the Mississippi formerly controlled by France. The Crown, however, desiring to keep these newly acquired lands as Indian country, forbade white settlement west of a line drawn along the crest of the Appalachians. That effectively stemmed the colonists' migration there. This changed when the Treaty of Paris that ended the American Revolution ceded these lands to the United States. The pent-up desire to move west led to a rapid settlement of these lands and to the discovery of the great earthworks of the "mound builders," constructions that had been little noticed when white interest in the region concerned the fur trade. Reports of these monuments drifted east, which in their turn fueled more interest in these archaeological remains.

At the same time, the new nation was seeking to establish its identity as one separate from England, as a country with its own history. Interest in its "antiquities" increased—antiquities which, although bearing some resemblance to those of the Old World, were in other ways unique. Reports on the mounds appeared in some journals, and learned societies such as the American Philosophical Society called for more from the western settlers, who were establishing their own major settlements where the older Indian ones had often been located. Description of these earthworks was also an opportunity not lost on the scholars of the day to prove that Americans were capable of doing science equal to that being done in Europe.

Although fewer in number than those to the west, some such mounds were found in New York State along with other Indian archaeological remains, and the history of the "discovery" and interest in these earthworks paralleled that in the Ohio region.[1] In 1788, the noted missionary to the Oneidas, the Rev. Samuel Kirkland, visited a half dozen of them while journeying from the Genesee to Buffalo Creek.[2] Three years later, while touring western New York State, a small party visited a site on the Seneca River, which they later said was "unequalled perhaps even by the celebrated vestiges at Muskingum."[3]

The rapid white settlement of the western part of the state during the next two decades brought to light a number of earthworks. They particularly interested the indefatigable De Witt Clinton. After having visited several in the central part of the state, he mentioned them briefly in an address in 1811, and described them more fully along with some mention of more western sites in an address in 1817.[4] These various notices of sites of the state were mentioned in Yates and Moulton's *History of the State of New-York* published in 1824.[5] Five years later, James Macauley repeated Clinton's observations in his history and appended a description of Fort Hill at Auburn.[6]

Not unexpectedly, then, when Schoolcraft, endeavoring to enhance his reputation, took the 1845 census of the New York Indians, he also collected data on their archaeological remains. At the time, the state made a decennial census of its own. At the urging of the New York Historical Society—and perhaps at Schoolcraft's suggestion—the state added to its 1845 census of citizens a census of the Indians residing within its boundaries. Schoolcraft was appointed to undertake it and to give a report on their present as well as their past condition. In preparation, he made a list of the sites mentioned in the literature so that he might visit them.[7] Later that summer he visited some of them, and in his report to the state, republished under the title *Notes on the Iroquois,* included sketch plans of four earthworks, including the one at Buffalo Creek (fig. 8).

He apparently did not visit Fort Hill in Auburn as he had intended. In October of that year, Stephen A. Goodwin[8] forwarded to him a plan made by James H. Bostwick (fig. 10). Goodwin was a member of the order, later succeeding Morgan as grand sachem, and Schoolcraft probably had met him in Aurora at the annual meeting of all the chapters of the order.

From Chester Dewey, principal of the Rochester Collegiate Institute and scientist of some note, Schoolcraft obtained a plan of Fort Hill at Le Roy (fig. 9). It was perhaps at Morgan's suggestion.[9]

Three years after Schoolcraft visited some of the "ancient monuments" of the state, Ephraim George Squier undertook a more intensive survey of them. Three years younger than Morgan, Squier became a journalist and editor first in Albany, New York, then in Hartford, Connecticut, and then in Chillicothe, Ohio. There he met Edwin Hamilton Davis, a medical doctor who had long been interested in the mounds of the region. Together they made a study of the earthworks, published in 1848 by the Smithsonian Institution.[10] Its comprehensive treatment and many plates attracted wide attention.

That fall, with financial support from the Smithsonian and the New York Historical Society, Squier undertook a somewhat similar survey of the archaeological sites of New York State. About halfway through his eight-week trip, he visited Morgan in Rochester, obtaining from him a sketch of the "fort hill" at Le Roy and information about other sites between Rochester and Auburn. Leaving Rochester, Squier went on to survey the sites at Canandaiga and Victor, then to Geneva where he located the sites Morgan had mentioned to him. Next he went to Auburn where he saw Fort Hill, and then to look for sites on the east side of Cayuga Lake.[11]

As published, Squier's report contained Morgan's plan of the Fort Hill near Le Roy as well as Squier's sketches of the plans of Kanadesaga and two sites near Kanadesaga, the Fort Hill at Auburn, and the Buffalo Creek cemetery[12]—all places visited by Morgan (see figs. 7, 12, 14, 16, 18, and 20).

Just before Squier's visit, Morgan had finished preparing his own ground plans of sites he had visited in previous years, drawings he intended to send to the regents of the University of the State of New York. In 1845, the regents had been placed in charge of the state's Cabinet of Natural History, itself created two years before to care for the collections of the state's geological and natural history survey (1836–41). In 1847, they received an appropriation for preserving and increasing the collections of the cabinet and hired a curator. At a meeting on May 28 that year, the regents passed a motion of Governor Young and appointed a special committee to make plans for a state antiquarian collection to be attached to the Cabi-

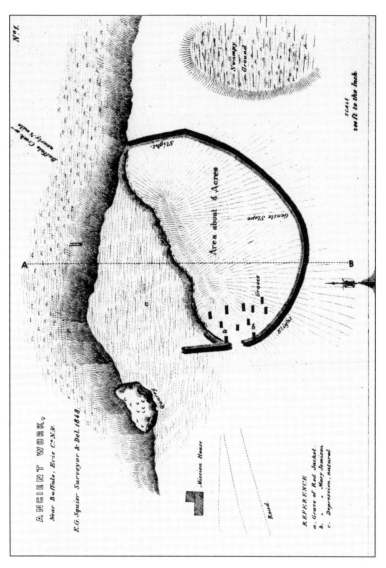

Figure 7. Ephraim George Squier's plan of the Buffalo Creek cemetery, in Squier, Aboriginal Monuments of the State of New-York, *Plate VII, no. 1.*

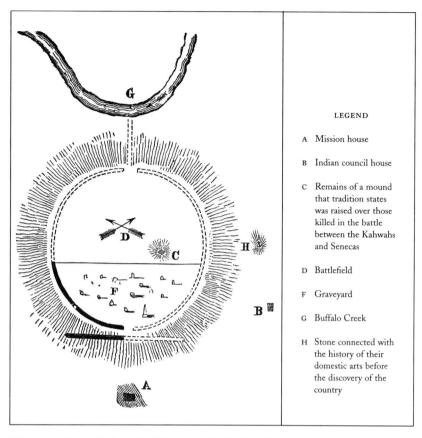

LEGEND

A Mission house

B Indian council house

C Remains of a mound
that tradition states
was raised over those
killed in the battle
between the Kahwahs
and Senecas

D Battlefield

F Graveyard

G Buffalo Creek

H Stone connected with
the history of their
domestic arts before
the discovery of the
country

Figure 8. Henry R. Schoolcraft's plan of the Buffalo Creek cemetery, in Schoolcraft,
Notes on the Iroquois, *1846 edition, p. 122; 1847 edition, p. 215.*

net of Natural History. The committee consisted of the Governor, John
van Schaick Lansing Pruyn, a member of the Board of Regents, and
T. Romeyn Beck, secretary of the Board.[13]

The regents' interest in expanding the state cabinet to include a historical and antiquarian collection had attracted Morgan's attention, and he offered his collection of "Indian antiquities and relics" to it. The regents accepted his offer at their meeting of October 27, 1848 (see fig. 21).[14] On
October 31, Morgan wrote a letter to the regents, an extract of which was
published in their annual report for 1848:[15]

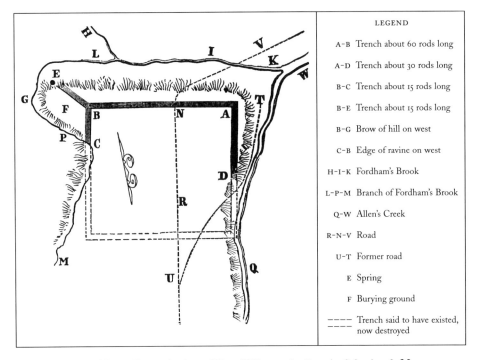

LEGEND	
A–B	Trench about 60 rods long
A–D	Trench about 30 rods long
B–C	Trench about 15 rods long
B–E	Trench about 15 rods long
B–G	Brow of hill on west
C–B	Edge of ravine on west
H–I–K	Fordham's Brook
L–P–M	Branch of Fordham's Brook
Q–W	Allen's Creek
R–N–V	Road
U–T	Former road
E	Spring
F	Burying ground
– – – –	Trench said to have existed, now destroyed

Figure 9. Chester Dewey's plan of Fort Hill near Le Roy, in Schoolcraft, Notes on the Iroquois, *1846 edition, p. 247; 1847 edition, p. 193.*

The vestiges of our Indian predecessors are very limited, and the utmost efforts of a single person would accumulate but a small cabinet. Numerous individuals in the State, however, have fugitive specimens, which singly have no particular interest, but which if accumulated would become valuable. There is every reason to believe that most of these would be cheerfully surrendered to a general cabinet, such as the Board of Regents propose to found under the patronage of the State, as an adjunct to that of Natural History. Such a collection, in the course of time, would enlarge into a respectable and interesting cabinet, and in after years would assume a deeply attractive character. If the specimens in our museums and private cabinets were at once brought into one collection, they would excite universal surprise by their variety and singularity. Such a cabinet would, it is true, contain but little to instruct; would seem to enlarge but slightly the bounds of human knowledge, yet it would be all it pretended—a memento of the Red Race who preceded us. If the scholar of after years should ask of our age an account of our predecessors, such a collection would be the most acceptable answer it could render. It would enable the Red Race to speak for itself through these silent memorials. As a private citizen, I feel personally indebted to the Board for taking this enterprise under their protection and patronage, and will not only willingly contribute what little I have, to promote the object, but will aid, so far as I may be able, in other ways.

Allow me to suggest that W. H. C. Hosmer, of Avon, Livingston county, has a small collection. Perhaps, if applied to, he would be willing to place it at the disposal of the Regents. J. V. H. Clark, Esq. of Manlius, Onondaga county, has devoted considerable attention to Indian matters, and I presume has some specimens. Charles P. Avery, of Owego, Judge of the county, has some Indian relics. Mr. Atwell, of

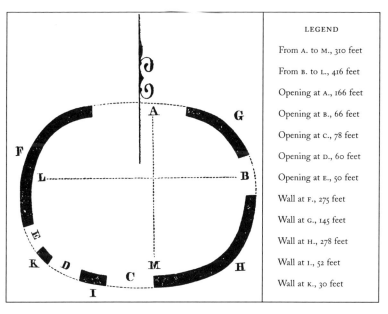

LEGEND

From A. to M., 310 feet

From B. to L., 416 feet

Opening at A., 166 feet

Opening at B., 66 feet

Opening at C., 78 feet

Opening at D., 60 feet

Opening at E., 50 feet

Wall at F., 275 feet

Wall at G., 145 feet

Wall at H., 278 feet

Wall at I., 52 feet

Wall at K., 30 feet

Figure 10. James H. Bostwick's plan of Fort Hill near Auburn, in Schoolcraft, Notes on the Iroquois, *1846 edition, pp. 106 and 241; 1847 edition, p. 215.*

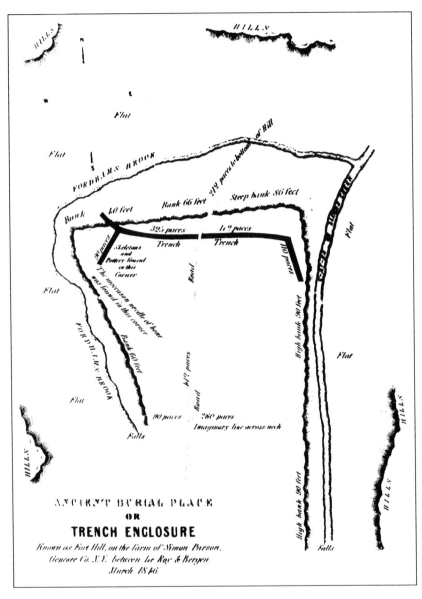

Figure 11. *Morgan's plan of Fort Hill near Le Roy, in second Regents report.*

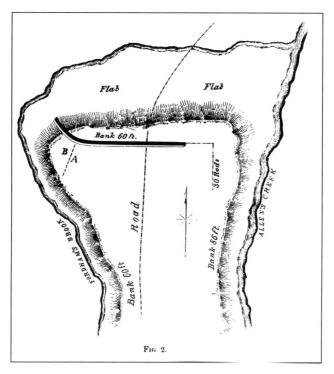

Figure 2.

Figure 12. Morgan's plan of Fort Hill near Le Roy, in Squier,
Aboriginal Monuments of the State of New-York, *Figure 1,*
p. 48.

Lima, Livingston county, has a pipe of black pottery, very large and perfect. It is the most perfect specimen of Indian pottery I have ever seen. Dr. Francis Moore, of Livingston county, now a resident of this city, has a stone or marble pipe of singular workmanship. I enclose drawings of these two pipes, which I made when I saw them in 1846. Dr. Sprague, of Pavilion, Genesee county, has also a stone vessel of singular design.

The day before, Morgan had written to Ely Parker. Parker had attended the annual council at Tonawanda in the fall of 1848. At Morgan's earlier request to take down Jemmy Johnson's speech "in full," he had made notes on it, as he later informed Morgan.[16] Morgan replied to Parker's letter on October 30, requesting various kinds of information on the collection he was preparing to send to the state cabinet:[17]

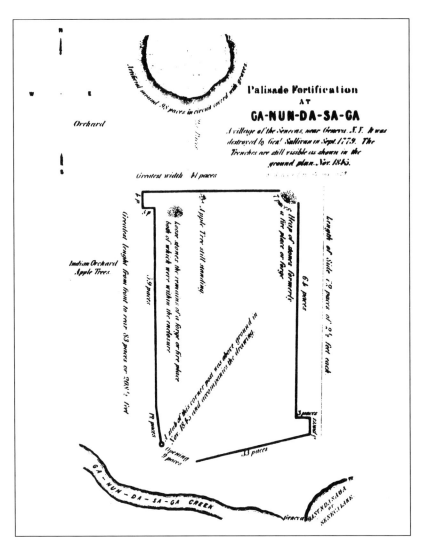

Figure 13. Morgan's plan of Kanadesaga, in second Regents report.

Rochester, October 30, 1848

Ely S. Parker, Esq.

Dear Sir,

    Your letter was duly received, and I am glad indeed to learn that you made copious notes on the proceedings of the late council. I am very impatient for a copy, but do not wish to hurry you at all. I would much rather wait any length of time and have a full report, including the speeches, than to have one abbreviated. So take it easy, but be sure and get it up in your customary style.

I am about to label my Indian relics, and curiosities such as I have to send them down to Albany to put in the "State Indian collection" which the Regents of the University are about to found under the patronage of the State. Numerous individuals have a few specimens, which in such small numbers do not possess much interest; but if all these could be accumulated, it would furnish an interesting collection.

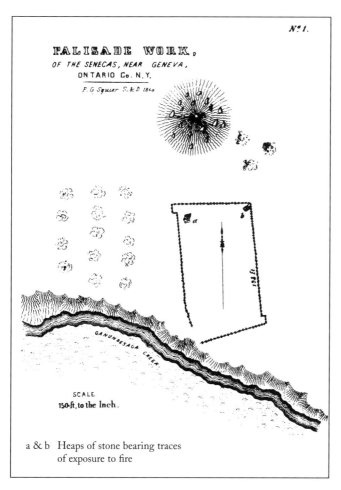

Figure 14. Ephraim George Squier's plan of Kanadesaga, in Squier, Aboriginal Monuments of the State of New-York, *plate xiii, no. 1.*

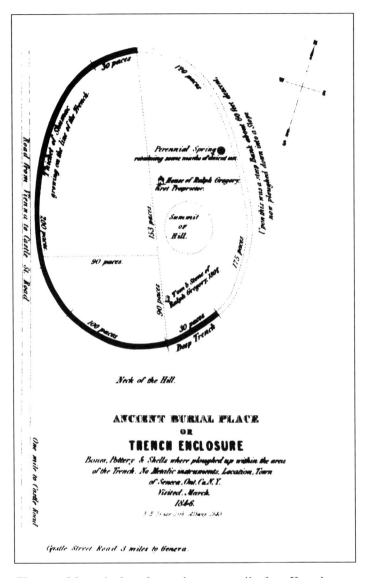

Figure 15. Morgan's plan of an enclosure two miles from Kanadesaga, in second Regents report.

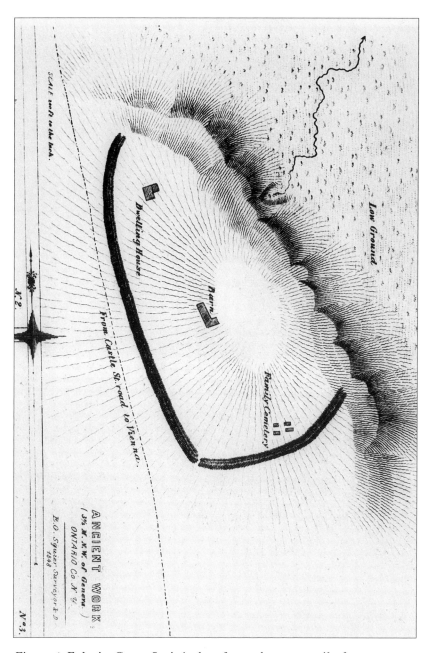

Figure 16. Ephraim George Squier's plan of an enclosure two miles from Kanadesaga, in Squier, Aboriginal Monuments of the State of New-York, *plate vii, no. 1.*

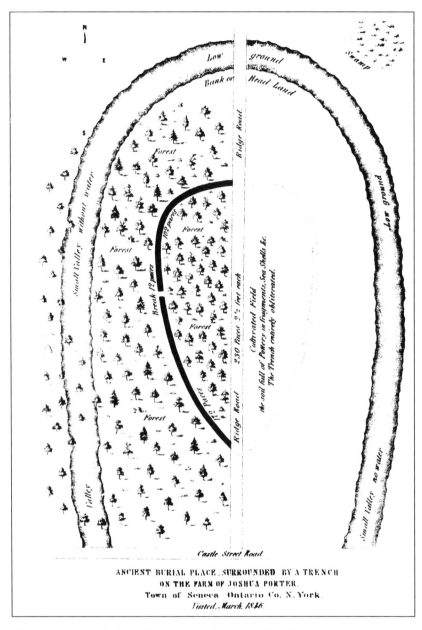

Figure 17. Morgan's plan of an enclosure four miles from Kanadesaga, in second Regents report.

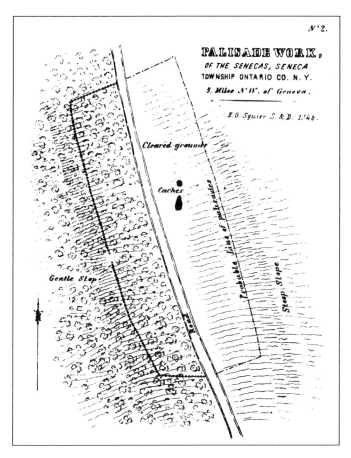

*Figure 18. Ephraim George Squier's plan of an enclosure four miles
from Kanadesaga, in Squier,* Aboriginal Monuments of the
State of New-York, *plate xiii, no. 2.*

The Regents have resolved to try and make a collection, and to make it
a department of the Geological Collection. It is a good idea and ought
to be encouraged. I wish to attach correct Indian names to all of mine
as it will be in better taste, and I must turn to you of course for the
names themselves. I enclose a list which I wish you would go over and
place the Indian name opposite and return it; giving me an explanation
of each in your answer if any should be necessary.

You must remember the large Indian mortar of stone, or corn mill,
which I showed you at Aurora in my collection. You gave an opinion

upon it I believe. I wish now to get its correct Indian name, and to ascertain that we must know its use. There are two cavities upon the face of the stone, a small and a large one. If the Indians ever used mineral paints I should be inclined to think it had been used for some such purpose. On the other hand it would be very easy to put around it some basket work and thus make it an excellent contrivance for pounding and grinding corn. The lower side of the stone had several cavities

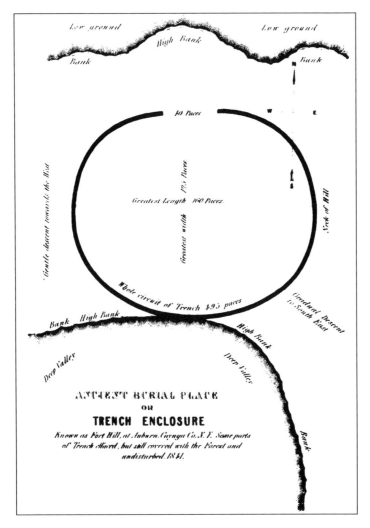

Figure 19. Morgan's plan of Fort Hill near Auburn, in second Regents report.

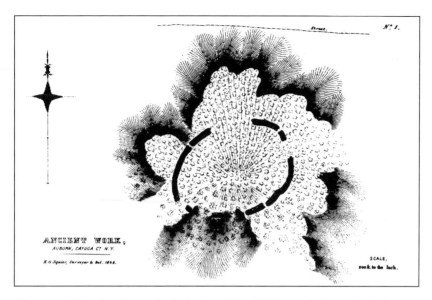

Figure 20. Ephraim George Squier's plan of Fort Hill near Auburn, in Squier, Aboriginal Monuments of the State of New-York, *plate v, no. 1.*

in it, worn into each other like this [small sketch here]. Stone pestles you know are often found, and they must have been used in stone mortars. I wish you would give me the name for a "stone mortar," and "corn mill"; and if possible tell me just what this is and give me its exact name. If you can give me no light on the question I shall call it a "stone mortar" for grinding corn, and let it go at that. It is at all events a "stone mortar" and you may give me that Indian name for that. The purpose for which it was used is another thing. Let me know its purpose if you can. I have also a stone gouge made in the fashion of a metallic chisel, convex on the outside and concave within. It must have been used to hollow out wooden vessels after fire had been applied. Give me the original name for that. We have two kinds of pipe, the stone, and the earthen, or burnt clay. Give me the names of each. I have the front part of the bowl of one having a wolf's head. It is of black pottery. Will you name that, if it would have a different name from a common pipe. I have some arrowheads unfinished or in the rough, and some finished. Send me the names of each. You remember our talk about the moccasin needle, which you told me was a small bone of deer. I have one of bone. Give me the Indian name of it and tell me where in the deer it is found. Levi gave me a stone with a hole bored through it. Perhaps you remember it. It was in this shape [small sketch here]. The hole is well drilled. It may have been used for a pipe by putting a reed in one end. Give me its name if it had any, and tell me its use. I have a small brass kettle taken from an Indian grave near Geneva. Did a vessel used for such a purpose have a peculiar name. If so send it. Earthen vessels were also buried as were brass [ones]. All the pottery we find pretty much was buried in this way. What is the name of these earthen dishes. Give the names both of the earthen and the brass. I have also a calumet, a long one about two feet. The stock is of wood, and covered with a case of bead work. It is from the west. Give me its name.

What would be a pretty name for a "Collection of Indian Antiques" or "Indian relics," or "Aboriginal Curiosities," or "Cabinet of Indian History," or "Indian Museum." If you can give me a fine name for the new collection, which is to be confined to our State principally [?], I will suggest it to the Regents. You know what I want. Think it over, and send me what would be your choice, with the translation. *One word* is to be preferred. It must all be in one word. Send me a number of names, with their meanings. This will be questions enough for you to answer, as I shall expect an answer for each.

I wish we could secure some relic of Red Jacket and Cornplanter and Farmer's Brother, Blacksnake, Johnson and Blacksmith for this collection. Could it be done. Red Jacket's tomahawk would be a great attraction.

Will you write an answer to this so that I may receive it next Tuesday a week from tomorrow, at the latest, as I wish to send my specimens down to Albany the last of next week.

One thing more. You have seen the stone chisel so often found in various parts of the state. It is a popular notion that they were used for skinning deer, that this was their object. Let me know whether this is true. It seems reasonable.

Figure 21. Letter of T. Romeyn Beck to Lewis H. Morgan, October 1848, in Morgan Papers. (Courtesy of the Department of Rare Books and Special Collections, University of Rochester Library.)

Lewis H. Morgan Esq.

Sir

Without any preamble, I beg leave to submit to your notice, a copy of the proceedings of the Regents of the University, at a meeting held Oct 27, 1848. I trust the matter needs no further explanation & I will only add my sincere wish that you may deem it advisable to comply with the wishes of the Board.

Very respectfully,
T. Romeyn Beck
Secy

At a meeting held as above

The Secretary informed the Board on the authority of Professor Emmons, that Lewis H. Morgan Esq of Rochester, was the owner of a large collection of Indian Antiquities & Relics, principally obtained within this State & that Mr Morgan had expressed a willingness to present the same to the "Historical Antiquarian Collection" founded under the authority of the Regents, provided other persons would also contribute.

Whereupon

Resolved that the Secretary, in behalf of the Regents, solicit from Mr Morgan, the donation of the above collection & in case that the same be presented, that the Standing Committee on the "State Cabinet of Natural History" take proper measures for its exhibition & safe keeping. —

Resolved further, in case said donation be made, that the Governor & Secy of State be advised & requested (if within their power) to present Mr Morgan with a copy of the "Natural History of the State of New York"

A true Copy
T. Romeyn Beck
Secy.

T[heodoric] Romeyn Beck

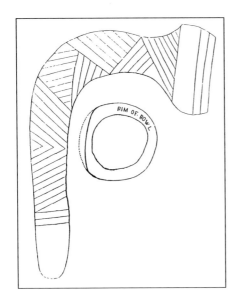

Figure 22. Morgan's sketch of a pipe in possession of Mr. Atwell, published in second Regents report, p. 83.

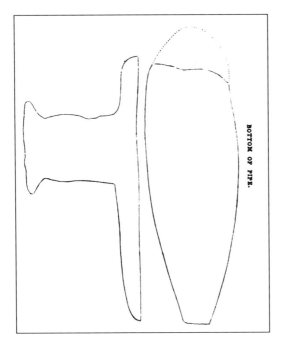

Figure 23. Morgan's sketch of a pipe in possession of Dr. Francis Moore, published in second Regents report, p. 82.

We should be glad to see you in Rochester when you can make it convenient. We are all well in this quarter. No news. Very quiet for a time so near a general election.

Yours

L.H. Morgan

Of the objects Morgan sent to the state in November—some forty in all—a few were of historic interest, such as a cross found at Tonawanda, a fragment of Red Jacket's gravestone, and a piece of the palisade at Kanade-saga. A few were ethnographic, as the headdress and war club from Tona-wanda. Most, however, were artifacts collected from various sites in the region (see list in appendix 1).

Morgan also sent the state some account of the specimens and their use, prefaced with some observations on the importance of collecting more such materials—that, for example, these manufactures "unlock the social history of the people from whom they come." With this letter Morgan also sent the site ground plans he had finished preparing shortly before Squier had visited him earlier that month. They were also published in the regents report (see figs. 11, 13, 15, 17, and 19) as well as the list of articles sent and Morgan's letter describing these objects.

5

. . . . .

Collecting for the State

Several weeks later Morgan sent six more archaeological objects to the state. The next year he sent eleven more and some ethnographic specimens: bows and arrows, mortar and pestles, a quantity of white corn, splint baskets, a bark tray, lacrosse sticks, and snow snakes (see appendix 1). In these two years, 1848 and 1849, the state collection was augmented by the purchase of archaeological specimens from William H. C. Hosmer and in 1849 also by the purchase of similar objects from Squier.[1] Of greater importance, however, was the large collection of ethnographic objects Morgan obtained for the state cabinet later that year.

After Squier had returned to New York City, he wrote to Morgan informing him, among other things, of his election as corresponding member of the American Ethnological Society, and asking him to write a paper on "the order of descent among the Iroquois" for an "Archaeological etc. Journal" then being planned.[2] To this suggestion Morgan replied:

> In relation to an article on the Iroquois Code of Descent, I like the idea very much, but should prefer to make some further investigations before writing it. I think I have a correct analysis of the system, but it would be necessary in a separate article upon this subject to go more into detail. It is my intention to visit Tonawanda and Cattaraugus during the winter, and I will then get at the bottom of the matter if possible, and send you a piece on the subject. In the mean time "possess yourself in patience."[3]

He also offered to make a large "Iroquois map of the State" for Squier's forthcoming volume. As Morgan wrote:

Another project has come into my head since the receipt of your letter which I will now proceed to unfold to learn what you think of it. Your forthcoming work will be entirely a New York matter, and will necessarily be a thin volume for a quarto. How would you like to have me furnish you with an Iroquois map of the State, including all the Indian trails, or routes of travel, to preface it with, and also with a condensed essay upon the geographical names, territorial boundaries and trails of the Iroquois, to illustrate the map. It would require but a few of the opening pages of the volume and if done correctly, would be a fit accompaniment of your aboriginal remains. . . .

. . . I have long entertained a desire for the publication of this map and would willingly do considerable work to have it done. I tried to get [George H.] Colton to publish it in the [American] Review, and have thought of urging the [New York] Historical Society to do it. I have also thought of republishing my Letters [on the Iroquois] with additions, and also with this map. But my determination to adhere to my profession will prevent me from doing the latter for some years. Such a map 30 by 20 inches or such a matter, colored, and marked with the boundaries and trails would be unique and attractive.[4]

Squier agreed and Morgan began working on it. In April he sent Squier the Seneca portion of the map, but not the essay. Of that he wrote:

I have done nothing yet. My law business at the last circuit drove me hard. At the May circuit also I shall be much occupied, but think by the middle of June I can write all I wish to publish, and then I am all done I hope. I am determined to give up this Indian fanaticism and attend to the law. It is more profitable, and at times a great deal more interesting.[5]

Nonetheless, some months later Morgan undertook another project. As he had written in his report on the objects sent in 1848:

It would be an easy matter to obtain full Iroquois costumes, male and female, together with the implements, weapons and utensils in common use among them. When collected, they would richly repay the cost and trouble. The birch bark canoe, the bow and arrow, tomahawk, belt, turtle-shell rattle, drum, wampum, war club, ball club, snow snake, and all other articles of this description should have a place in the "Historical and Antiquarian Collection" of the State.[6]

He now proposed to make such a collection. As the regents noted in their annual report for 1849:

A few months since, Mr. Lewis H. Morgan, of Rochester, whose liberal gifts have been enumerated in a former report, and who has continued them during the present year, suggested the propriety of endeavoring to bring together a full exhibition of the manufactures of the Indian tribes still remaining within our State, and thus to show, as it were, their transition condition, in the union of their ancient and rude constructions, with the improvements received through the whites. Mr. Morgan added, that he would with pleasure superintend the disposition of any appropriation that might be resolved upon. The Regents could not hesitate to agree to his offer. So rapid, indeed, is the progress of change, with the ancient lords of the soil, that what is to be done must be done quickly. A sum of money was accordingly placed at the disposal of Mr. Morgan.[7]

The sum given was $215.[8]

To make the collection, Morgan enlisted the aid of the Parker family. In fact, the project became essentially that of the Parker family, involving in one way or another all its members. They made or obtained most of the objects, receiving a considerable portion of the $215 allotted by the regents, and supplied the objects' Indian names and descriptions of use.

William Parker (fig. 24) was the father of what Morgan later called "the most talented family of the Iroquois stock."[9] Parker had been born about 1794 on the Allegany reservation and had moved as a youth to Tonawanda with his family. When Indian assistance was requested during the War of 1812, Parker enlisted along with a large number of other Iroquois, and he was wounded. After he returned he married Elizabeth (fig. 25), niece of Jemmy Johnson.[10]

In 1849, six of their children were still living. All had apparently received their early education at the Baptist mission school, and all except Ely (fig. 26) were then residing on the Tonawanda reservation. The oldest was Spencer H. Cone, who had returned not long before to Tonawanda from the West, where he had been a miller, among other things.

At the time, whites often named Indians after noted white Americans. Spencer's name, that of a well-known Baptist minister of the day, was probably given to him at the mission school. Throughout most of his life he was known as Spencer Cone; only around this time did he sometimes use the Parker surname. The others of the family in order of age were Levi (fig. 27), Nicholson (fig. 30), Ely, and Caroline (figs. 28, 29). Newton (fig. 31), then about sixteen, was the youngest.[11]

Just when and how Morgan made arrangements with the Parker family to supply the articles is not known, but something of their nature is indicated in a surviving letter of Morgan's to Caroline Parker:[12]

Rochester, November 13, 1849

Dear Friend

Your letter came this morning and Newton's yesterday, and I was glad to hear that the articles are doing so well, and being collected so fast. I am sorry that the beads were not as fine as you wished. Still I think they will look well. As Thursday the 29th inst. is Thanksgiving day, I have concluded to change the day of starting for Tonawanda to Friday the 30th of November when I will meet you and Levi in Batavia about noon. The train leaves here at 9 A.M. Tell Levi that I have changed the day to Friday November 30. I will write to Ely, and see if he will be home.

I send you $1.00 as you requested, and $2.00 for your mother towards the baskets. Remember whatever you use for materials of any kind is a separate thing from the prices for making, and you must let me know whenever you want materials that I may send you money.

I enclose $3.00 also for Newton. Tell him he must try his best to get one turtle shell rattle. As to the 150 feathered arrows, I suppose he will soon have them done. I think Newton has done exceedingly well to secure so many of his articles so quickly. Write again next week.

Yours etc.
L.H. Morgan

Figure 24. William Parker. Photograph of a
daguerreotype, in Arthur C. Parker, The Life of
General Ely S. Parker, *facing p. 40.*

As he had written Caroline, Morgan did go to Tonawanda on Friday
the 30th. He took the opportunity while there to collect some information
on religious practice, notably that of the New Year's ceremony, and interviewed Jemmy Johnson on Handsome Lake, obtaining from him an abbreviated version of his annual speech. On Monday night Morgan attended a
War dance, at the time a popular diversion. But his principal purpose in
going to Tonawanda was to collect articles and to obtain information on
their use.

Of the articles he took back to Rochester, most had been purchased, but
a few were gifts. Among them was a gift of a catlinite pipe from William
Parker that he had used for some years. In return, Morgan gave a German
silver tobacco bag. Mrs. Printup (Da-wä-ke-was, "She goes not out to

Figure 25. Elizabeth Parker. Photograph of a daguerreotype, in Parker, The Life of General Ely S. Parker, *facing p. 40.*

war") of the Hawk clan gave Morgan a bark bowl about 40 years old and two baskets. In return, he gave her "a beautiful testament."[13]

Morgan did not, however, bring back all the articles that the Parker family was to furnish, as evident by his letter to Newton dated December 19, 1849:[14]

Tell Caroline that I should be glad to receive her articles by the 3rd of January if she can get them ready without much inconvenience. You may tell her also that I will send her $2.00 about that time to meet any contingent expenses she may be at in finishing them including the moccasins. I may have about the same sum to send to Nic for the silver ware at the same time, but I cannot tell just yet how the money account will come out. [See fig. 32.]

Neither had Morgan received all the names of the articles; in a post-script to this letter, he wrote:

Caroline forgot to send me the names which I wrote for. Ask her to send them to me by the 3rd of January. I add a few to the list. Have Nic help spell them out.

Needle book
Pounder for corn
Steel and flint for striking fire
New Year's shovel

Figure 26. Ely S. Parker. Photograph probably taken in 1855. (Courtesy of the Western Reserve Historical Society, Cleveland, Ohio.)

Figure 27. Levi Parker wearing articles of clothing Morgan collected for the state in 1849. Engraving in Morgan, League of the Iroquois, *frontispiece.*

Ribbon for hair
Scalping knife
Wild potato
Knot pitcher
Pin cushion

On the first of January Morgan went to Albany.[15] Before he left, however, he exhibited his objects in Rochester as is indicated by his brother-in-law, Charles T. Porter, in a letter of January 20, 1850, to Caroline.[16]

Figure 28. Caroline Parker wearing articles of clothing Morgan collected for the state in 1849. Photograph of a lost hand-tinted daguerreotype. (Courtesy of the Southwest Museum, Los Angeles, California [photo no. N.24963].)

Rochester, January 20, 1850

My Sister,

Many thanks for your note of the 3rd, and your kind present, very beautiful and acceptable. They had a journey to Albany, for Lewis was there, and they were sent to the cabinet of the State, with the rest of the curiosities. They soon found their way back however, and Lewis brought them up to us one morning. We could not open the purse for a good while, it is very ingenious. I shall value it very much indeed. Your sister Harriette is very much pleased with the basket, which she will put her fine work in; and the bead work case, which hangs up on a pin in our parlor. We shall remember you, and days gone by, always when we see them. We thank you for them very much, and next opportunity which we have we will try to send you something which we hope will be equally acceptable.

Lewis exhibited all his curiosities from Tonawanda at his office the day after he got home, or rather the day but one, for the next day was Sunday; he invited a great many ladies to see them, and his office was full all the afternoon. They were beautiful particularly the bead work, which the ladies admired very much, and the baby-frame. Harriette is

Figure 29. Caroline Parker wearing articles of clothing Morgan collected for the state in 1849. Engraving in Morgan, League of the Iroquois, *following p. 147.*

very much obliged to her mother for the handsome and convenient covered basket which she sent her. It was a very acceptable present indeed. I am glad to hear that you are so well and enjoying yourself so well in Tonawanda. Do you have books as many as you want? Have you got a good school at the station. I was sorry to hear that the missionary's wife was dead some time ago. I love sleigh riding very much, but get only a very few rides, for we live in the city where it costs a good deal to enjoy a sleigh-ride, and we are not very well off, and have

Figure 30. Nicholson Parker as a student at the Albany State Normal School. Photograph in Parker, The Life of General Ely S. Parker, *facing p. 262.*

Figure 31. Daguerreotype of Newton Parker (probably) wear-
ing articles Morgan collected for the state. (Courtesy of Rare
Books and Manuscripts Division, The New York Public Library,
Astor, Lenox and Tilden Foundations, New York, New York.)

to be very economical, so we generally walk. I should love to take some
of those sleigh-rides with you in Tonawanda woods. I remember them
very well, the pine woods, the oak woods and openings, and how deep
it is down, down, under the falls. I should love to visit there again in
pleasant summer time. I hope to very much. Perhaps I shall. If I was
not so poor I certainly should go next summer, perhaps I may as it is,
for I want to see you all.

Good bye, your sister sends you many thanks and much love, and so
does your brother

Charles

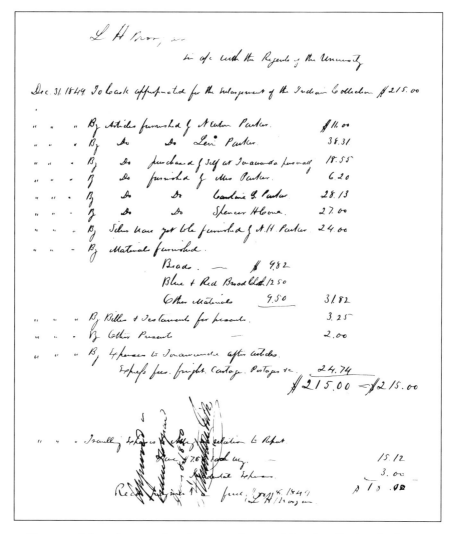

Figure 32. Morgan's accounting of expenses for assembling the collection for the state in 1849. Manuscript in Morgan Papers. (Courtesy of the Department of Rare Books and Special Collections, University of Rochester Library.)

Give much love also to my father and mother. I would send a belt of wampum with this if I had it.

C.

Before Morgan left for Albany, he wrote up a report on the objects he had obtained from the Parker family, using in part the information he had gathered while on his visit to Tonawanda. In his report of the previous year, Morgan had described the articles in the order they appeared in the list he had prepared. His 1849 report, however, does not follow that practice, and the list of articles sent does not provide an index to the report.

There is some evidence that this list of articles sent is a kind of running account of articles he received from the Parkers and thus reflects the order in which Morgan received them. The first items on the list are: three Indian drums, two turtle rattles, and four squash rattles. Only the turtle rattle is mentioned in Morgan's field notes, and this only a brief description of how the rattle is made. Since these articles are not described in field notes, it may be conjectured that Morgan received them before going to Tonawanda.

The same is true for the next items on the list: articles of clothing and those items more recently introduced, at least some of which were of types manufactured for sale to whites—pin cushions, needle books, work bags, and pocketbooks. These latter, those "of a mixed character," Morgan observed, "are not without a particular interest" as they "furnish no slight indication of artisan capacity."[17]

On some occasions, for the most part ceremonial ones, the Iroquois still dressed in "Indian costume," and Morgan made a particular effort to obtain two such complete outfits, one for a man and one for a woman. His desire to do so was dictated by his intent in making the collection: to provide examples of then-manufactured objects of Indian invention. Nonetheless, it may also be supposed that Morgan's interest was also influenced by his experience in the Grand Order of the Iroquois. At their meetings, as has been noted, members of the order dressed in Indian costume. This, in fact, Morgan regarded as essential, as he noted in a letter to a newly organized chapter:

In relation to costume, you are aware that every association, as Masons, Odd Fellows, fire and military companies, etc. all prepare uniforms;

they seem to lend dignity and interest to the organization, and in my way of viewing the subject, an Indian costume is indispensable and one of the most interesting departments of the order. Have the whole equipage, dress, bow, tomahawk, and head dress of feathers; the bow next to the coat goes the farthermost.[18]

"Indian dances" were also danced at the meetings of the order, and this may account for Morgan's interest in the dance so evident in *League of the Iroquois*.[19] Whatever the case, it is possible that Morgan obtained the complete costumes and some other articles as well as the drums and rattles before he went to Tonawanda in November 1849. It is also possible that the next items on the list were also obtained early. The baby frame, for example, is not described in his field notes, but like his descriptions of the dances, obviously was described based on personal observation of its use.

Most, if not all, of the articles listed in the middle half of the schedule (beginning with the implements for playing games and ending with the specimens of plants grown by the Seneca) are those that Morgan obtained by Tonawanda. The objects listed at the end, however, may be those that the Parkers sent after Morgan had returned to Rochester.

In the report itself, the objects are described in a different order than either that of the schedule of articles or in the field notes. No particular logic is apparent other than that objects of certain classes—the implements for playing games and those instruments used in dances, for example—are considered as a group. The order seems merely to be one of convenience.

Morgan apparently finished writing the report the day before he left for Albany: as published, it is dated December 31, 1849. In Albany, he promptly set about arranging the collection, revising the report, and instructing the engraver as to the wood cuts that were to accompany it.[20] The date of this trip seems to have been occasioned by the opening of the legislature. While there, Morgan had introduced into the state legislature a bill for the support and education of Indian students at the state normal school at Albany. The bill passed, and in June three Indians from Tonawanda—including Caroline and Newton Parker—were enrolled.[21]

While in Albany, Morgan may have also talked with the regents about enlarging the Indian collection. Whatever the case, the regents purchased Cornplanter's tomahawk from Ely Parker for $20.00.[22] Parker supplied a description of it in June (see appendix 2). The regents also advanced Morgan, on June 17, the sum of $250 for the purchase of another collection of

Indian manufactures. Later that month Morgan shipped to Albany a model of an Iroquois house made by William Parker and a large canoe.[23]

That year also Morgan determined to publish his "Letters on the Iroquois" with some additions—as he had mentioned to Squier he might sometime do. It was an idea that George Colton, editor of *The American Review*, had suggested to him when he accepted the "Letters" for publication.[24] It was perhaps with this in mind that Morgan had in the next years collected more information on Iroquois religion—a subject of only one of the "Letters."

He also now had his description of the objects he had collected for the state cabinet, which the regents had published in their third annual report with engravings of some of the objects by Richard H. Pease of Albany. Squier did not publish Morgan's Iroquois map in his *Aboriginal Monuments of the State of New York*, perhaps because in April he was appointed chargé d'affaires to Guatemala and left the country before Morgan finished it. Consequently, Morgan made arrangements with Pease to have a large engraving of the map made.

He also had Pease engrave two plates, undoubtedly from daguerreotypes: one of Levi Parker dressed in male costume and one of Caroline Parker dressed in the Indian costume she had made for the state collection (figs. 27 and 29).[25] In anticipation of their inclusion in Morgan's report on objects he was to collect in 1850, Pease also made engravings of the canoe and house model made by William Parker that had been sent to Albany.

With these materials Morgan proceeded to fashion a book on the Iroquois. He rearranged his "Letters on the Iroquois," adding information from his description of the objects collected in 1849 at Tonawanda and the illustrations from that report. He also added Parker's report on the 1848 council at Tonawanda that Parker had finally sent him, and wrote some new material including an introductory and concluding chapter.[26]

The book, *League of the Ho-dé-no-sau-nee, or Iroquois*, was published early in 1851. It did not include information Morgan gathered on two field trips that he had undertaken in the fall of 1850 to collect articles for the state. The first trip was to the Six Nations Reserve on the Grand River in Ontario. Morgan, accompanied by Ely Parker, left Rochester on the evening of October 28 and arrived at the reserve on the 30th. They stayed with Peter Smith, a Mohawk who was interpreter for the Six Nations council and a prosperous farmer, and his wife, Charlotte Brant, granddaughter of Joseph Brant.

While on the reserve, Morgan obtained a number of objects, some from noted individuals, but little information on their use. He obtained a shell breastplate from Peter Fishcarrier, who was in his sixties and the son of the noted nineteenth-century Cayuga chief, Fish Carrier. From John Jacobs, a leading Cayuga chief then in his seventies, Morgan purchased a carved cane, a fine burden strap, silver beads, and a plume of white heron feathers. From Catherine John, then a widow about sixty years old, he bought a quantity of wampum that had belonged to her father, the famed Mohawk chief Joseph Brant. These he later had made into a wampum belt at Tonawanda. Morgan also bought from her for $3.00 a copper breastplate mounted with silver—a relic he did not send to the state but kept for himself—that also had belonged to her father (see figs. 33 and 34).[27]

Morgan had arranged with the Parkers to supply him with articles, and on November 20 he wrote to Caroline, then attending Albany Normal School, about some of them.[28]

Figure 33. Gorget that belonged to Joseph Brant purchased by Morgan from Brant's daughter Catharine John in 1850. (Courtesy of the Rochester Museum and Science Center, Rochester, New York.)

*Figure 34. Portrait of Joseph Brant painted by Charles
Willson Peale, 1797. (Courtesy of the Independence National
Historical Park Collection, Philadelphia, Pennsylvania.)*

Rochester, November 20, 1850

Dear Friend

Your letter came yesterday. I enclose $2.00 as you requested, and
will send you $5.00 more sometime next month. As to the green over-
dress, as you have it with you, you may make it up as part of my dress.[29]
If you wish anything from Tonawanda, you must write to Maria
[Spencer Cone Parker's wife] to give it to me in December when I go
up there, and I will then send it to you by express.

I have some business with Mr. Pease in Albany but I cannot tell
when I shall go down. Tell Newton I am much obliged to him for his
letter, and hope he will mind [?] himself. He should attend to his writ-

ing and composition. Now is the time for him to learn to write our language, and he must take the greatest pains to be accurate. His grammar is not very correct as yet, but he will improve with practice.

> Your friend
> L.H. Morgan

In December Morgan went to Tonawanda as he had planned. He left Rochester on Christmas morning and arrived in time to have Christmas dinner with the Spencer Cone Parkers. He stayed with the William Parkers, and as he had the previous year, obtained information on the manufacture and use of the objects purchased.[30]

After returning to Rochester on December 30, Morgan shipped the objects he had collected that fall to Albany. They had not arrived by January 9, and the regents could only note in their annual report to the legislature that they "are understood at the date of this report to be on their way to this city" and that Morgan had promised a report on them.[31]

At the time Morgan was working on his report. It began, as had his two previous ones, with some general observations on the importance of making collections of ethnographic objects, followed by descriptions in no particular order of articles sent. Some of these were further examples of types of objects already furnished. Others were examples of types not previously sent.

Morgan completed his report on January 22 and sent it to the regents in time for their January 24 meeting, as the minutes of this meeting note:[32]

A report by Lewis H. Morgan, Esq. of Rochester, on the fabrics, inventions, implements and utensils of the Iroquois was presented, accompanied with a schedule of articles of Indian manufacture and art added to the Historical and Antiquarian Collection of the State Cabinet up to the present date.

Mr. Morgan, in a letter accompanying said Report, intimated a wish that it might be illustrated with engravings, as was done with his communication of last year, and it was understood that he had furnished an artist in this city, (Mr. R. H. Pease,) with a list of the same, a copy of which was presented.

Whereupon it was *Resolved* that the report of Mr. Morgan with the accompanying schedule of articles not actually in the State Cabinet or

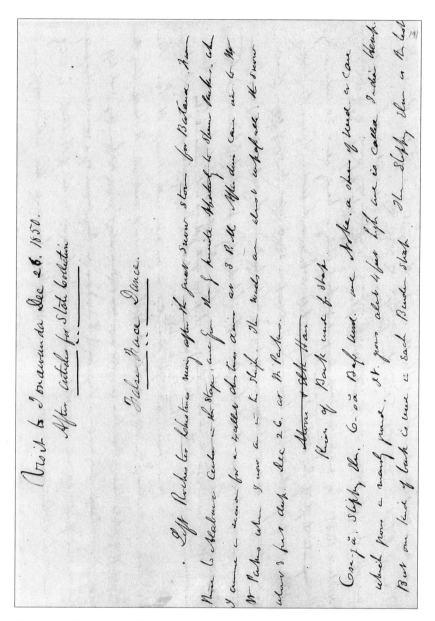

Figure 35. First page of Morgan's 1850 Tonawanda field notes. (Courtesy of the Department of Rare Books and Special Collections, University of Rochester Library.)

presently expected, be communicated to the Hon. the Senate, with a request that the same be appended to their Annual Report on the State Cabinet and considered part of it.

The Chancellor was further requested to intimate the wish of Mr. Morgan to the Legislature that his report might be illustrated with engravings, and that the list of these now before the Board be also communicated.

The senate rejected the regents' request in 1851. Only in the session the following year did they appropriate funds, which permitted publication of the Morgan report as an appendix to the regents' annual report for 1851.[33]

The appearance of the report marked the completion of Morgan's ethnographic study of the Iroquois begun in Albany eight years before when he first met and interviewed Ely Parker and Jemmy Johnson. With the publication of *League of the Iroquois* the previous year, Morgan wrote that he "laid aside the Indian subject to devote my time to my profession."[34] In August of that year he married his cousin, Mary Elizabeth Steele of Albany, and for six years did no further ethnographic work.

But Morgan's fascination with the Iroquois never left him. When in 1857 he took up again the study of ethnology, beginning the extensive comparative research that resulted in the publication of his monumental *Systems of Consanguinity and Affinity of the Human Family* and *Ancient Society,* it was to answer a question posed by his earlier field work: Why should the Iroquois have the kinship terminology and the clan organization they did? And when in 1881 he published *Houses and House-Life of the American Aborigines,* it was, in part, to answer the question: Why should the Iroquois have constructed the communal longhouses that they did?

During these years the state added little to its Indian collection. James Hall, who had been appointed curator of the cabinet in 1865 and director when the State Cabinet of Natural History became the New York State Museum of Natural History, was little interested in Indians; he preferred to devote his considerable energy and ability to his great love, paleontology. Hall resigned as director in 1894. Two years later, in 1896, the state leg-

Figure 36. Accounting of expenses in Morgan's 1850 Tonawanda field notes. (Courtesy of the Department of Rare Books and Special Collections, University of Rochester Library.)

Minnie's Schedule			List of Caubri	
1 Necklace of Beads	$1.50		1 Kilt Uhn. woman	5.00
1 Kilt Uhn. for child	4.00		1 Pair Leggins to model	1.50
1 Pr Leggins " do	1.50		1 Breech clouth	1.50
1 Breech clouth " do	1.50		1 small Kilt girl	4.00
2 Pair Moccasins 2/ each	4.00		1 Pair Leggins do	1.50
" for Material	.88		1 Breech clouth do	1.50
" Making Moccasin Belt	.75			15.00
for Band	$14.13			

		Levi Parker	
		1 Stone Pipe	0.50
		1 Stem Powder	.13
		1 Bow	.25
		" Timber for bow & making of	.38
1.25		1 Arming stone made f.A.A	6.25
25		1 do f Nichan	1.00
25		18 Arrows made f Nichan	.75
1.75		1 Bunches Feathers	.25
		1 Pipe Stem	.25
		1 Ayer Catch	.06
		1 Ayer Catch	.24
13.38		Mrs Sam Parker	8.04

Horace C Parker			Mrs William Parker	
1 Bail Frame Belt	$1.00		1 Bark Band	$1.50
1 do Red	1.00		1 do "	1.00
1 Red Mourn cloth case	.50		1 do "	.75
1 Satchell Blue Beaded	4.00		1 Sash Iron 8/	1.00
1 Pair Cushion	.50		1 " do 7/	.88
" for Materials	.38		1 do do 6/ 1 do of 12 3/	1.50
1 Deer Skin Kilt	8.50		1 Pair Husk Moccasins	.75
1 Pair Deer Skin Leggins	5.50		1 Holy Art. Skhir	.75
1 Belt Deer Skin	2.50		3 Ropes 6/ each	2.25
1 Pair Moccasins	3.00		2 Bark Ladles	.13
1 Do Plain	.75		5 Skin Skff. thn	.75
Extra allowance for Deer Skins	3.00		2 Bail Frames 8/	.25
1 Deer Skin belt for Shoulder with beads			1 Deer Hair Belt Red	1.25
1 Sheaf for Arrows	3.00		1 Bunches Shafts	1.00
1 Hair Ornament	1.50		1 Do Iron	.38
1 Shot Pouch	.30		1 Piece of Wampum	1.00
			6 Baskets	.75
1 Bark Pocket	.88		1 Tray injured	.25
	38.51		4 Sup. Stich. 11	.50
1 Bail Frame Band	1.00		2 Strips of corn. Red & White	.25
1 Bow	.75		1 Bunch of Split Corn	$6.75
10 Bunches 8/	1.25		2 do Split frine	
	$41.51		1 do Long frine	
	20.00		1 Burnt Stubby Orn Cornelie A $10.47	
	$21.51		3 Baskets	
	.25		1 Hoof	
	$21.76 Paid up		6 Baskets	.75
Silver Beads	1.50		Pk Corn Seive	
Beaded Material	2.00			7.87
Basket + Ladle	1.00			
Beaded 4 Child	.50			
	$1.76		Mrs Sam Parker 7/6	
	1.25			
	33.01			

12.37	30.00
14.13	18.76
$32.00	48.76
	15.00
74.00	63.76
32.00	
106.00	
43.00	

islature passed an act establishing an Indian section of the state museum, appropriating $5,000 for making and arranging the collection. An unsalaried honorary curator was appointed to do this work. Appropriations in subsequent years provided for the purchase of additional materials and for the publication of a series of monographs by William M. Beauchamp.[35]

This work was furthered by Nicholson Parker's grandson, Arthur C. Parker, who was born on the Cattaraugus reservation in the year Morgan died. Arthur's family moved to White Plains, New York, when he was about eleven, and he graduated from high school there in 1897. Two years later, intending to become a minister, he entered Dickinson Seminary in Williamsport, Pennsylvania, but left in 1903 without graduating. During these years, he frequented the American Museum of Natural History in New York City and had become friendly with the staff. One was the eminent anthropologist Frederick Ward Putnam, curator of the Peabody Museum and professor of American archaeology and ethnology at Harvard, who at the time was also curator of anthropology at the American Museum. In the summers of 1903 and 1904, Parker participated in archaeological expeditions under Putnam's direction. Then, in 1904, he began working for the New York State Department of Education, receiving a fee for manuscripts on the Iroquois sent to the state library and for specimens collected for the state museum. Two years later he became archaeologist at the state museum, a civil service position.[36]

Parker had more than a casual interest in the collections made by his family in 1849 and 1850, and in 1910 had these and others installed in exhibition cases in the fourth-floor corridors of the Capitol building. The move was to have disastrous consequences. Early in the morning of March 29, 1911, a fire broke out in the assembly library. It spread to the state library and from there to other nearby rooms. Although not all the building burned, the Morgan collection was largely destroyed (see fig. 37). As Parker later reported it:

> In the New York State Capitol conflagration of March 29 the archaeological and ethnological collections of the State Museum were almost totally destroyed by fire and water. The collections were installed in vertical wall and square alcove cases about the corridors at the head of the western staircase. The location seemed to insure singular protection from fire, there being nothing inflammable in the vicinity save the molding that held the cases together. The damage seems to have been

Figure 37. Fourth-floor corridor on the southwestern staircase of the New York State Capitol building after the 1911 fire. The heat of the fire caused the stones to fall from the sides and ceiling. The cases contained Indian artifacts. (Courtesy of the New York State Temporary State Commission on the Restoration of the Capitol, Albany, New York.)

done by the long sheets of flame that burst through the large corridor windows of the library bindery on one side and of the Education Department offices on the other. The immense amount of inflammable material there fed the flames once established and the draft caused by the breaking of the heavy plate windows that opened out into the hall about the staircase carried the blast directly against the cases, shattering the glass and exposing the specimens within. The archaeological cases suffered most from breakage brought about by the crumbling of the sandstone ceilings that had been subjected to the intense heat. The falling of the ceilings in great blocks broke the shelves that had so far resisted the fire and spilled the specimens into the water and debris. The continual dropping of masses of cracked rock from the walls made work of rescuing valuable objects most hazardous. However, despite the choking smoke, the sudden bursts of heat, and the falling walls the majority of the more valuable objects, untouched by the fire, were carried to safety.

The ethnological exhibits consisted principally of three large collections; one made by Lewis H. Morgan before 1854 and embracing some 200 objects, the Harriet Maxwell Converse collection of about 350 specimens, and the collection made by Arthur C. Parker embracing nearly 200 rare objects, exclusive of silver ornaments. The famous Morgan collection of old Iroquois textiles and decorated fabrics went up in the first blast of flame, and the cases were burned to their bases. About 50 Morgan specimens were in the office of the archaeologist of the museum for study purposes, and fortunately have been preserved. The Converse collection of silver articles was rescued intact.

Many of the less inflammable objects were rescued during the fire and carried out of the danger zone. None of the wampum belts of the Six Nations was injured.

One of the odd features of the calamity was that hardly a single object connected with the ceremonies of the Iroquois totemic cults or the religious rites was injured. The hair of the 30 medicine masks that hung in a line across the westernmost cases was not even singed.

Of the 10,000 articles on exhibition, including about 3500 flints, only 512 have been identified by their catalog numbers. One thousand other articles, more or less ruined by the action of flame and water, will entail a great deal of work to identify. In this connection it is interesting to note that catalog numbers applied directly to the surface of the stone, bone, or clay specimen with waterproof ink, withstood the action of fire and water better than the numbers painted on white varnish or on paper labels. Even when the object had been considerably heated the ink number on the surface was still legible. Paper labels proved valueless especially those with typewritten numbers. Those with numbers written in waterproof ink came through better.[37]

Fortunately, Morgan's descriptions are also preserved, as valuable in their own way as the objects themselves.

II
. . . . .

The Morgan Collection

6
· · · · ·

Classification of Articles
in the Collection

Written information on the approximately five hundred objects that Morgan sent to the state in the years 1848–1850 is contained in three types of sources: (1) the lists of articles sent that were published in the several Regents reports; (2) the long reports, also published by the regents in their annual reports, that Morgan wrote describing the articles sent in each of his three major shipments (herein referred to as Regents reports); and (3) Morgan's field notes, now in the University of Rochester Library, of his trips to Tonawanda in 1849 and 1850 and his trip to the Six Nations Reserve in 1850 to collect articles for the state. The lists of articles sent are in appendix 1, the field notes are in chapter 7, and the Regents reports are in chapter 8.

Each of these sources contains some information not in the others. Most if not all of the lists of articles sent apparently represent a kind of shipping list that Morgan sent with the objects and provide an inventory of the articles in the collection. In these lists the ethnographic specimens are grouped into categories ("species"): the Seneca name for the type of article is first, then the English name, followed by the number of specimens sent. Many of Morgan's field notes and reports are similarly organized, with the Seneca and English names of objects serving as headings for their descriptions. Although some of these descriptions contain information on size, material, and manufacture of objects, they are more often accounts of the uses of the objects. The descriptions in the reports are not identical to those in the field notes. In writing these reports, Morgan did not merely copy his field notes, but described each type of object anew.

The sheer number of objects Morgan collected and the fact that information on any particular type of artifact appears in several places makes some classification imperative. The anthropological study of material culture has yet to produce its Linnaeus, and there is no generally accepted system of classification. In fact, such classifications as have been devised can scarcely be said to be systematic ones at all. For the most part, they are ad hoc classifications—a listing of convenient categories employing no consistent criteria and lacking logical plan.[1]

Morgan's data suggest that the articles of Iroquois manufacture that he obtained can be conveniently divided into two principal kinds, both broadly defined: "containers" and "tools." The category "containers" can be subdivided into two types on the basis of what they "contain": those for people (houses, cradleboards, and dress) and those for objects (trays, baskets, bags, and the like). The category "tools" can be subdivided into eight types on the basis of what functional activity they are used for (war and hunting, transportation, fire-making, smoking, food preparation, singing, gaming, and religious ceremonies).[2]

This taxonomy underlies the Classification List of Articles in the Collection, that, among other things, serves as an index to the next section, Synopsis of Ethnographic Articles Sent to the State. This synopsis gives for each "species" of object the number of specimens of that species sent and when—information taken from the lists of articles sent. It also indicates where the objects are illustrated and described in Morgan's field notes and Regents reports; for this reason, it serves as an index to the field notes in chapter 7 and Regents reports in chapter 8.

Synopsis of Ethnographic Articles Sent to the State

This synopsis lists all of the ethnographic articles Morgan sent to the state in the years 1848–50. Types of objects are listed in the order given in the classification list (opposite). The Seneca name and English translation recorded by Morgan for each type of object is given first. In brackets immediately following is a modern transcription of the Seneca word and English translation as provided by Marianne Mithun and Wallace Chafe. (Some Seneca words Morgan recorded are not now known and some cannot now

Classification List of Ethnographic Articles Sent to the State

House
Cradle and cradleboard
Dress
   Traditional dress
   Basic items of dress
      Breechcloth
      Kilt
      Overdress
      Skirt
      Blanket
      Leggings
      Pantalettes
      Moccasins and moccasin-making
      Headdress
   Bands
      Belts
      Knee, wrist, arm, and hair bands
      Hat bands
      Wampum strings and belts
   Ornaments
      Necklaces
      Grass shoulder ornament
      Medals and breastplates
      Silver crosses
      Silver brooches, earrings, and finger rings
      Hair ornament
Containers for things
   Containers of bark and wood
   Containers of basketry
   Containers of skin
   Containers of cloth
War and hunting tools
   Weapons
      Spear
      War club
      Tomahawk

Classification List (continued)

       Scalping knife
       Bow and arrows
       Quiver
       Blowgun and darts
     Traps
       Bird trap
       Fish trap
   Transportation tools
     Cane
     Snowshoes
     Corn-husk overshoe
     Rope and burden straps
     Burden frame
     Saddle
     Canoe and paddles
   Fire-making tools
   Smoking tools
     Tobacco
     Pipes
   Cooking tools
     Food
     Mortar and pestle
     Ladles and spoons
     Hominy stirrer
     Bread turner
   Singing tools
     Drum
     Rattles
       Turtle rattle
       Squash rattle
       Horn rattle
       Knee rattle
     Flute
   Gaming tools
     Peach stones and bowl
     Bone dice

Lacrosse stick and ball
Snow snake
Snow boat
Javelin
Ceremonial items
    False Face mask
    New Year's shovel
Miscellaneous
    Ax handle
    Splint broom
    Eye showerer
    Finger catcher

---

be determined from Morgan's transcription. In such cases, no modern transcription and translation is given.)

The entries under each name include the following information: number of objects of this type sent; year sent; and whether or not the object is illustrated and/or described in Morgan's field notes and Regents reports, and if so, in which ones. Additionally, if the description of the object in *League of the Iroquois* is identical or almost identical to that in the third Regents report, the reference to *League* is enclosed in parentheses. For example, "Described in the 1849 report (*League* pp. 390–91)" indicates that the wording of the description of this type of object on pages 390–91 of *League of the Iroquois* is identical or almost identical to that in the third Regents report. If the two descriptions are not identical, the reference to *League* is not enclosed in parentheses. For example, "Described in 1849 report and in *League,* pp. 263–64" indicates that the wording of the description in *League of the Iroquois* is not the same as that in the third Regents report.

Illustrations in *League of the Iroquois* are not indicated. Almost all the plates and cuts in *League of the Iroquois* are used in the third Regents report, with these exceptions: the plate illustrating the bark house and that of a bark canoe, both of which later appeared in the fifth Regents report; the engraving of Levi Parker and Caroline Parker in costume (see figs. 27 and 29); illustrations of two pipes in the second Regents report (see figs. 22 and 23); and illustrations of an "earthen vessel" (p. 357) and a "stone tomahawk" (p. 359).

Synopsis of Ethnographic Articles Sent to the State

HOUSE

Gä-no-sote, or bark house [*kanǫhso:t* 'house']

Bark house model made by William Parker sent in 1850. Illustrated in 1850 report, Plate 20. Bark house sketch in 1849 field notes (see fig. 40 this volume). Described in 1850 field notes and in 1850 report (*League*, pp. 317–19).

CRADLE AND CRADLEBOARD

Ga-yuh, or splint cradle [*ka:ǫyǫ'* 'setting cradle']

Splint cradle sent in 1849. Neither illustrated nor described.

Ga-on-seh, or baby frame [*kę:ǫshæ'* 'cradleboard']

Baby frame sent in 1849. Illustrated in 1849 report, Plate 16. Described in 1849 report (*League*, pp. 390–91).

Baby frame sent in 1850. Illustrated and described in 1850 report.

Gä-swä-hos-ha, or baby frame belt [probably, *ka:wáhashæ'* 'belt,' or literally, 'it is tied around the waist'] and Ga-nose-gă, or baby frame belt [*kanǫhsęhka:h*, literally, 'it has a tie on it']

Baby frame belts described in 1850 field notes.

Three baby frame belts sent in 1850. One illustrated in 1850 report, Plate 2. Described in 1850 report.

DRESS

Traditional dress

Complete men's costume illustrated in *League*, frontispiece (fig. 27 this volume). (Engraving is of Levi Parker wearing articles collected in 1849 that are separately illustrated and described in 1849 report and in *League*.)

Complete women's costume illustrated in *League*, following p. 148 (fig. 29 this volume). (Engraving is of Caroline Parker wearing articles collected in 1849 that are separately illustrated and described in 1849 report and in *League*.)

Men's and women's dress described in 1849 report. Men's and women's former dress described in 1850 field notes. Beadwork described in 1850 field notes.

Basic items of dress

Gä-kä, or breechcloth [*ka'kha:a'* 'skirt']

Breechcloth sent in 1849. Illustrated in 1849 report, Plate 15. Described in 1849 report.

Gä-kä-ah, or kilt [*ka'kha:a'* 'skirt']

Kilt sent in 1849. Illustrated in 1849 report, Plate 7. Described in 1849 report and in *League*, pp. 263–64.

Kilt sent in 1850. Illustrated in 1850 report, Plate 9. Described in 1850 report.

Ah-de-a-dä-we-sä, or overdress [*atyá'tawí'shæ'* 'smock']

Overdress sent in 1849. Illustrated in 1849 report, Plates 6 and 6a. Described in 1849 report and in *League*, pp. 385–86.

Overdress for adult and overdress for child sent in 1850. Neither illustrated nor described.

Gä-kä-ah, or skirt [*ka'kha:a'* 'skirt']

Skirt sent in 1849. Illustrated in 1849 report, Plate 5. Described in 1849 report and in *League*, pp. 384–85.

Two skirts sent in 1850. One illustrated in 1850 report, Plate 17. Described in 1850 report.

E-yose, or blanket [*i:yo:s* 'blanket, shawl']

Broadcloth blanket described in 1849 report (*League*, p. 386), but not on list of articles sent.

Broadcloth blanket sent in 1850. Illustrated in 1850 report, Plate 16. Described in 1850 report.

Gise-hă, or legging [*káishæ'* 'leggings']

> Pair of leggings for male sent in 1849. Illustrated in 1849 report, Plate 8. Described in 1849 report and in *League,* pp. 264–65.

> Deerskin leggings sent in 1850. Illustrated in 1850 report, Plate 10. Described in 1850 field notes and in 1850 report.

Gise-hă, or pantalette [*káishæ'* 'leggings']

> Pair of leggings for female sent in 1849. Illustrated in 1849 report, Plate 4. Described in 1849 report and in *League,* p. 385.

> Two pairs of leggings for female sent in 1850. Neither illustrated nor described.

Ah-tä-quä-o-weh, or moccasin [*ahtáhkwa'ǫːweh* 'native shoe, moccasin']

> Two pairs of decorated moccasins sent in 1849: pair of moccasins for male, illustrated in 1849 report, Plate 1; pair of moccasins for female, illustrated in 1849 report, Plate 2. Described in 1849 report (*League,* pp. 359–62) and *League,* p. 265.

> One pair of decorated moccasins sent in 1850. Illustrated in 1850 report, Plate 11. Described in 1850 field notes and in 1850 report.

> Two pairs of plain moccasins sent in 1850. Illustrated and described in 1850 report.

O-je-she-wä-tä, or deer's brains and moss [*ojí'syǫwǫhta'* 'brain']

> Cake of deer's brains and moss for tanning deerskin sent in 1849. Description of tanning deer skins in 1849 field notes.

Gä-wä, or moccasin awl [*kęːwęː'* 'awl' also 'wire, pin, needle, nail']

> Moccasin awl sent in 1850. Illustrated and described in 1850 report.

O-ha-dä, or porcupine quill [*ohé'ta'* 'porcupine quill']

> Porcupine quills sent in 1850. Illustrated in 1850 report, Plate 14. Described in 1850 field notes and in 1850 report.

Gus-to-weh, or headdress [*kastoːwæ'* 'headdress']

> Headdress sent in 1848. Neither illustrated nor described.

Headdress sent in 1849. Illustrated in 1849 report, Plate 3. Described in 1849 report (*League*, p. 264).

Headdress sent in 1850. Illustrated and described in 1850 report.

Bands

Gä-geh-tä, or belt [*kakéhta'* 'sash']

Three belts sent in 1849. One illustrated in 1849 report, Plate 9. Described in 1849 report and in *League*, p. 265.

De-con-deä-da-hust-tä, or belt for female costume [Seneca word not recognized now]

Belt sent in 1849. Neither illustrated nor described.

Yunt-ka-to-dä-tä, or shoulder belt [*yǫtkéhtotæːhta'* 'shoulder belt,' or literally, 'one uses it to put over the shoulders']

Shoulder belt sent in 1850. Illustrated in 1850 report, Plate 12. Described in 1850 field notes and in 1850 report.

Da-yunt-wä-hos-tä, or waist belt [*teyǫthwahástha'* 'waist belt,' or literally, 'one uses it to tie around oneself']

Waist belt sent in 1850. Illustrated in 1850 report, Plate 13. Described in 1850 field notes and in 1850 report.

Gä-gë-ne-as-heh, or knife and belt [*kakánya'shæ'* 'knife']

Knife and belt sent in 1850. Illustrated and described in 1850 report.

Gä-geh-tä yen-che-no-hos-ta-ta, or knee band [*kakéhta'* 'sash'; *yǫtsínǫhǫstha'* 'legband,' or literally, 'one uses it to tie around the leg']

Pair of knee bands sent in 1849. Illustrated in 1849 report, Plate 10. Described in 1849 report and in *League*, p. 265.

Yen-nis-ho-quä-hos-ta, or wrist band [*yęnęsho'kwáhastha'* 'bracelet,' or literally, 'one uses it to tie around the wrist']

Pair of wrist bands sent in 1849. Illustrated in 1849 report, Plate 10. Described in 1849 report and in *League*, p. 265.

Pair of silver wrist bands sent in 1849. Neither illustrated nor described.

Pair of wrist bands of beads sent in 1850. Neither illustrated nor described.

Gä-geh-tä yen-nis-hä-hos-ta, or arm band [*kakéhta'* 'sash'; *yęnęshahástha'* 'arm band,' or literally, 'one uses it to tie around the arm']

Pair of arm bands sent in 1849. Illustrated in 1849 report, Plate 10. Described in 1849 report and in *League,* p. 265.

Arm band of deer tail described in 1850 field notes.

To-do-war-she-so-wä, or ribbon for hair [Seneca word not recognized now]

Ribbon for hair sent in 1849. Neither illustrated nor described.

Dä-yase-ta-hos-ta, or silver hat band [Seneca word not recognized now]

Silver hat band sent in 1849. Neither illustrated nor described.

Silver hat band sent in 1850. Neither illustrated nor described.

Da-ya-he-gwä-hus-ta, or hat band of brooches [*teyéhikwáhastha'* 'one uses it to tie around the hat']

Hat band of brooches sent in 1850. Neither illustrated nor described.

Ote-ko-a, or string of wampum [*otkóæ'* 'wampum (string)'] and Gä-sweh-dä ote-ko-ă, or wampum belt [*kaswęhta'* 'wampum, wampum belt'; *otkóæ'* 'wampum (string)']

String of wampum and wampum belt sent in 1850. Illustrated in 1850 report, Plate 1. Described in *League,* pp. 387–88, in 1850 field notes, and in 1850 report.

Wampum necklace sent in 1849. Neither illustrated nor described.

Ornaments

Gä-de-us-ha, or necklace [*katę'ashæ'* 'what one puts over oneself']

Necklace sent in 1849. Neither illustrated nor described.

Wampum necklace with silver cross sent in 1849. Illustrated in 1849 report, Plate 3. Described in 1849 report and in *League,* p. 387.

Glass bead necklace sent in 1850. Illustrated in 1850 report, Plate 7. Described in 1850 report.

O-sta-quä, or bead necklace [*ostéo'kwa'* 'bead']

Bead necklace sent in 1850. Neither illustrated nor described.

O-wis-tä-no-o o-sta-o-qua, or round silver beads [*o:wistano:o'* 'silver,' or literally, 'precious metal'; *ostéo'kwa'* 'bead']

Round silver beads sent in 1850. Illustrated in 1850 report, Plate 7. Described in 1850 field notes and in 1850 report.

Ont-wis-tä-ne-un-da-qua, or silver beads [*yǫthwístaniyǫtáhkwa'* 'silver beads, pendants,' or literally, 'one uses it to hang metal/silver']

Silver beads sent in 1850. Illustrated in 1850 report, Plate 6. Described in 1850 field notes and in 1850 report.

Gä-te-äs-hä gä-a-o-tä-ges, or grass shoulder ornament [Seneca words not recognized now]

Grass shoulder ornament sent in 1850. Illustrated in 1850 report, Plate 8. Described in *League*, p. 387, in 1850 field notes, and in 1850 report.

Gä-nuh-sä, or sea-shell medal [Seneca word not recognized now]

Sea-shell medal sent in 1849. Illustrated and described in 1849 report (*League*, pp. 388–89).

Tuesh-tä-ga-tas-tä, or tin breastplate [Seneca word not recognized now]

Tin breastplate sent in 1849. Illustrated in 1849 report. [In *League*, p. 388 this breastplate is identified as being made of silver and as having the Seneca name Ont-wis-da-ga-dust-ha (see Seneca word for Brant's and any medal in 1850 Grand River Field Notes, chapter 7.)]

Gä-no-sä, or conch shell breastplate [Seneca word not recognized now]

Conch-shell breastplate sent in 1850. Illustrated in 1850 report, Plate 14. Described in 1850 field notes and 1850 report.

Da-gä-yä-sont, or silver cross [*tekáyahsǫ:t* 'cross']

Four silver crosses sent in 1850. One illustrated in 1850 report, Plate 4. Described in 1850 report.

An-ne-as-gă, or silver broach [*ę:nyáskæ:*' 'brooch']

> Forty-six brooches of various sizes sent in 1850. One illustrated in 1850 report, Plate 5. Described in 1850 report.

Ah-was-hă, or earring [*a'wáshæ:*' 'earring']

> Pair of earrings sent in 1849. Illustrated and described in 1849 report.

> Pair of earrings sent in 1850. Illustrated in 1850 report, Plate 5. Described in 1850 report.

Au-ne-ä-hus-ha, or finger ring [*ę'nyáhashæ*' 'finger ring,' or literally, 'what one ties around the finger']

> Four finger rings sent in 1850. Illustrated in 1850 report, Plate 5. Described in 1850 report.

A-ne-us-hä-nen-dok-tä-quä, or hair ornament [Seneca word not recognized now]

> Hair ornament sent in 1850. Neither illustrated nor described in 1850 report. Described in 1850 field notes.

CONTAINERS FOR THINGS

Containers of bark and wood

Gä-o-wä, or bark tray [*ka'ǫ:wǫ*' 'tray, trough']

> Bark tray donated in 1849. Neither illustrated nor described.

> Three bark trays sent in 1849. One illustrated in 1849 report. Described in 1849 report (*League,* p. 367).

> Six bark trays sent in 1850. Not illustrated. Described in 1850 report.

Gä-na-quä, or bark barrel [*ka'nǫhkwa*' 'barrel']; Gä-snä gä-ose-hă, or bark barrel [*kasno*' 'bark' *ka'áshæ*' 'basket']

> Bark barrel sent in 1849. Not illustrated. Described in 1849 report and in *League,* pp. 366.

> Three bark barrels sent in 1850. One illustrated in 1850 report. Described in 1850 field notes and in 1850 report.

Gä-oo-wä, or bark sap tub [*ka'ǫ:wǫ'* 'tray, trough']

> Three bark sap tubs sent in 1849. One illustrated in 1849 report. Described in 1849 field notes and in 1849 report (*League*, 369–70).

> Bark sap tub sent in 1850. Neither illustrated nor described.

Containers of basketry

> Basket-making described in *League*, pp. 382–83, in 1850 field notes, and in 1850 report.

Splint baskets

> Two splint baskets donated in 1849. Neither illustrated nor described.

Gase-hǎ, or covered basket [*ka'áshæ'* 'basket']

> Covered basket sent in 1849. Neither illustrated nor described.

> Covered basket sent in 1850. Neither illustrated nor described.

Ta-gase-hǎ, or market basket [*teká'ashæ:oh* 'cross basket,' or literally, 'crossways']

> Market basket sent in 1849. Neither illustrated nor described.

> Market basket sent in 1850. Neither illustrated nor described.

O-gä-kä-ah, or open-work basket [*okáhkao'* 'it has bigger holes in it']

> Three open-work baskets sent in 1849. Neither illustrated nor described.

> Open-work basket sent in 1850. Neither illustrated nor described.

Ne-us-tase-ah, or basket sieve [Seneca word not recognized now]; Yowonk-tä, or basket sieve [*yǫwǫ:ktha'*, literally, 'one uses it to sift']

> Basket sieve sent in 1849. Not illustrated. Described in 1849 field notes.

> Basket sieve sent in 1850. Neither illustrated nor described.

O-ne-ose-to-wa-nes, or basket sieve [*o'néyostowanǫs* 'coarse kernels']

> Basket sieve sent in 1849. Not illustrated. Described in 1849 field notes.

Yun-des-ho-yon-dä-gwat-hä, or pop corn [parched corn] sieve [Seneca word not recognized now]

Pop [parched] corn sieve sent in 1850. Illustrated in 1850 report. Described in 1850 field notes and in 1850 report.

Gä-nose-hă, or husk and flag basket for coarse meal [Seneca word not recognized now]

Four husk and flag baskets sent in 1849. Not illustrated. Described in 1849 field notes and in 1849 report.

O-no-ne-ä gos-ha-dä, or corn-husk salt bottle [*ono:nya'* 'corn husk'; *kashé'ta'* 'bottle']

Two corn-husk salt bottles sent in 1849. Illustrated in 1849 report. Described in 1849 field notes.

Ya-nuh-ta-dä-quä, or toilet basket [*yenǫhtatáhkwa'* 'comb basket,' or literally, 'one uses it to put comb(s) in']

Toilet basket sent in 1849. Neither illustrated nor described.

Containers of skin

Gis-tak-he-ä, or skin bag [*ojísta'thya'* 'speckled fawn']; Gis-tät-he-o gä-yä-ah, or fawn skin bag [*ojísta'thya'* 'specked fawn'; *kaya:a'* 'bag']

Speckled fawn skin bag sent in 1849. Neither illustrated nor described.

Speckled fawn skin bag sent in 1850. Illustrated and described in 1850 report.

Bearskin bag (mislabeled on 1849 list as Gis-tak-he-ä) [*ojísta'thya'* 'speckled fawn']

Bearskin bag sent in 1849. Neither illustrated nor described.

Yun-ga-sa, or tobacco pouch [*yǫke:shæ'* 'pocket']

Four tobacco pouches sent in 1849. One illustrated in 1849 report. Described in 1849 report (*League,* p. 380).

Tobacco pouch made of the foot and leg of a snapping turtle sent in 1850. Neither illustrated nor described.

A-squă-dä-qua, or shot pouch [Seneca word not recognized now]

Shot pouch sent in 1850. Neither illustrated nor described.

Containers of cloth

Gä-yä-ah, or work bag/satchel [*kaya:a'* 'bag']

Five work bags sent in 1849. One illustrated in 1849 report, Plate 11.

Work bag sent in 1850. Not illustrated.

Satchel sent in 1850. Illustrated in 1850 report, Plate 18. Described in 1850 field notes (identical description in 1850 report).

Got-gwen-dä, or pocketbook [*katkwę'ta'* 'pocketbook, wallet, purse, suit-case']

Six pocketbooks sent in 1849. One illustrated in 1849 report, Plate 14.

Ya-wa-o-dä-quä, or needle book/pin cushion [*yę:wéotahkwa'* 'needle book, pin cushion,' or literally, 'one stands pins/needles with it']

Five needle books sent in 1849. One illustrated in 1849 report, Plate 12.

Three pin cushions sent in 1849. One illustrated in 1849 report, Plate 13.

Two pin cushions sent in 1850. One illustrated in 1850 report, Plate 19.

WAR AND HUNTING TOOLS

Weapons

Gä-se-gwă, or spear [*kahse:kwa'* 'spear']

Spear sent in 1850. Illustrated and described in 1850 report.

Ga-neah, or war club [Seneca word not recognized now]

War club used in war dance donated in 1848. Described in 1848 report.

Gä-je-wä, or war club [*kají:wa'* 'war club, hammer, mallet']

Four war clubs with ball heads sent in 1849. One illustrated in 1849 field notes (see fig. 39 this volume). Two illustrated in 1849 report. Described in 1849 field notes and in 1849 report (*League*, pp. 362–63).

War club with ball head sent in 1850. Neither illustrated nor described.

Gä-ne-u-ga-dus-ha, or war club [*kanǫ'kéotashæ'* 'horn war club']

> Two war clubs with deer horn spike sent in 1849. One illustrated in 1849 field notes (see fig. 39 this volume). Another illustrated in 1849 report. Described in 1849 field notes and in 1849 report (*League*, p. 363).

> War club with steel blade sent in 1850. Illustrated and described in 1850 report.

O-sque-sont, or tomahawk [*a'skwíhsa'* 'axe'; *a'skwíhsǫ:t* 'ax is attached to it']

> Two tomahawks (one used in bear hunt) sent in 1849. One illustrated in 1849 report. Described in 1849 report (*League*, pp. 363–64).

Da-ya-no-a-quä-tä gä-ga-neä-sä, or scalping knife [*teyenǫehkwatha'* 'one scalps with it'; *kakánya'shæ'* 'knife']

> Two scalping knives sent in 1849. Neither illustrated nor described.

Wä-a-no, or bow [*wa'ę:nǫ'* 'bow'] and Gä-no, or arrow [*ka'nǫ'* 'arrow']

> Two bows and six arrows donated in 1849. Neither illustrated nor described.

> Six bows and fifty arrows sent in 1849. One bow and four arrows illustrated in 1849 report. Described in 1849 report (*League*, pp. 305–07).

> One bow and eighteen arrows (in quiver) sent in 1850. Neither illustrated nor described.

> One arrow with deer horn point sent in 1850. Illustrated and described in 1850 report.

Gä-däs-hă, or sheaf for arrows [*ka'ta:shæ'* 'quiver']

> Sheaf for carrying arrows sent in 1850. Illustrated in 1850 report. Described in 1850 field notes and in 1850 report.

Gä-ga-an-dä, or air gun [*káeo'ta'* 'blowgun, gun'] and Gä-no, or arrow (for air gun) [*ka'nǫ'* 'arrow']

> Air gun (blowgun) and two arrows (darts) sent in 1849. Blowgun and one dart illustrated in 1849 report. Described in 1849 field notes and in 1849 report (*League*, p. 379).

Traps

Bird trap

> Bird trap for catching quails sent in 1850. Illustrated and described in 1850 report.

Yont-kä-do-quä, or basket fish net [*yǫtkéhtahkwaˀ* 'shoulder basket,' or literally, 'one uses it to carry over the shoulders']

> Basket fish net sent in 1850. Illustrated in 1850 report. Described in 1850 field notes and in 1850 report.

TRANSPORTATION TOOLS

Ah-dä-dis-hă, or cane [*atáˀtishæˀ* 'cane,' or literally, 'what one leans on']

> Two canes sent in 1850. One illustrated in 1850 report. Described in *League*, p. 384 and in 1850 report.

Gä-weh-ga-ă, or snowshoe [*oːwę́ˀkæːˀ* 'wood, splint'; *teyéːwę́ˀkeotáhkwaˀ* 'snowshoe, ski']

> Three pairs of snowshoes sent in 1849. One snowshoe illustrated in 1849 field notes (see fig. 41 this volume) and in 1849 report. Described in 1849 field notes and in 1849 report (*League*, pp. 376–77).

O-tä-quă-osh-ha, or snowshoe of splint [*ahtáhkwaˀ* 'shoe']

> One pair snowshoes of splint sent in 1849. Neither illustrated nor described.

O-no-ne-ä-dä-quä, or corn-husk overshoe [*oːníyehtáhkwaˀ*, literally, 'it is used for making it solid']

> One pair of husk moccasins sent in 1850. Not illustrated. Described in 1850 field notes.

Ose-hä, or O-să, or basswood [*oːosæˀ* 'basswood']

> Skein of basswood bark strings sent in 1849. Not illustrated. Described in 1849 field notes and in 1849 report (*League*, pp. 364–65).

Strips of basswood bark and one skein of basswood filaments sent in 1850. Skein of basswood filaments illustrated in 1850 report. Described in 1850 report.

Ose-gă, or slippery elm [*ó:skæ*' 'slippery elm']

Skein of slippery elm strings sent in 1849. Not illustrated. Described in 1849 field notes and in 1849 report (*League,* pp. 364–65).

Strips of slippery elm bark, one skein of slippery elm thread, one skein of colored slippery elm thread, and one skein of slippery elm thread twisted into strings sent in 1850. Skein of slippery elm filaments illustrated in 1850 report. Described in 1850 field notes and in 1850 report.

Gä-sken-dä or Gä-a-sken-dä, or bark rope [*káiskę'ta*' 'it is braided']

Bark rope of slippery elm sent in 1849. Not illustrated. Described in 1849 field notes and in 1849 report (*League,* pp. 364–65).

Three bark ropes sent in 1850. One illustrated in 1850 report. Described in 1850 field notes and in 1850 report.

Deer's hair

Deer's hair used for making burden straps, etc., sent in 1850. Neither illustrated nor described.

Gus-hä-ah, or burden strap [*kasha:a*' 'strap, halter, cord']

One burden strap of basswood and one burden strap of slippery elm sent in 1849. One illustrated in 1849 report. Described in 1849 field notes and in 1849 report (*League,* pp. 364–65).

One burden strap of basswood, one deer hair burden strap, one moose hair burden strap, two bark and moose hair burden straps, and one bark and worsted burden strap sent in 1850. Moose hair burden strap illustrated in 1850 report, Plate 3. Described in 1850 field notes and in 1850 report.

Gä-ne-ko-wä-ah, or burden frame [Seneca word not recognized now]

Burden frame sent in 1850. Illustrated in 1850 report. Described in 1850 field notes and 1850 report.

Ah-da-dä-quä, or saddle [*atætahkwa'* 'saddle,' or literally, 'one uses it to perch on']

> Saddle sent in 1849. Illustrated in 1849 field notes (see fig. 38 this volume) and in 1849 report. Described in 1849 field notes and in 1849 report (*League,* pp. 377–79).

Ga-snä gä-o-wo, or bark canoe [*kasnǫ'* 'bark'; *ka:ǫwǫ'* 'boat']

> Bark canoe sent in 1850. Illustrated in 1850 report, Plate 15. Described in 1849 field notes and in 1850 report (*League,* pp. 367–69).

Gä-gä-we-sä, or paddle [*kakáwihsa'* 'shovel']

> Six paddles sent in 1850.

FIRE-MAKING TOOLS

Dä-ya-yä-dǎ-ga-ne-at-hä, or bow and shaft for striking fire [Seneca word not recognized now]

> Bow drill for making fire sent in 1849. Illustrated and described in 1849 report (*League,* pp. 381–82).

Gä-gis-dä, or steel, flint, and punk for striking fire [*kaji:sta'* 'spark, fire, ember, coal']

> Steel, flint, and punk for striking fire sent in 1849. Neither illustrated nor described.

SMOKING TOOLS

O-yeh-quä-ä-weh, or Indian tobacco [*oyę'kwa'ǫ:weh* 'native tobacco']

> Indian tobacco sent in 1850. Not illustrated. Described in 1849 report (*League,* pp. 374–76) and in 1850 field notes.

Sumac

> Bunch of sumac sent in 1850. Not illustrated. Use described in 1849 report (*League,* pp. 375–76).

Ah-so-guä-tä, or pipe [*ashókwahta'* 'pipe']

> Pipe made from a cyathophyllum sent in 1849. Illustrated in 1849 report, Plate 17.

> Five pipes sent in 1850. Three illustrated and described in 1850 report.

COOKING TOOLS

> Quantity of white corn donated in 1849. Neither illustrated nor described.

> Seventeen small square baskets numbered 1 to 17 containing specimens of several varieties of corn, beans, squashes, tobacco, dried corn, etc. raised and prepared by the Senecas sent in 1849. Described in 1849 field notes.

1. O-nä-o-ga-ant, or white corn [*onęokę:t* 'white corn,' or literally, 'white corn']
2. Tic-ne, or red corn [*tekhni:h* 'two']
3. Ha-go-wä, or white flint corn [*héhko:wa:h* 'flint corn, hominy']
4. O-nä-dä, or charred or roasted corn [*onę:'ta'* 'charred or roasted corn']
5. O-go-on-să, or baked corn [*oko:sæ'* 'baked corn']
6. O-si-dä, or long-vine bean [*osáe'ta'* 'bean']
7. Gwed-dä-a o-si-dä, or red bean [*kwęhtæ:'ę:'* 'red'; *osáe'ta'* 'bean']
8. Te-o-gä-ga-wä o-si-dä, or speckled bean [*tekaka:wa'* 'trout'; *osáe'ta'* 'bean']
9. Ta-gä-gä-hät, or short-vine bean [*teká:ka:ha:t*, literally, 'it is lying with legs apart']
10. Ah-wa-own-dä-go, or red-flower pole bean [*awęǫta:kǫh*, literally, 'deep-colored flower']
11. Hä-yoke, or cranberry pole bean [*ha:yok* 'Roman bean, cockleberry bean']
12. O-yä-gä-ind, or gray squash [*o'yáka:ęt* also 'anus']
13. Gä-je-ote, or big-handle squash [*kajé:ot*, literally, 'it has a handle on it']
14. Sko-ak, or toad squash [*sko'æk* 'frog']

15. O-ne-ä-sä-ä-weh, or small squash [*o:nyá'sa'* 'neck, throat, squash, or gourd with neck']

16. O-yeh-quä-ä-weh, or Indian tobacco [*oyę'kwa'ǫ:weh* 'native tobacco']

17. O-sa-wa, or parched corn pounded into flour with maple sugar [*oshǫwe:'* 'mush']

Two ears of white corn, two ears of red corn, and two ears of white flint corn also sent in 1849.

To-an-jer-go-o o-no-no-do, or groundnut (*Apios tuberosa*) [*onǫnǫ'ta'* 'potato']

Groundnuts sent in 1849. Described in 1849 report and in *League*, p. 376.

Gä-ne-gä-tä, or mortar [*ka'nékahta'* 'mortar'] and Gä-nih-gä-dä, or pestle [*ka'nékahta'* 'mortar']

One mortar and two pestles donated in 1849. Described in 1848 report.

Two mortars and two pestles sent in 1849. One mortar and pestle illustrated in 1849 report. Preparation of corn described in 1849 report (*League*, pp. 370–74).

Ah-do-gwä-seh, or ladle [*atókwa'shæ'* 'spoon, ladle,' or literally, 'the thing that scatters, spreads out']

Four ladles sent in 1850. Illustrated and described in 1850 report. Described in *League*, p. 383.

Bark ladle sent in 1850. Illustrated and described in 1850 report.

Wooden spoon sent in 1850. Neither illustrated nor described.

Gät-go-ne-as-heh, or hominy blade [*katkónya'shæ'* 'stirring instrument, paddle, oar, ladle,' or literally, 'it stirs']; Ah-de-gwas-ha, or hominy blade [*atókwa'shæ'* 'spoon, ladle,' or literally, 'the thing that scatters, spreads out']

Four hominy blades sent in 1849. Neither illustrated nor described.

Four hominy blades sent in 1850. Two illustrated and described in 1850 report.

Ya-ă-go-gen-tä-quä, or bread turner [*yéæhkoję́htahkwa'*, literally, 'one scoops up bread with it']

Bread turner sent in 1850. Illustrated and described in 1850 report.

SINGING TOOLS

Drums

Gä-no-jo-o, or Indian drum [*ka'nǫhkǫ:ǫh* 'water drum,' or literally, 'covered keg']

Three drums sent in 1849. One illustrated in 1849 report. Described in 1849 report.

Rattles

Gus-dä-wa-să, or rattle [*kastáwę'sæ'* 'rattle']

Two turtle-shell rattles sent in 1849. One illustrated in 1849 report. Described in 1849 field notes, in 1849 report, and in *League*, p. 280.

Two turtle-shell rattles sent in 1850. Neither illustrated nor described.

Four squash-shell rattles sent in 1849. Two illustrated in 1849 report. Described in 1849 report and in *League*, p. 288.

O-no-gă gus-dä-weh-să, or horn rattle [*onó'kæ:'* 'horn'; *kastáwę'sæ'* 'rattle']

Horn rattle sent in 1850. Illustrated and described in 1850 report.

Gus-dä-wa-sä yen-che-no-hos-ta, or knee rattle of deer hooves [*kastáwę'sæ'* 'rattle'; *yǫtsínǫhǫ́stha'* 'legband,' or literally, 'one uses it to tie around the leg']

Pair of knee rattles of deer hooves sent in 1849. Illustrated in 1849 report. Described in 1849 report and in *League*, pp. 265–66.

Knee rattle of deer hooves sent in 1850. Neither illustrated nor described.

Ya-o-dä-was-tä, or Indian flute [*ye:o'táwastha'* 'flute,' or literally, 'one blows with it']

Flute sent in 1849. Illustrated in 1849 report. Described in 1849 field notes and in 1849 report (*League*, p. 380).

Two flutes sent in 1850. Neither illustrated nor described.

GAMING TOOLS

Gä-jih, or bowl [*kaję*' 'bowl, dish'] and Gus-ka-eh, or peach stones [*kaskę'ę̨*' 'seed, pit']

Bowl for game with peach stones and six peach stones (dice) sent in 1849. Illustrated in 1849 report. Described in 1849 field notes, in 1849 report, and in *League*, pp. 307–12.

Gus-ga-e-sa-tä, or deer buttons [*kaskę'isé:htǫh* 'deer buttons']

Eight deer buttons (one set of dice made of deer bone) for game sent in 1849. Illustrated in 1849 report. Described in 1849 field notes, in 1849 report, and in *League*, pp. 302–03.

Gä-ne-ah, or ball bat [*ka'hnya*' 'stick, club'] and O-nus-quä ah-hose-hä, or knot ball [*onǫskwæ:*' 'knot (in rope or tree)'; *ę'ho:shæ*' 'ball']

Two ball bats (lacrosse sticks) donated in 1849. Neither illustrated nor described.

Four ball bats and two knot balls sent in 1849. One ball bat illustrated in 1849 report. Described in 1849 field notes, in 1849 report, and in *League*, pp. 294–98.

Ball bat sent in 1850. Neither illustrated nor described.

Gä-wä-sä, or snow snake [*ka:wa:sa*' 'snow snake']

Two snow snakes sent in 1849. Neither illustrated nor described.

Four snow snakes sent in 1849. One illustrated in 1849 field notes (see fig. 42 this volume) and in 1849 report. Described in 1849 field notes, in 1849 report, and in *League*, p. 303–05.

Five snow snakes sent in 1850. Neither illustrated nor described.

De-ya-no-tä-yen-dä-quä, or snow boat [*teyenotayętáhkwa*', literally, 'they use it for putting down a reed or flute']

Snow boat sent in 1849. Illustrated in 1849 field notes (see fig. 44 this volume) and in 1850 report. Described in 1850 field notes and in 1850 report.

Gä-geh-dä, or javelin [*kake:ta'* 'javelin, dart']

Eighteen javelins or shooting sticks for game sent in 1849. Javelin and
ring illustrated in 1849 report. Described in 1849 field notes, in 1849
report, and in *League,* pp. 298–302.

Javelin or shooting stick sent in 1850. Neither illustrated nor described.

CEREMONIAL ITEMS

Gä-go-sä, or False Face [*kakǫhsa'* 'face, false face']

False Face mask sent in 1849. Neither illustrated nor described.

False Face mask sent in 1850. Illustrated in 1850 report. Described in
1850 field notes and in 1850 report.

Gä-ger-we-sä dun-daque-quä-do-quä, or New Year's shovel [*kakáwihsa'*
'shovel']

New Year's shovel sent in 1849. Neither illustrated nor described.

MISCELLANEOUS

Got-kase-hä, or axe helve [*katke:sha'* 'handle, as of an ax']

Ax handle sent in 1849. Neither illustrated nor described.

Skä-wä-ka, or splint broom [*yeskæ:wa:ktha'* 'broom,' or literally, 'one
sweeps with it']

Splint broom sent in 1849. Neither illustrated nor described.

O-dä-da-da-one-dus-tä, or eye showerer [Seneca word not recognized
now]

Eye showerer sent in 1850. Not illustrated. Described in 1850 field
notes.

Go-yo-ga-ace, or finger catcher [Seneca word not recognized now]

Finger catcher sent in 1850. Neither illustrated nor described.

7

. . . . .

Morgan's Field Notes

Morgan's field notes of the three collecting trips he made for the state are preserved in volume two of the *Manuscript Journals* (the volumes of manuscript notes Morgan himself had bound and so titled) now in the Morgan papers in the University of Rochester Library.

These field notes are written in four lined booklets, approximately eight inches by six inches in size. Two of these booklets contain Morgan's field notes for his trip to Tonawanda in 1849, one headed with the date of November 30, 1849, and the other December 7, 1849 (designated nos. 4 and 5 respectively in the "Descriptive Table of Contents" prepared by the University of Rochester Library). A third (designated no. 6) contains his notes on his trip to the Grand River Reserve in 1850, and the fourth (no. 7) contains his notes on his trip to Tonawanda later that year.

They are printed here in their entirety with the exception of the 1849 Tonawanda field notes, which contain some materials not directly relevant to the present study. The omitted sections, which are indicated by asterisks, are: a list of Indian village names; a description of a War dance Morgan attended while at Tonawanda; notes on a conversation with Jemmy Johnson on the New Religion (Newton Parker was interpreter with Dr. Sanford assisting); notes on a conversation with William Parker on the "Allegany idol"; and notes on the New Year's ceremony (informant unspecified). For the principles used in editing these manuscripts, see Editorial Notes.

Extracts from 1849 Tonawanda Field Notes

. . . . .
. . .
.

Moccasins—Tanning Deer Skins

Originally the Iroquois made their moccasins from the skin of the elk which covered the gamble joint. They cut the skin above and below the joint, sewed up the lower part, and thus the natural bend of the skin was adopted to the foot. When the art of moccasin making was first known they do not pretend to say. The deer skin is usually scraped immediately after it was taken off, the grain of the skin being scraped off together with the hair with a stick over a cylindrical stick a foot in diameter, like the currier's beam. It was then pulled and stretched to give it softness. In tanning they used deer's brains. These they were in the habit of mingling with moss, and then drying them before the fire. Afterwards they were made into cakes and this preserved for years in a dried form if necessary. When the deer skin was ready a cake of this was boiled in a kettle of water, the moss thus removed. Then the skin was dipped in this solution and thoroughly soaked for several hours. It was then wrung out dry, and afterwards pulled and stretched until it became soft and pliable, when it was ready for use. In taking off the hair sometimes it was necessary to soak the skin in water to soften it, after which with a stick the hair and grain of the skin were rubbed off. The outside of the skin was still the hair side. After the tanning and before use it is necessary to smoke the skin to complete the work. This is done by stretching the skin over a kettle or tin pail in which a lot of corn husks or cobs are set asmoking. The skin is turned that both sides may be smoked. The color of the skin is thus changed from white to brown, which is the color of all Indian moccasins.

For tanning the brains of a dog or any animal are as good as those of the deer. The brains of one animal are more than sufficient to tan one skin. They sometimes use eggs to tan with. It does not make as good leather as the other.

There is a tradition that the discovery of this method of tanning deer skins was accidental as follows. A stiff deer skin was one day walking around from house to house through an Indian village frightening everyone it visited. At last it went to the house of a man who was boiling deer's brains for a vomit. He did not propose to be frightened by this mysterious skin out of his house, and therefore he poured the hot water solution of deer's brains upon the stiff skin which at once softened it down, took away from it all power of motion, and flattened it to the floor. The people in fright had been shooting it with arrows. After it was softened they began to pull it and thus resulted the tanned deer skins.

The Indians sometimes use the backbone of the elk for the purpose of tanning deer skins. It is pounded up and boiled in water, and the skin is then soaked in this solution.

To this day the Senecas tan their deer skins with the brains of animals and they have never resorted to any other system of tanning. In making they used deer sinews for thread, and a bone needle taken from the deer.

Bear Skin. Gä-ne-ä-guise-tä.

This skin is not tanned but scraped on the flesh side until soft. It is then dried.

Indian Flute. Ya-o-dä-was-tä.
[*ye:o'táwastha'* 'flute,' or literally, 'one blows with it']

The word Ya-do-dä-was-tä means a blow pipe. They are usually about 18 inches in length and one inch in diameter, made of red cedar, and having six finger holes equidistant. Like the clarinet [written over word: flageolet] you blow in the end. Like the whistle the sounding part is constricted, or on the same principle. About five inches from the mouth piece is a seventh hole with a movable slide tied partly above it. The flute can make but six consecutive notes, although you can make 4 others losing one intermediate note. It is a wind instrument of Indian invention, but it contains no new principle that I know. As played by the Indian it affords an interesting sort of music, wild and peculiar, like all their musical notions. On trying the flute it seems to make but 9 notes instead of 12. It makes 6 regularly, then loses the 7, but makes the 8, 9, and 10.

Indian Ball. Ă-hose-hă. and Ball Bat.
[*ę'ho:shæ'* 'ball']

The Indian ball was formerly made of wood, of knot usually, which was ground down and polished on a rough stone. The ball bat at that time was of a small tree with a crooking root, the root turning up in such a way as to make a bat. The ball was then knocked along the ground. The rules of the game the same as at present. The present ball bat has been in use but a few years. To-do-da-ho[1] invented the game of ball, also the snow snake, also Gä-jih, or game of bowl and peach stones.

Indian Bark Canoe. Gä-snä Gä-o-wä.

[*osnǫ'* 'bark'; *ka:ǫwǫ'* 'boat']

The Indian canoe is made usually of birch bark which is the most valuable. But as this is found only in Canada, the New York Indians often made them of elm bark and also of bitternut hickory. The birch bark canoe was often from 35 to 48 feet long, or 8 times the length of a man's arms from fingers to fingers. The bark is all one piece. For the rim they take ten sticks of limber [?] wood, black or white ash of the width of the hand, and having placed one upon each side of the bark, they sewed them through and through into the bark itself. They sew with bark thread. Next for ribs they take black or white ash and cut it into strips and set them a foot or so apart along the bottom, with the ends fastened under the rim. The bow is rounded and turned up. It has a wooden beak or prow which is made by setting upon the outside a round piece of timber about 2 or three inches in diameter and about a foot and a half long. Some portion of the bark is cut away and the bark is sewed to the beak in such a way as to give to the front a gradual line from the keel. The stern is made in the same manner, so that it can go either way. The birch bark always keeps its place without warping, is light and durable. The hickory and elm is heavier and is apt to warp. A birchbark will last good several [?] years. After using it is taken out of the water and dried.

Paddles. Gä-gä-we-sä.

[*kakáwihsa'* 'shovel']

Two usually paddle the large canoes, one at the bow and the other at the stern. If more, they are arranged on alternate sides between them. A party of 10 in a canoe of good size started at night when the lake had become still from the mouth of the Oak Orchard Creek. They paddled all night, but at daybreak turned ashore, and waited until the next night when they resumed, and reached the mouth of the Genesee river at midnight, about 18 hours in all.

Ah-da-dä-qua, or Indian Saddle

[*atætahkwa'* 'saddle,' or literally, 'one uses it to perch on']

The word signifies a seat to sit on. It is the original Indian saddle, and is still used by the western Indians, and also by the Mexicans. The saddle of the latter race being not much unlike this. It consists of four pieces of wood. Two side pieces about 18 inches long by 6 inches wide, and about 12 inches in thickness at the thickest place, but coming to a sharp edge above and below. On the lower side they are about 10 or 12 inches apart, and at the top about 3 inches so that the backbone of the horse was up between them. In front is a high pommel rising about 5 inches above the side pieces. It is a crotch piece of timber about three inches in diameter at the top and spreading out so as to pass down the outside of the two side pieces nearly to the bottom, thus including them, and determining the spread of the saddle. On behind was another crotch piece passing over and embracing the two side pieces, and holding them in their place. It was about 5 inches above the side pieces, and descends nearly to the bottom of them. The outer rim is elliptical, and must be 20 inches around. Where it crosses the center it is hollowed out, so that the backbone of the animal will not hit it. Over it all is stretched rawhide which is sewed with rawhide or with the sinews of animals at the ends and on the upper sides. One piece of the skin covers the whole, the sides, the pommel and the rear piece. Sometimes this skin is stained or colored a dark color with hemlock bark. On the sides are hair hangers for the stirrups, which are of wood and were formerly suspended by bark rope or rope made of buffalo hair. Another is attached behind. For a surcingle a strap descends from the pommel around which it is wound, and another from the stern [?] piece. This went below the side piece in the center and are fastened into a ring. Into this ring also the surcingle is fastened.

[For sketch here, see fig. 38.]

Gus-hä-ha. Bark Head Strap for Carrying Burdens.
[*kasha:a'* 'strap, halter, cord']

The Indian uses a bark rope about 14 feet long for carrying baskets and other loads. In the center is a broad strip about 4 inches wide and 18 long braided into a flat surface like a belt. The residue is a three strand rope about half an inch in diameter, but flattened. It is made out of basswood bark. The strands are peeled off, and immediately boiled in ashes and water. After this they are dried. Then it is peeled off into fine strings by hand. It was with the grain and strings several feet long are easily obtained. It is then ready for braiding into ropes or strings. The Gus-hä-ha is frequently made of slippery elm which makes a softer rope.

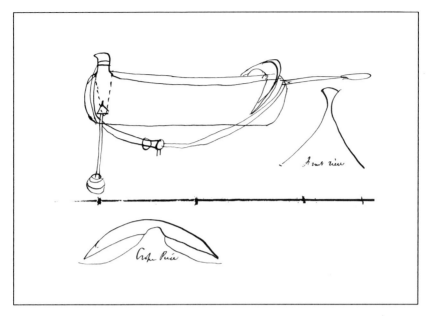

Figure 38. Sketch of an Indian saddle in Morgan's 1849 Tonawanda field notes. (Courtesy of the Department of Rare Books and Special Collections, University of Rochester Library.)

Gă-sken-dä. Bark Rope.
[*kaískę'ta'* 'braid']
They make bark ropes for clotheslines 40 feet long, and for other purposes.

Ne-us-täse-ä
Yo-wonk-tä, or Sieve Basket.
[*yęwǫ:ktha'*, literally, 'one uses it to winnow']
This beautiful basket is made of black ash splints and is used to sift Indian meal after it has been pounded in the mortar. The Indians always sift their meal before they use it. This basket therefore is a substitute for a bolting machine. Used for sifting white corn. It is fine. The O-ne-ose-ta-wa-nes [*o'nę́yostowanes* 'coarse kernels'] is coarse, and used to sift white flint corn.

Basket for Coarse Meal. Gä-nose-hă.

This basket is used to receive the coarse meal which could not pass the sieve. It is made very ingeniously of corn husks and blue flag (O-no-dä) [*ono:ta'* 'reed'] which grows in swamps, a round flag which grows from 4 to 6 ft. high. The bottom is entirely of corn husks, and so also are the ribs, but the sides are made of flag. Rim [?] of corn husks. Flags are not as good as husks, but they are larger, and therefore better for the sides.

Gus-ha-dä, or Bottle.
[*kashé'ta'* 'bottle']

Bottles are made of husks and flags, for holding salt.

Ga-je-wä or War Club.
[*kají:wa'* 'war club, hammer, mallet']
[*For sketch here of ball-headed club, see fig. 39.*]

This is the name of the war club with a round ball of knot upon the end. It is about 2-1/2 feet long, the ball about 5 inches in diameter, and it was the ancient war club of the Iroquois. It was used in close combat, and before the tomahawk came into use. The head would be the chief point of attack but not exclusively. They wore it [on] a belt on either side. It is usually made out of ironwood.

Ga-ne-u-ga-o-dus-ha. War Club.

Another kind of war club, about the same length, or about 2 feet and made of hardwood was much used. It had a handle and blade something like a sword blade, or Turkish sword. The peculiar feature of this club is a sharp deer's horn about 3 inches long inserted on the edge side. It was a formidable weapon for inflicting deep wounds.

[*For sketch here of toothed club, see fig. 39.*]

The Indians never used the lance or the spear.

•　•　•　•　•

O'-nă-da, or Charred Corn
[*oné:'ta'* 'charred or roasted corn']

To char corn, the Indians built long fires, in green corn time, and roasted it when at the right age for roasting. Afterwards it was shelled from the cob and dried hard in the sun. It would keep for years in this condition. The Indians were doubtless in the habit of digging pits or caches in which they

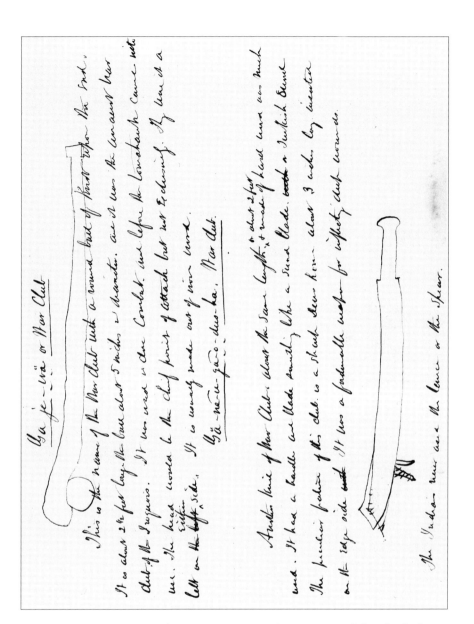

Figure 39. Page from Morgan's 1849 Tonawanda field notes containing sketch of war clubs. (Courtesy of the Department of Rare Books and Special Collections, University of Rochester Library.)

buried and covered this corn. We find traces of these caches to this day in the vicinity of their ancient villages. The Senecas are still in the habit of charring corn for domestic use. They put it up in bark barrels and use it in succotash and in soups except those made of meat. The charred corn now found in old pits on analysis will doubtless be found identical with the present[2] red corn of the Senecas.

Ose-ho-wa, or Corn Meal Mixed with Sugar
[*oshǫwęʼ* 'mush']

The Indian white corn will not pop. The red corn is preferred to char.[3] It is burned or charred in the fire after it is ripe and hard. This is done by putting it in the ashes and stirring it up until blackened. After this it is pounded into flour and then mingled with maple sugar, they being pounded in together. This pulverized corn is often the only subsistence of the Indian hunter, or the war party for days together. It is prepared expressly for such uses. It is eatable dry or not with water and is both pleasant and nutritious. The Senecas still use it, and keep in their families.

Gä-oo-wä, or Bark Sap Tub.
[*kaʼǫ·wǫʼ* 'trough']

The art of making sugar from the sap of the maple is a very ancient one. They collected the sap in numerous tubs of bark. The tree is cut with the axe and a basswood bark inserted in the cut. Above the cut the bark is then cut away. After the bark has dried a little it curls up on the outside, and this makes a softer conduit for the sap into the tub. The sap is afterwards collected and boiled down and poured off into dishes in the same manner as the sugar is now made by the whites. How they made sugar before axes and kettles came into use, they do not know.

Na-o-geh-o-wä, or Venison.
[*neokęʼ* 'deer'; *oʼwáʼ* 'meat']

Venison was cured by baking or drying before the fire. The bones were carefully removed, and the meat was then baked, or dried hard. In this state it would keep for years. In winter it can be dried in the sun without first roasting. Unlike the white man, the Indian saved every part of the deer, even to some parts of the intestines. They found use for the flesh, the skin, the sinews, the horns, the hooves. When a hunting party had been successful, and took more venison then they needed, they took the best parts and baked them as above described, and then made a tight small blockhouse 6 or 8 feet long by 3 high and 2 wide, in which they deposited the surplus for the benefit of all the families of the party. Deerskins were put on the bottom of the pen and on all sides of the meat. It was brought home first to the village of the party.

Bear's meat (Ne-ar-guy-e-o-nä) [*nyakwai'* 'bear'] is always roasted first both in winter and summer, and then dried before the fire, after which it is put away in the same manner as deer's meat. There is frequently a great accumulation of bear's grease, which they used to eat upon their bread and wild potatoes in the same manner as they now use pork grease. When they had a surplus they would fall a tree and split it, and having made a deep trough in one side by burning it out they would pour in a barrel or two of bear's oil and then put on the other half. In this way it would keep a year or two. They also had a way of skinning the deer, shaving off the hair, and making a bottle for bear's oil of his skin. Fruits like berries, plums etc. were dried in the sun.

· · · · ·

Gus-ga-e-sa-tä. Indian Game Played with Deer Buttons.
[*kaskę'isé:htǫh* 'deer buttons']

This is an Indian game. Eight buttons are made of elk horn about 7/8 of an inch in diameter. Both sides are rounded and smooth alike but one is burned to make it black or nearly so while the other is white. Two, three or more can play the game. Beans are the articles won or lost. If two play 50 beans would be enough for a good game. If three or four about 100 would be necessary. The parties set down around a blanket. The beans are placed on one side. One of the party takes the 8 buttons and having shook them turns them onto the blanket. It is not necessary to shake them but you can take them up in the hand and throw them down. If all come up white or black except two, the person wins two beans, which he takes at once from the general heap. He continues to throw as long as he wins. If the next throw all come up white or black except one he wins 4 beans, which he takes as before from the general heap. If on the next throw all come up white or all black it counts 20 beans, which the winner takes as before. This is the highest number which can be won at one throw. Two also is the smallest. There are but three wins. If the buttons turn up 3 white and 5 black, or four white and 4 [black], or 5 white and 3 black the person fails to win and the next person takes the throw. It would be the same if the colors were reversed. The players continue until all the beans are won. After that the forfeit is paid jointly by those who are playing. If three are playing and one wins two, each of the others pays one, and so on. If four play, and one wins two, each of the three pays one, so that in fact he wins three. If he wins 4, they pay him 2 each. If all turn up the same he wins 10 from each of the three. But if three are playing, and all turn up [the same] he wins 20, or 10 from each. Two may play together as partners, and throw in their regular turns, or the one who is playing may choose a friend. They usually lend this person 6 beans, and this one plays until he loses the 6. All that he wins goes into the other one's lot. When you make two, it is called on-ne-a-ä ['onyo:'ah, literally, 'almost wild']. If he wins four it is called Gä-ne-ä-shon-dä, or a pumpkin ['onyǫhsa' 'squash']. If he wins 20, it is called O-gine-dä-a or a field ['okáęta:e', literally, 'it came up with all six identical' cf. another name for this throw, 'o:ęta', literally, 'planted field']. This is a very old game, and is more a game for females than males. I have played it and become quite interested. After a person has lost all his beans he has two throws to get in again. If he fails he is out.

Gus-gä-a, or Indian Game with Bowl and Peach Stones.
[kaskę̓ę̓ 'seed, pit']

This is a favorite Indian game, and often played at councils. The bowl is usually made of knot, about a foot in diameter at the bottom and about 6 inches high. The bowl is called De-a-yun-dä-guä Ga-jih, or the basin used in this game [teǫyętáhkwa, literally, 'one uses it to bet with'; kaje̓ 'bowl, dish']. The peach stones are called Gus-gä-a [kaskę̓ę̓ 'seed, pit']. Hence the game may be known by either name. 6 peach stones are filed down to about the size of a plum pit. The meat or fruit is removed from the shell. One side is burned black. The other is left in its natural color. They are put in the dish and the players set down upon a blanket. It is played by but two. 100 beans is the number for a full game but 50 makes a good game. The people at councils especially at the Indian New Year's Feb. 1 divide by tribes [clans].[4] The four brothers against the four cousins. Wolf, Turtle, Beaver, and Bear [clans] on one side. On the other the Hawk, Snipe, Deer, Heron [clans]. The Deer tribe is in two divisions, and hence they say there are five tribes on this side. The bowl is shook and to win it is necessary to turn up 5 of one color. If 5 are turned [up one color], it counts one and the winner takes one bean. If he turns up all of one color, it is the highest count which can be made and counts 5. The winner takes 5 beans. There are but two wins. It seems that one overseer is appointed for each side. Two persons set down to commence the play. The 100 beans are in one pile before them. 5 beans are given to each by the overseers. As soon as one loses his five he gives his seat to another person appointed by the overseer appointed to arrange the order of succession [on his side]. The one who wins the other five retains his seat, but the 5 go into the pile belonging to his side, and not into his. The next person receives 5 beans as the first and plays until he loses the 5. All that either win goes into a pile by itself. As soon as one is broke another takes his place and thus the play continues until the 100 beans or the 75 [50 is intended] beans are won by the two sides. If it is kept in mind that all the beans won go into one pile belonging to the side of the player, and that the player only keeps his seat until he loses his 5, no matter how many he may win, the matter will be clear. As soon as the beans are thus divided, the next business is to see which side can win the whole and the beans are now in two piles, one to each side. Before they were in 5 piles: one to each player, one to each side of the beans won, and the original general pile. In the second part of the game the course is just the same. Each one plays until he loses 5, and then he yields his place, no matter how many he may win. It often takes a whole day to play a game with 100 beans. They bet of course everything which they have if they get into the real spirit of it. It is a regular betting game. They bet money and silverware and trinkets, and whatever little valuables they have. They often become much excited. The game was invented by To-do-da-ho, and is very ancient, and a great favorite.

O-tä-dä-jish-guä-age, or Ball Game.

They divide by tribes as in the above game, four against 4. The gates are usually 40 or 50 rods apart. The number of players usually 6 or 8 on a side. The object of one party is to drive its ball through one gate, the other to drive it through the opposite gate. The gates are two poles about 2 rods apart set on opposite parts of the field. They commence in the center. The 6 players stand opposite nearly naked. Both parties strive to carry or kick the ball to his own end. Sometimes the ball is carried in the network of the ball bat by the player in a full race. When overtaken he throws the ball towards his gate over his head. 7 is the highest number for a great game, and 5 the smallest. The party who carries the ball through his gate 7 times before the other does as many wins. Thus they may stand 6 to 6, and the last game [goal is intended] determines who wins. It is a great game. They bet

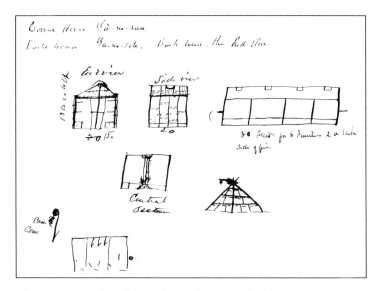

Figure 40. Page from Morgan's 1849 Tonawanda field notes containing sketches of bark house. (Courtesy of the Department of Rare Books and Special Collections, University of Rochester Library.)

of course and become greatly excited. I have seen it played, and can readily see how they can become so much enlisted.

Received yesterday a present of a bark bowl about 40 years old, and two baskets from one of my relations of the Hawk tribe. Her name, Da-wä-ke-was, or Mrs. Printup. I gave her in return a beautiful testament. The name signifies that "She goes not out to war."

· · · · ·

[*For sketches here, see fig. 40.*]

· · · · ·

Snowshoes. Gä-weh-ga-ă.
[*o:węˀkæ:ˀ* 'wood, splint']
[*teye:węˀkeotáhkwaˀ* 'snowshoe, ski']
[*For sketch here, see fig. 41.*]

An Indian invention. They are about 18 inches in length, by 10 or 12 inches in greatest width, coming in front, swelling towards the center, and coming

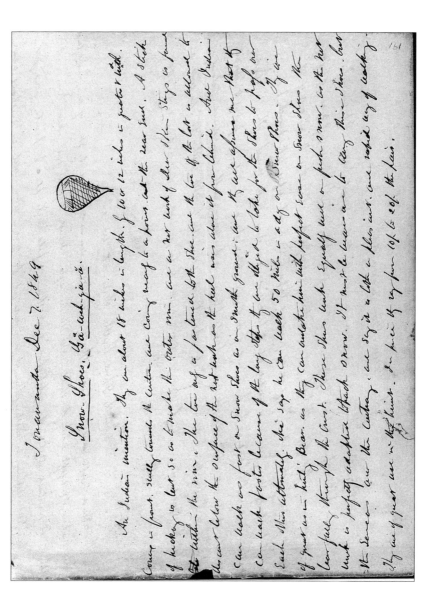

Figure 41. Page from Morgan's 1849 Tonawanda field notes containing sketch of snowshoe. (Courtesy of the Department of Rare Books and Special Collections, University of Rochester Library.)

nearly to a point at the rear end. A stick of hickory is bent so as to make the outer rim, and a network of deer skin strings is found within the rim. The toe only is fastened to the shoe, and the toe of the boot is allowed to descend below the surface of the network as the heel arises above it from behind. An Indian can walk as fast on snowshoes as on smooth ground, and they all assure me that they can walk faster because of the long steps they are obliged to take for the shoes to pass over each other alternately. Nic [Parker] says he can walk 50 miles in a day on snowshoes. They are of great use in hunting bear, as they can overtake him with perfect ease on snowshoes the bear falling through the crust. These shoes work equally well on fresh snow, as the network is perfectly adapted to pack snow. It must be wearisome to carry these shoes, but the Senecas aver the contrary, and say it is both a pleasant, and rapid way of walking. They are of great use in the hunt. In price they range from 10/- to 20/- the pair.

Air Gun. Gä-ga-an-dä.
[*káeo'ta'* 'blowgun, gun']

An Indian invention, and is used for killing small birds.[5] It consists of a long hollow tube or barrel about 7 feet in length perfectly straight. It is usually made of alder. The heads are worked off with lead. One orifice is larger than the other, the one out of which the arrow is discharged. There is a gradual taper from the outer orifice to the mouth piece. A delicate but strong arrow is inserted into the barrel and run down to the mouth. Thistle down is then put in the barrel at the lower end of the barrel between the mouth and the foot of the arrow, and the individual taking sight over the barrel blows out the arrow with considerable velocity. An arrow may thus be thrown 8 or 10 rods. Birds can also be shot with it, as well as with the bow and arrow. The arrow is put in at the large end. One orifice is a little larger than the other.

Turtle Shell Rattle. Gus-dä-wa-sä.
[*kastáwę'sæ'* 'rattle']

The mud turtle shell is used. After the animal is removed, and the skin of his head and neck were taken off and left with the shell, the skin is again sewed together with deer skin. A stick is inserted within the outstretched neck skin, and held to its place by splints. Some yellow corn is put within to rattle. Thus it is made fit for use. The rattle is principally used to mark time with in the Religious Dance.[6] They can be bought for 3/- to 12/-.

Gä-was-sä-yă-duk, or Game with Snow Snakes.
[*ka:wasyę:tak* 'snow snake game,' or literally,
'let it be used for laying down a snow snake']
[*For sketch here, see fig. 42.*]

The snake is a piece of hickory from 5 to 10 feet long, with a round leaded head, bent up from the ground like a snake's head, with a flat belly about an inch wide, and 1/2 of an inch thick. This they throw on the snow with great rapidity, and it runs to the distance often of 60 rods. The point is to see who can throw the farthest. Tribe plays against tribe when a set game is made as in the ball and peach stone games. Betting also is common. They play from 3 to six on a side, and each one has from 2 to 4 snakes. These are rubbed with beeswax on the bottom to make them glide over the snow more easily. The game is usually from 6 to 10. Any player can leave and a new one take his place. If there are 5 on a side, and 7 be the game, they count like this. If the 5 snakes on one side are all ahead of the other 5, it would count five. If four came out ahead of the other 5, it would count 4, if 3, 3, if 2, 2. If 1, it would count one. If four on one side are ahead of 4 on the other, and the last snake on the last side goes ahead of all, it counts one for that side. This is repeated until the game is decided. The snake is held in the right hand with the forefinger against the small end, and it is then thrown longitudinally.

Gä-na-gä-o.[7] Game with Shooting Sticks, or Javelins.
[*kanó'ka'o:*' 'hoop and javelin game']

A game of Indian invention. Two persons can play, or sides with 15 to 30 on a side. They can play by tribes as usual with all games. The javelin, or shooting sticks are of hickory, maple, alder, or any kind of hardwood.[8] The shaft must be straight and slick [?], and are from 5 to 6 feet long. Each player usually has from 3 to 6 as previously agreed. The sticks are the forfeit, and the game is won when all the sticks are taken by one side. A ring about 6 inches in diameter is made, and wound with splint so as to be a solid wheel. A line is decided upon on which the ring is to be rolled. The players stand on one side of this line. The other side then roll the ring by them. This party throw their javelins at the ring. If one hits the ring, then the other party are obliged to come and in turn standing in the precise place where the person stood who hit the ring, throw their shooting sticks at the ring. The javelins which hit the ring are saved from forfeit. Those which do not hit the ring are then taken by the other side and shot at the

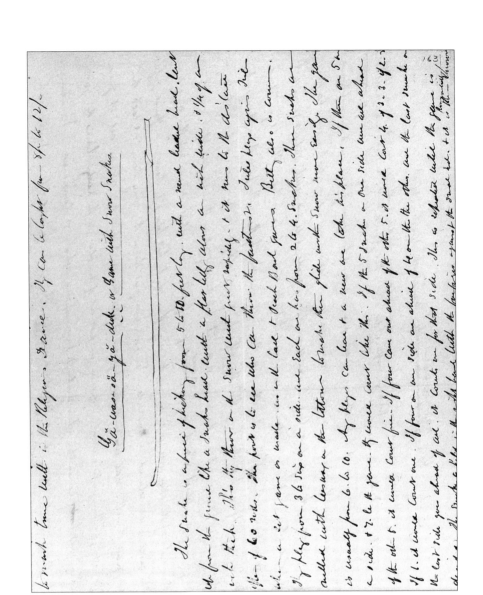

Figure 42. Page from Morgan's 1849 Tonawanda field notes containing sketch of snow snake. (Courtesy of the Department of Rare Books and Special Collections, University of Rochester Library.)

ring. Those which hit belong to them as a final forfeit. The residue are returned to the other side. The party who first shot at the ring then roll back
the ring past the other side who shoot at it as before. If neither party hit
the ring at all it goes for nothing. The javelins which are worn are put out
of the play, and the party loses the game which first loses the whole number of javelins with which it commenced. Sometimes an open ring is used
instead of a solid wheel. The javelin is held like the snowsnake, and that
horizontally, or is thrown over the head, or from the side as the player may
prefer. The name of the ring Gä-na-gä [*kanó'kæ:*' 'hoop' also 'poplar'], of
the javelin Go-ga-dä [*kake:ta*' 'javelin, dart' also 'hoop and javelin game'].

> Gä-ga-dä-yan-duk. Game with Javelins.
> [*kaketayę:tak* 'javelin game,' or literally,
> 'let it be used for laying down a javelin']

In this game sumac sticks are always used because of their lightness. The
sticks are called shooting sticks as those in the other game. They play by
sides, and the game is from 10 to 25. They have any number on a side, usually 5 to 10, each with 4 to 6 sticks. A stick is laid on the ground or raised a
little above it. The shooting stick is held like the snow snake and in shooting must be brought down to the cross stick and shot over it. By shooting
it down upon the cross stick, the head of the javelin is thrown upward into
the air. The point is to see which can throw through the air the greatest
distance. The rule of counting is exactly the same as in the snow snake
game. On it they usually all bet, and play by sides. Boys play this game as
that of snow snakes in pairs. The party who has the throw determines what
stick or log shall be thrown over, and whether it be at the foot, or a rod or
2 rods distant from the shooter. When that throw is decided the other
party then decides upon what stick they will throw over, or whether they
will throw through the air as they may. Thus the game is conducted until
one side has gained the requisite number of points. The game being won
the bets which were of course put up, are divided.

• • • • •

The wild potato still grows at Tonawanda, and as large as a hen's egg.

Varieties of Indian Corn, Beans, Squash, Melon, and Dried Corn Basket

No. 1. O-nä-o-ga-ant. White corn [*onẹoke̞:t* 'white corn']. This is the favorite corn of the Indian and takes the same place with them that wheat does with us. It is used for corn bread. Sometimes the remains not passing the sieve called the heart is used for hominy, but seldom. It is used for corn bread principally. It is also the corn for succotash, or corn and beans. It is planted in hills. It ripens the 3rd corn, the white flint first, the red corn second, the white corn third, and the sweet corn last.

No. 2. Tic-ne. (it means 2). [*tekhni:h* 'two']⁹ This is the red corn of the Indian. It has a large and fair [?] ear. It ripens next after the white flint. This corn is used for succotash, never for hominy. This is also the corn which is charred, and thus kept for years. It is white when green. When the corn is green, they roast it before a log fire built in the field. The fire is made in a trench, and the principal log raised above the ground. The ears are stood up in rows leaning against the log. It is rather dried than roasted. That is, it is not roasted enough to eat, although perhaps burned or charred in places. As soon as it cooks they shell it by hand and dry it in the sun. It thus shrinks about half by roasting and drying. It is then carried out by hunting parties it being light and small in bulk. It is dried in part for this purpose. It is also used for bread, for succotash, to char, and to pound green, and then bake and dry. This is the next to most valuable corn. Nearly every Indian however raises these two kinds of corn.

No. 3. Ha-go-wä. White flint corn [*hẹhko:wa:h* 'flint corn, hominy']. This ripens first, and is used for hominy. It is the favorite corn for this last article of Indian food. It is also used for hulled corn soup or succotash. It makes bread when the white corn is out, but is not good for bread.

No. 4. O-nä-:dä. (Roasted corn.) [*onẹ:'ta'* 'charred or roasted corn'] This is the name of the corn after it is roasted or charred as above described. A few bushels, 3 or 4, are usually thus roasted and dried by every family. The red corn is used. It is used for succotash and hominy.

No. 5. O-go-on-sä. (Baked corn.) [*okọ:sæ'* 'baked corn'] It is usually red. It is shaved off green, and then baked in an oven or before the fire. After this it is dried in the sun, and then broken up into fragments. It is used for soup, for succotash, and for hominy sometimes. The roasted corn is however preferred.

No. 6. O-si-dä. (Bean.) [*osáe'ta'* 'bean'] A long vine bean. It ripens first of all, and two crops can be raised in one season. It has been done at Tonawanda. It is used for many uses. They can be used alone, or with bread, or in hominy, or with pork, or pork [?] meats [?]. It yields largely. The color is singular. A regular Indian bean.

No. 7. Gweh-dä-ă O-sid-dä. (Red bean.) [*kwę́htæ:'e:'* 'red'; *osáe'ta'* 'bean'] This is called the red bean. Is put to all uses. It is middling early. It yields well. It is a pole bean.

No. 8. Te-o-gä-ga-wä O-si-dä. (Speckled bean.) [*tekaka:wa'* 'trout'; *osáe'ta'* 'bean'] It is middling early, yields pretty well, is used for all purposes.

No. 9. Ta-gä-ga-häät. (Short vine.) [*teká:ka:ha:t*, literally, 'it is lying'] This is a short vine bean. It ripens early and yields well. It is used for all purposes.

No. 10. Ah-wa-own-dä-go. (Red flower.) [*awę́ǫta:koh*, literally, 'deep colored flower'] This is called the red flower bean. It is a pole bean. It ripens late, but yields liberally well.

No. 11. Hä-yoke. (Cranberry bean.) [*ha:yok* 'Roman bean, cockleberry bean'] This is a pole bean. It is good to eat for green beans. This is its principal use. It ripens early. It yields largely.

No. 12. O-yä-gä-ind. [*o'yáka:ęt* also 'anus'] It is a large squash. Short handle. The head or eye is peculiar. The color gray. It ripens late. The seeds have two colors but are the same.

No. 13. Gä-je-ote. (Big handle.) [*kajéo:t*, literally, 'it has a handle on it'] This is the large handle squash. Color white with black spots. It grows large, and ripens late.

No. 14. Sko-ak. (Toad.) [*sko'æk* 'frog'] This we should call the toad or frog squash. Its color is yellowish like a frog's belly, striped with black. It ripens late rather. Is very large.

No. 15. O-ne-ä-sä-ä-weh. (Small and thick.) [*o:nyá'sa'* 'neck, throat' 'squash or gourd with neck'] This is a small squash and grows thick. Ripens the first of all. They are of all colors, some white, some red, some yellow.

No. 16. O-yeh-quä-ä-weh. (Tobacco. The only tobacco.) [*oyę́'kwa'ǫ:weh* 'native tobacco'] So called because they had no other. The Senecas still raise it at Tonawanda. It is raised from the seed, which is planted in the spring. It ripens early. The leaves are picked off and dried. It sheds its seed after the leaves are picked, and comes up the next year spontaneously after it is sowed or planted once. After that it takes care of itself. Only if after a few years it grows too thick the leaves become too small, they then thin it out. It grows vigorously. They hoe it a little, and cut up. When the leaves begin to grow yellow they are picked off, and dried, and put away for use. It is a very mild tobacco. Anciently they smoked it alone. They do not chew it now. It is a mild tobacco. They dry sumac and when they smoke they then mix them together.

No. 17. O-so-wa. (Parched corn flour.) [*oshǫwę:*' 'mush') It is made of white corn. The corn is baked or parched (it will not pop). It was parched in the ashes, it is then pounded into flour, sifted close [?], and is then pounded again with maple sugar. It is the great food of the hunter and of the war party. Upon this alone they could travel for miles. They carried it in their hunting bags. It swells in the stomach. They still use it, and prepare it as of old. They make [of] it a charred corn.

1850 Grand River Field Notes

. . . . .
 . . .
 .

Left Rochester with E. S. Parker Monday evening for Buffalo, and the next morning for Hamilton, Upper Canada, via Niagara Falls and Lewiston. Had a fine view of the falls from the cars, and also of the Suspension Bridge a mile below. Reached Hamilton at 6 in the evening. Stopped at Davis's Hotel, and immediately after tea took the stage to Demorex Hotel about 20 miles on the road to Brantford. This is a fee road constructed by the government. It is macadam for about 14 miles and the rest of the way a plank road. This road passes on to Brantford, London, and thence to Lake Erie. The plank road is sadly out of repair, but it has been a noble road. We reached Demorex Tuesday night at 12, and Wednesday morning October 30 were upon the reservation on Grand River, in the midst of a beautiful country.

Peter [Fish Carrier]
Gä-no-sä, or Conch Shell Breastplate

Purchased this shell of Peter Fish Carrier, son of Ho-jä-ga-ta or Fish Carrier whose family resided at Cayuga. This was made for him at Niagara in 1802, and cost him four dollars. I paid $5.00. Such ornaments were formerly much worn. Fish Carrier with the Cayugas retired to Niagara after the invasion of Sullivan in 1779, but subsequently Hise-tă-jue (Steeltrap) and some others returned. But Fish Carrier retired to Buffalo and lived there until he died, when Peter now 60 was a young man. Fish Carrier left 3 children—Peter Fish Carrier (So-ace), another brother now dead, and a sister now dead. They all have children living on Grand River.

Sister of John Brant

Saw the daughter of Joseph, and sister of John Brant at the house of his niece Mrs. Peter Smith on Grand River near the Onondaga Council House. She is a widow apparently about 60, very genteel and fine looking. She has quite the air of a lady from long familiarity with the whites. She is a widow, and her name is Mrs. John. She showed us a likeness of her father taken in London when he was a young man.

O-dä-da-ŏne-dus-ta
Self [?] Blower

An implement designed for showering the eye, and for cooling it when inflamed. It is designed to shower water into the eye by blowing into one end after it is filled either with cold water or medicinal water. An Indian invention used for some years.

> Ah-was-ha [*a'wáshæ:'* 'earring']
> or earring   10/-
> Necklace   7.00
> Burden strap   1.25
> Three [?] ladles   .75
> Canoe   1.00

John Jacobs, a Cayuga, 74 years of age. [His Indian name is] Jote-ho-weh-ko.[10] He was born at the Cayuga village three miles south of Springport on the Deep Gully creek. The council house of the Cayugas was a mile and a half from the lake. The village was scattered along the creek. It was called Gă-yä-gä-an-ha. Springport was called Ge-wä-ga, a neck of land, and means the point north of Springport. The name of the Indian village means "inclined" referring to the rapid descent of the ground. He says there were abundant springs upon the bank so that it was not necessary to go down to the creek for water.

Ne-o-däk-he-ät was the name of the head of the Cayuga lake. It means simply "the end"; with the word lake added it would be described as "the end of Cayuga." There is a legend in relation to one of the falls on the east side of the lake, either Clifton or Paine's creek falls, that it was the "place where the snake fell off." It was called Sä-wees-tă-o (where the serpent fell).

Iris-ge-ne-un-dä-quä
or Silver Beads
[*yǫthwístaniyǫtáhkwa'* 'silver beads, pendants,'
or literally, 'one uses it to hang metal/silver']

It means "hanging" or "pendant." It is worn around the hat, in the hair, or dangling down before, where the dress opens.

Dä-de-trä or Cane
[*atá'tishæ'* 'cane,' or literally, 'what one leans on']

This singular cane was carved by an Indian and presented to John Jacobs.

Gä-a-o-tä-ges

or Male or Female Shoulder or Neck Ornament

[*ka'éohta:kęs*, literally, 'smelly grass']

The word signifies "sweet smelling grass" because the strands are made of a long wiry grass which grows in marshy ground, and emits a sweet smell when worn at certain times. They made a very pretty ornament.

Ose-ca wild flax. Ain't got any.[11]

An-ne-us-kă or Silver Broach

[*ę:nyáskæ:'* 'brooch']

These broaches which are of all sizes are worn by the Indian women, on their overdress and sometimes in strings around their hats.

Wampum belt Gä-sweh-ta [*kaswęhta'* 'wampum, wampum belt'][12]

Wampum beads Ote-ko-ah [*otkóæ'* 'wampum (string)']

Burden strap Gus-hä-ä [*kasha:a'* 'strap, halter, cord']

Burden strap worked with porcupine quills Da-gä-ha-dä-ugh-ha Gus-hä-ä

Porcupine quill O-ha-dä [*ohé'ta'* 'porcupine quill']

Bread turner Ya-ă-go-jen-tä-quä To take out bread with [*yéæhkojęhtahkwa'*, literally, 'one scoops up bread with it']

Baby frame Gä-us-heh Ga-ose-hă Gä-us-hă [*kę́:oshæ'* 'cradleboard']

Brant's medal Ont-wis-dä-ga-dust-hä and means any medal

Spear Gä-se-gwă [*kahse:kwa'* 'spear']

Spear for fighting Gä-se-gwă, Na, Ong-wa, Yun-dä-dä-gä-tä-quä which signifies a spear to pierce men with

Soup stirrer Gät-go-ne-äs-heh [*katkónya'shæ'* 'stirring instrument, paddle, oar, ladle,' or literally, 'it stirs']

Knee rattles Gä-so-ă and may be either tin or deer's hoofs [*kastáwę'sæ'* 'rattle']

Ladle ä-do-gwä-seh [*atókwa'shæ'* 'spoon, ladle,' or literally, 'the thing that scatters, spreads out']

Finger ring ă-neä-hus-hä [*ę'nyáhashæ'* 'finger ring,' or literally, 'what one ties around the finger']

Silver band Da-yä-ese-tä-hus-tä

Necklace Gä-teäs-hă Any necklace [*katę́'ashæ'* 'what one puts over oneself']

Tä-yen-dä-ná-ga. Joseph Brant. Two sticks lying side by side[13]

Total number of Iroquois on Grand River 2310, as follows

Mohawks	700
Tuscaroras	300
Onondagas	400
Cayugas	700
Oneidas	
Senecas, and	210
Chippeways	

This estimate was given to us by Peter Smith, a Mohawk at Grand River. He further told us that there were about 500 Mohawks about 30 miles above Kingston on the northern side of the lake on a fine [?] reservation [i.e., Tyendinaga reserve or Deseronto]. Besides this there are a number at Caughnawaga below Kingston and also at St. Regis.

Brant's Descendants

There are now living two daughters of Brant. The youngest Catharine is now 57 years of age, a widow, having the name of Catharine John. She resides at Brantford. The other is Margaret, residing also near Brantford. Elizabeth Kerr, the third daughter died in 1845, at Wellington Square.

Catherine has one son living, a dissolute man. He has four children. Elizabeth left six children. Margaret I believe has none. John Brant left no children, was never married. Jacob, the brother of John and Catharine etc. left children. One of them the wife of Peter Smith we stayed with at Grand River. She has 6 children. From which it is apparent that the Brant family will not soon disappear.

Catharine is a fine looking, and ladylike woman. We purchased of her a quantity of wampum which belonged to her father, and also a copper breast plate mounted with silver which belonged to her father. This relic of the great captain we purchased for $3.00. The wampum for $4.00 about 2000 beads. It used to sell she told us at 4/- per hundred bead. We paid at the rate of 2/-. They are usually in strings of several strands each, and about 3 feet long. A string of six strands was the value of a life,[14] but it was of the white kind, or a mixture of white and purple. This wampum is now scarce, as it contains their laws and usages.[15] It used to be abundant, but as it is customary to bury portions of it with the dead and none is now manufactured, it has become scarce and valuable. We heard of but two or three belts of wampum, and these were valued as near as we could ascertain at $25 or $30.

Grand River Reservation

Originally they had 100 miles by treaty on Grand River extending from above Brantford towards the mouth of the river. It is greatly reduced by sales to the government. The Indians mostly reside on the west side of the river where the reservation reaches back 6 miles from the river, and runs about 20 or thirty miles from Brantford down. They have some hundreds of acres reserved upon the east side of the river. Smith told me that in all they had about 50,000 acres, but there must be more than this. The Mohawks are at the upper end of the reserve, and are mostly Christianized. Next are the Onondagas, and next and last the Cayugas. These two nations are almost entirely pagan and adhere to their dances, and ancient customs. The land on this river back from the bottom land, which is small, is hard to till, and suffers for water. The Indian mode of tillage is also peculiarly exhausting, as they seldom or never seed down their lots after ploughing. These Indians are in a fair condition of progress, and will eventually turn out some free [?] men.

Fish Carrier

So-ace or Peter Fish Carrier, the son of Ho-jä-ga-ta, or Fish Carrier, the celebrated Cayuga sachem who resided at Canoga [on the west side of Cayuga Lake] is now about 60 or 70 years old. He is fine looking, intelligent, and sociable. We had a pleasant time with him. At the time of Sullivan's invasion, 1779, his father removed with the Cayugas to Niagara, and from thence to Buffalo [Creek] where he remained until his death. Fish Carrier did not return to Cayuga after Sullivan's invasion. Steeltrap, Hise-tă-je, with a large number of Cayugas did return, and so did Fish Carrier to attend the treaties of 1795, etc. After the death of Fish Carrier, when his son was about 13 years old, the family removed to Grand River where they have since resided. Fish Carrier has a flourishing family, is now quite independent, and a member of the Christian party, which perhaps accounts for his living at the upper end of the reserve among the Mohawks. We bought his seashell medal for $5.00 which he had made at Niagara.

John Jacobs. Jote-ho-weh-ko.

Jacobs was by far the finest looking man we saw on the reservation. He is a Cayuga sachem, and 70 or 80 years old, very pleasant and sociable. He is a pagan in his customs and habits, and when we saw him last was on his way to attend a False Face dance. We obtained of him the names or tribes of the Cayuga, Oneida, and Mohawk sachems, which are given on another paper.[16] He says the Oneidas and Mohawks never had but three tribes. We bought of him the curiously carved cane and the best new burden strap. Also the silver beads, $7.00. Also the plume [?] of white heron's feathers.

Grand River

This river is made navigable by means of dams and locks from Brantford to its mouth, and a small steamer runs up and down each alternate day. The river at the Onondaga council house or rather at [the] English [Anglican] Church some 10 miles below Brantford is a quite beautiful river and the scenery upon its banks very attractive. There are no bridges over the stream as it ranges from 15 to 40 rods in width, but there are numerous [?] canoes along the bank which are public to anyone, and occasionally a boat ferry for teams. At this season of the year at least, the fogs are a great inconvenience. The fog is constant in the morning and lasts until towards 10 A.M. Along the bank of the river is a regular towpath, with bridges over the marshy grounds so that vessels are towed up and down loaded with lumber and grain. Large quantities of pine wood [?] are carried from this river in boats and in rafts to our side, and some of sent even to New York. The river was made a canal about 20 years ago.

1850 Tonawanda Field Notes

. . . . .
. . .
.

Visit to Tonawanda, Dec. 26, 1850
After Articles for State Collection

———— • • ————

False Face Dance

———— • • ————

Left Rochester Christmas morning after the great snowstorm for Batavia. From thence to Alabama Center in the stage, and from thence by private opportunity to Spencer Parker's, where I arrived in season for an excellent Christmas dinner at 3 P.M. After dinner came over to Mr. W. Parker's where I now am in his sleigh. The roads are almost impassable, the snow almost 3 feet deep. Dec. 26 at Mr. Parker's.

Kinds of Bark Used for Strap

Ose-gă, Slippery elm [*ó:skæ'* 'slippery elm'], O-să, Basswood [*o:osæ'* 'basswood'], and Noke, a species of reed or cane which grows in marshy ground [*kano:ta'* 'reed, flute']. It grows about 4 feet high and is called Indian hemp. But one kind of bark is used in each burden strap. The slippery elm is the best and most used as it is the most pliable, and has the strongest and finest thread. They take off the bark in small strips about three feet long and having boiled it in ashes and water and after drying it they run it off into small filaments or strips, which they put up in skeins (see woodcut). To make the strap they first make by twisting or braiding about 20 cords, or strips the length of the central part or band. In making the belt or band in the center they use their hands alone. The filling or thread which is braided in with the warp is small, about the size of coarse thread. This is twisted by hand as it is passed over and under, and braided in with warp cords one by one. It is braided from right to left and then back again, after which the filling is pushed back by hand, and worked up until it becomes solid and compact. Although woven by hand it is done so closely that in the finer specimens you cannot see through them any more than in cloth. After the band is done, the cords are continued by new filaments to the requisite length, and are then braided into ropes. The filling is colored some dark color.

Hair Burden Strap

The finer specimens are often ornamented on one side with moose or elk hair. Near the rump of the moose (O-yen-dä-ne) [*oyętani'* 'moose'] between the hip bones, and near the neck between the shoulder bones there is a tuft of white hair. These hairs are fine and round, and about four inches long, each tuft yielding about a handful, but more in a large one. These hairs are then dyed red, blue, and yellow, and [they] use some white or uncolored. Sometimes one side of the strap is entirely covered with this hair worked in various [?] patterns or speckled here and there with small figures. It is done in this way. The thread used as filling when it comes up on the face of the strap is wound round with hair of the color selected. Four hairs are used together in winding, but are wound parallel and not as one. After the cross thread is passed through to the underside, it shows only [on] back surface. This work is so neatly and ingeniously done that the moose hair appears only upon one side of the strap, and the other at the same time is uniform and precise. The elk (Jo-na-dä) [*jonǫ́ętaʼ* 'elk'] yields the same kind of hair but not in as large quantities as the moose. The Iroquois used this hair for no other purpose. The Chippewas use it on birchbark in a great variety of fancy work. The name of moose hair is O-yen-dä-ne-o-eh-dä [*oyętaniʼ* 'moose']. It would take 6 or 8 days to make a strap of the best kind.

Common Burden Strap
(woodcuts)

Another burden strap is made in a more hurried [?] manner. The warp or main cords are prepared as in other cases, about the size of common twine. A cord smaller in size is then run through each cord between the strands of it by means of a bone needle having an eye like a large darning needle. In this manner the warp cords are brought close together, and held firmly in their places. It is not made so tight however, but that you can see through in places. After the band or strap is made of the requisite length, the warp is continued by catching new plaits until the entire length of the strap is made. Then these are braided into ropes.

Still another kind of burden strap is made of basswood, braided like splint basketwork. It makes a durable but not as good an article as the slippery elm.

Ropes
(woodcut)

In making ropes, basswood bark is used as it is the coarsest. The bark is taken off in long strips, boiled in ashes and water, washed and dried. It is then stripped off in long filaments as long as they will run, and tied up into skeins, when it is ready for use.

In making rope these strands only are used. They are braided by hand without twisting. When the filaments run out, others are added, and thus the rope is continued to any length.

Coloring Bark Thread

They color in various ways by boiling the skeins of thread in some solution. They used both vegetable and mineral substances, and sometimes combine them. The filling of all the finer burden straps is colored in this way, while the warp and the ropes at the ends are uncolored, and therefore light. The best quality of slippery elm bark is of a light stone [?] color, but the most of it has a reddish tinge. In ancient times they made hunting bags of slippery elm thread and also many other articles. (Both 1.50)

Ancient Costume

In ancient times the women wore deerskin moccasins and pantalets, the latter worn tight to the skin, and went down over the moccasins. No embroidery was used. The skirt also was of deerskin, and made in the same style or fashion as at present. The overdress was also made of the same material. But the blanket was dressed with hair on, the women and men both using the deer and bear skin blanket. The male costume consisted of deerskin moccasins without ornament at a very early day. The legging was also of deerskin and tight to the legs. In ancient times they used the breechcloth instead of the kilt, the kilt being modern. When they began to use cotton shirts they laid aside the breechcloth and wore shirts down to the knee. Mrs. Parker thinks the kilt is not of Indian origin, at least it did not originate with [the] Iroquois. They may have had a deerskin shirt. The kilt however never was worn as a common article of apparel, but merely in the dance. Perhaps it may have been of Scotch origin.

Basket Making

But one kind of splint is used. It is black ash (Gä-o-wo same as canoe) [*ka:ǫwǫ*' 'boat']. They usually take trees about a foot in diameter, sometimes less. They cut a tree free from limbs, and then take off [the] clear part cutting [it] into strips about 6 feet long. They then pound off the bark and pound the log itself lightly to make the splints run. They then strip off as long as the splints will run. In other words, they commence at the lower end and mark [?] a strip about 3 inches wide, and pound from the butt to the upper end. They then strip it off as it readily peels. They thus go around and round the tree until they take all of the white part off. The heart is useless. They then scrape this with a knife on both sides, and cut this of the requisite width, which can be easily done, running with the grain. For fine work the splint is then split with a knife. This gives it a white and smooth surface. For heavy baskets or coarse work, the splints are used without splitting. This is an original Indian art.

The yellow color is made by boiling the yellow oak bark in water with a handful of ashes and a little alum. The splints after they are split and ready are stained upon one side. They are always stained before the basket is made. The red color is made by boiling the bark of the O-sto-dese-kă, a shrub or bush which grows along the creek in water with a handful of ashes. Blue is made from indigo. Green. The name of splint is O-weh-gă [*oːwęʼkæ* 'wood, splint']. Open work basket O-gä-kä-ah [*okáhkaǫ* 'it has bigger holes in it']. Market basket Da-gäs-ha [*tekaʼashǽːǫh* 'cross basket,' or literally, 'crossways']. Back basket Yunt-ga-tos-tä [*yǫtkéhtastha*', literally, 'one uses it to carry over the shoulder']. Covered basket Nä-dä-was-yas. Comb basket Ya-nó-tä-dä-guä [*yenǫhtatáhkwa*', literally, 'one uses it to put comb(s) in'].

Yont-kä-do-quä or Fish Basket-net
[*yǫtkéhtahkwa*' 'basket you carry over your back and shoulders,'
or literally, 'one uses it to carry over the shoulders']
(woodcut)

This is made of splint in the shape of a conical basket. It is about two feet and a half long by twelve or fifteen inches in width at the mouth. To take fish they stand in the rapid shallow water of the creek and manage by means of a stick to direct the fish into it as they shoot down the creek. As soon as one is heard to flutter in the basket, it is raised from the water, and the fish secured. In early times when fish abounded in every stream, it was a convenient and ready method of taking them.

Ken-dä-ah, or Arm Band of Deer Tail

They stripped up the skin from the root of the tail sufficiently to fasten over [?] the arm and then let the tail hang down above the elbow. In the same manner they wore it hanging down from the back of the head,

A WAR DANCE

Figure 43. "A War Dance" by David Cusick, in Cusick, Sketches of the Ancient History of the Six Nations *(1848). (Courtesy of the Department of Rare Books and Special Collections, University of Rochester Library.)*

the band or string going around the forehead. See Cusick's pamphlet [see fig. 43].[17]

O-no-ne-ä-dä-quä, or Cornhusk Overshoe
[*o:níyehtáhkwa'*, literally, 'it is used for making it solid']
woodcut

As the fastening which holds the foot to the snowshoe would soon imitate the foot in consequence of the weight of the shoe, the contrivance in question was made to obviate this difficulty. It is made of cornhusks held in their places by cords of slippery elm thread by means of which the husks are bound together. Before lashing the moccasin to the snowshoe, this cornhusk overshoe is passed over it and the fastenings are then secured around it. This relieves the foot from the pressure of the strings and at the same time adds to the warmth of the foot.

Indian tobacco. O-yeh-gwä-a-weh.
[*oyé'kwa'o:weh* 'native tobacco']

Sumac. Ote-ko-dä.
[*otkó'ta'* 'sumac']

Gä-go-sä, or False Face

[*kakǫhsa'* 'face, false face']

In an[cient] times there was a regular band or society in each Indian village called False Faces. They had a species of initiation, regular forms and ceremonies, and a regular method of laying down a membership. The superstitious notion which prevailed on a great many subjects in Indian society are fully exemplified in the office and costume of the False Faces. Among other things they professed the power of curing diseases, but were sagacious enough to confine themselves in this respect to those which were comparatively harmless. The legend says that False Faces were seen wild in the woods in ancient times, and had medicinal powers. The idea of becoming one of the False Faces always originated in a dream, which they regarded as a species of supernatural visitation. Anyone dreaming he was a False Face had only to signify his dream to the proper person, and give a feast to be at once initiated and so on the other hand anyone wishing to give up his membership had to dream that he had retired from the band, and give a feast, and his exit was completed. The members were called False Faces from the fact that they wore a false face of the kind represented in the figure on all occasions when they appeared in character. Their masks were diversified in style and color, agreeing however in one respect, that of being equally hideous. The members of the band were all males save one who was a female, and the master of the band. She was called Gä-go-sä Ha-wun-nas-tase-tä, or Keeper of the False Faces. She not only had charge of the regalia of the band, but was the only one with whom any person could communicate with the False Faces, whose names were a secret. If anyone dreamed that he was a False Face to her he made known the dream and from her received directions to prepare an entertainment and the time when at which the False Faces appeared, and the ceremony of initiation was performed. If anyone was sick of either of the diseases which the False Faces could cure, and dreamed he saw a False Face, this was an evidence that they were to perform his cure. Information was communicated to the keeper, and the time by her immediately appointed to visit the invalid, who was directed to have a certain kind of a feast prepared. At the time appointed, which was always in the daytime, the False Faces, each one masked, with arms bare, and a tattered blanket over his shoulders, marched in procession, headed by the woman, to the house of the invalid. When they came near to the house the woman pointed it out whereupon they all ran to the door and commenced shaking their turtle shell rattles, which each held in his hand. Soon the woman came up and entered alone. When the patient was ready within she informed those without who opened the door and the first one entered. Falling down upon the floor he rolled himself up to the fireplace, and commenced stirring up the ashes with his hands. With his hands hot and full of ashes he turned to the patient who was made to stand up in the room, and sprinkled the ashes over his or her head and face. The others came in in the same manner, and went through the same process. After they had thus covered the invalid with ashes, and had stroked down his hair and face they commenced the False Face dance. If well enough the patient continued in the dance with them to the end, but if not, he was led around once, and then allowed to be seated while they finished the dance, which usually lasted about half an hour. After the dance was concluded, a small vessel carried by each person was filled with the article [?] (pudding) prepared for the occasion, after which they all departed. Anyone was allowed to be present. Toothache, nosebleed, inflamed eyes, and swellings are the curable diseases. Sometimes burns [?] and other disorders were included.

During the New Year's, on the second day, the False Faces go around from house to house and stir the ashes, strewing them over the floor unless appeased with tobacco. When the plague appears like the cholera, or smallpox the False Faces turn out and visit every house and dance, and throw around the ashes to drive away the plague. This was done as recently as [the] summer before last among the pagan part of the population at Tonawanda.

In ancient times there was a supernatural being called a False Face. It was merely a face, as was seen in the trees, darting from point to point, sometimes attached to the trunk, sometimes to the limb. If anyone chanced to see one it produced such a fright as to make their nose bleed. They are supposed[18] to have the power of inflicting disease and pestilence, but they had no power of speech. They are held in the highest terror. To this day a certain class believe in their present existence implicitly, they having been seen within a few years. For this reason the False Face band is supposed to propitiate the False Faces, and is kept up for that purpose.

Needlework, Bead

In this work the eye is the chief reliance. They never work from patterns, or drawings, except as they may have seen them in print. They imitate natural objects, like flowers, with great accuracy. The art of flowering as they call it is the most difficult of any part of beadwork, for the reason that in addition to an accurate knowledge of the flower at the stage in which it is to be represented, they must be able to imitate closely. In combining colors they never seek for strong contrasts, but choose those which most harmoniously blend with each other. White beads are most used, and usually to separate other colors. In making up their combinations the following general rules are observed: light green and pink go well together with white between, dark blue and yellow also with white between, red and light blue with white between, dark purple and light purple with white between. For flowering dark green are used for stems with white glass, pink glass and green glass, and pale yellow glass for the flowers.

Porcupine Quills. O-ha-dä.
[*ohë'ta'* 'porcupine quill']
(woodcut)

The name of the porcupine is Gä-ha-dä [*kahë'ta'* 'porcupine']. His quills have been used from an early day for ornamental purposes by the Indian female. These quills are from one to three inches in length, the outer end or about one-third being black or brown, and the lower part or that nearest the body being white. These quills are dyed yellow, blue, and red, and are then used for embroidering moccasins, and other articles of apparel. To flat[ten] them down they are soaked and compressed between the finger nails. In this condition they make the broad quill sewn in the outer border of this moccasin. The others are used round, and secured by thread which is stitched round and round the quill at short intervals as seen in this moccasin. The quills are spliced by inserting one into the other. No patterns are used, but the eye and the taste furnished their only guides. In dyeing they use different kinds of roots. The darker end of the quill is not changed by the color. Consequently this part is cut off and thrown away. The porcupine is of a dark color, as the outend [outer end] of the quill alone is seen. In working these quills red and blue are used with white between. Yellow is placed between two blues.

Satchel. Gä-yä-ah.
[*kaya:a'* 'bag']

This beautiful article is of Seneca manufacture. Upon one side the lower figure is designed to represent a rosebush, with its flowers at different stages of maturity from those [which] are just opening to those [which] are in full bloom. The success of the imitation although not perfect by any means is yet quite striking. It is quite easy to detect the opening rose in the bud at the left. The same thing is attempted on the rose at the top. On the reverse side are two stars, which as specimens of fancywork are certainly very tastefully and ingeniously made. It is an imitation of the ordinary travelling bag of the whites, and not an Indian article.

Knee rattle of tin. Ga-so-ă.
Splint. O-weh-gă. [*o:wę'kæ:'* 'wood, splint']
Finger catcher.[19] Go-yo-ga-ace.
Wrist bands[,] bead. Yen-nus-ho-gwa-hos-ta. [*yęnęsho'kwáhastha'* 'brace-let,' or literally, 'one uses it to tie around the wrist']

Table Spread[20]

5 bunches small white beads 15 cts. bunch				75
3	Do	"	white glass "	45
3	Do	"	pink glass "	45
3	Do	"	green beads "	45
3	Do	"	red " "	45
3	Do	"	light blue "	45
3	Do	"	dark blue "	45
3	Do	"	pink "	45
3	Do	"	gold color "	45
1/2 pound of coarse white beads				50
1 bunch of lilac				15
				− 5.10
1 1/2 yards of blue broadcloth $5.				7.50
6 yards of ribbon at 6 @				.13
" making				7.50
				———
				$20.13

Sheaf for Arrows. Gä-däs-hă.

[*ka'ta:shæ'* 'quiver']

This is an Indian invention and of great antiquity. It is made of deerskin flat on the back and curved in front, a mere sack in which the arrows are placed with the feathers out. The ordinary sheaf would hold from fifteen to twenty-four arrows. It was worn on the back, inclining from the left shoulder down towards the belt on the right side of the body. It was secured around the waist below, or to the belt usually worn by the Indian, while at the top it was fastened by a small belt passing around the neck and under the left arm. The arrows projected slightly above the left shoulder, and were drawn out of the sheaf with the right hand. In ancient times when the bow and arrow were shot, the former [was] about three and the latter about two feet in length. In modern times when the bow and arrow are used for ornament, and consequently the muscular strength not as great, both the bow and the arrow are made longer, the bow being from three to four feet, and the arrow from two to three. They used to use the skin of a wolf or an otter entire for a sheaf having the tail on hanging down.

Hair Ornament. A-ne-us-hä-nen-dok-tä-quä.
(woodcut)

This is designed purely as a female ornament for the hair. The body is made of wood, which is covered with deerskin. It is fastened to the knot of hair behind by means of a loop in the center of it through [which] the string which ties up the knot of hair is passed. Silver-headed nails are then driven in around the border of the article. The Indian female gathers her hair behind, and ties it up something in the fashion of the cue, except that it is doubled up from below. The ornament in question runs as high as the level of the ear, and descends halfway to the bottom of the knot of hair. In ancient times it was much worn.

Sioux. Squäw-ke-hä.
Osages. Wä-sä-sa. [*wasa:se'*] } Spencer C. Parker

Shoulder Belt. Yunt-ka-to-dă-tä.
[*yotkéhtotê:hta'* 'shoulder belt,'
or literally, 'one uses it to put over the shoulders']

Whether the Indian custom of wearing a belt over the left shoulder was an ancient fashion of theirs or an imitation of the sash in our own military costume is uncertain. The Senecas are of [the] opinion that the practice persisted among them from an early day. This belt is of deerskin and ornamented with beadwork. In ancient times porcupine quills were used instead of beads. In some instances another belt was passed around the neck from behind and passed down in front between the arms and was tied behind.

Waist Belt of Deerskin. Da-yunt-wä-hos-tä.

[*teyǫ́thwahástha'* 'waist belt,'

or literally, 'one uses it to tie around oneself']

This belt is in the ancient style, and to be distinguished from the bead and worsted belt Gä-geh-tä [*kakéhta'* 'sash'] described in the last report. It is embroidered with porcupine quills in a tasteful manner. The center [?] width [?] is entirely of porcupine quills. It is put on from the front back, and the ends brought around in front again and tied. This kind of belt was laid aside when the worsted and bead belt came into use.

Deerskin Leggings. Got-ko-on-dä Gise-hă.

[*káishæ'* 'leggings']

This is also the ancient legging. In ancient times as elsewhere stated the costume of the Iroquois consisted of the moccasin, legging, waist cloth, and blanket. When the shirt of the whites came into use after the discovery, the waist cloth was laid aside for the shirt. The naked Indians on the plains in the Indian territory still wear the moccasin, the leggings, and the waist cloth. In the winter they add the buffalo blanket. This was doubtless the American Indian costume from the earliest day down to the discovery. The kilt is thought to be a modern article, invented, or adopted merely as a fancy article to use in the dance. It was never an everyday article of apparel. The leggings are perfectly plain except upon the sides, which project beyond the seam. A border of porcupine quillwork extends up and down the sides, and still outside of this is a fringe of deerskins. This is in the old style in every respect.

Moccasins. At-tä-quä-o-weh.

[*ahtáhkwa'ǫːweh* 'native shoe, moccasin']

In ancient times the moccasin was entirely plain, but it soon came to be ornamented, as the tastes of the people improved. First came the porcupine quill, the most ready article to be found for embroidery, and it is at least equally beautiful with the bead, and to the Indian eye much more so. The above specimen is genuine in every respect, being entirely of deerskin and porcupine quill, and embroidered after the ancient fashion. It is truly beautiful, and the more closely it is examined the better it looks.

Shot Pouch. A-squă-dä-qua.

Silver Beads. O-wis-tä-no-o O-stä-o-guä.
[*o:wístano:o'* 'silver,' or literally,
'precious metal'; *ostéo'kwa'* 'bead']

This string contains 41 silver, and 9 blue glass beads of the antique kind. It was worn by the mother of Spencer C. Parker's wife. Beads of this description are now very rare.

Baby Frame Belt. Ga-swä-hos-hă.
[probably *ka:wáhashæ'* 'belt,' or literally,
'it is tied around the waist']

The red and the blue belts or bands are both called by this name. The red one commences under the chin and winds down. Next comes the blue belt with points, which is short and called Gä-nose-gä [*kanǫhsęhka:*, literally, 'it has a tie on it']. After this comes the blue one which comes out at the foot-board. These bands are passed under deerskin strings which are secured to the bottom of the frame. Over the bow is drawn the shawl or veil called Yun-dus-ho-dä-quä, which entirely conceals the face of the infant. Hanks [?] are laid upon the bottom of the frame, and the child is thus covered entirely with the exception of the face. In ancient times they used for the baby frame the broad spreading horns of the moose, which are well adapted to this purpose. The veil is usually hung with silver ornaments as also other parts of the strapping [?].

Gä-nó-sote.
[*kanóhsǫ:t* 'house']

All the families who occupied the same house held their stores in common, no matter how many families. They usually had one fire to about four families, that is, one for every two partitions, a family living on each side of the fire. They had regular times for cooking in which they got up food for the whole household. The principal cooking was in the morning. After it was cooked it was handed around among all, and if any was left it was put aside. In the evening or near night they usually cooked their hominy. Bread was made in the morning. The morning was the only regular meal. After that they partook as they felt disposed. Mrs. Parker remembers being in a bark house with two fires, and eight families, four on each side.[21] The partitions were sometimes the length of but one person, at others of two, depending on the size of the family. One or two spaces between partitions were set apart for storerooms, where they put their bark barrels, corn etc.

Mrs. Parker had never heard of a house with more than three fires in her day. All within the house were relatives or near friends. Their stores were all in common. If anyone took anything by the chase it went into the common stock for the whole establishment. The same with their corn. It was all in common. It is probably that Mr. Greenhalgh was mistaken about his 12 or 13 fires in the houses at Dä-yö-de-hok-to in 1677.[22] Still he may not have been. The bark used for this kind of house is black ash.

Wampum Belt. Gä-sweh-dä Ote-ko-ă.

[*kaswę̆hta'* 'wampum, wampum belt'; *otkóæ'* 'wampum (string)']
Wampum [belts] were usually three fingers wide, but sometimes they were six inches wide. The ordinary length of the belt was from four to six feet. They used it also for shoulder belts, also for wrist bands, and also for a species of collar around the neck. The belt was after all of any length or width depending upon its use. In ancient times wampum was a species of money, that is, everybody wanted it, and it was convenient to [use as] change [?].[23] All Indian ornaments are their currency, and they change hands like our money. White wampum was no more valuable than purple. They used it mixed, and either color pure, just as circumstances suggested. They made a treaty with the Cherokees many years ago by which it was agreed the council fire between the two nations should be in the territory of the Cherokees. A belt of white wampum was given at the making of this treaty several inches wide. It was used as a ransom for murder. In the belt made at the formation of the League[24] [the design] was made with five men standing with joined hands representing each nation. This is now at Grand River in the hands of an Onondaga chief by the name of Skä-no-wan-de (Hill) who has lots of it.[25] Subsequently a sixth was added to represent the Tuscaroras. Figures of men were often woven into their belts, but Parker does not know as he ever saw or heard of animals being thus woven. They got wampum from the English and Dutch. It was also used in the confession of sins.[26]

Bark Barrel. Gä-snä Gä-ose-hă.

[*kasnǫ'* 'bark'; *ka'áshæ'* 'basket']
The barrel was used for a great variety of purposes, to store corn, charred corn, beans, etc. It was also used to put corn in before it was buried in pits or caches. Mrs. Parker says in the War of 1812 when the British were expected over, the Senecas at Tonawanda buried their corn in barrels, covered

them over with bark and then with earth. Bark barrels formerly were to be found in every family and in numbers. The Senecas think that the corn was always shelled and put in barrels, and the charred corn also was put in barrels before it was buried, and not poured into bark repositories as others have believed. These bark barrels are always made of black ash, the trays of red elm, sap tubs [of] red elm. In the barrel the grain runs round the barrel. If taken care of the barrel will last a hundred years. They were used as a species of chest or bureau for clothes and personal ornaments. The uses of the barrel are infinite.

Burden Frame. Gä-ne-co-wä-ah.

This is a very ancient contrivance to assist in carrying burdens. It will carry bark, or wood or meat, or game, or a child, anything in fact which can be carried about by hand can be carried with this frame. Hunters use this as well as women at home. A basket may be set on the frame. 80 or 100 pounds can be carried by a stout man or even more. All that he can carry can be carried on this frame. It is made of hickory or other tough timber. Two straps are attached to the frame, one passes around the forehead, and the other across the shoulders and chest. They are inserted in the frame at the same point. The frame consists of two pieces of hickory. The bottom part is arched around in a bow, and an eye or socket formed [?] at each end by shaving it down and bending it back. The part which is lapped is fastened with hickory bark. The upright part is of the same size and shape but longer. The two ends pass through the eyes made in the lower part at right angles which are cut away some so as to be held firmly. Basswood bark strips are then passed between the bows both ways, and fastened to the rims by being inserted under the bark. The bark is preferred to splints because it is more durable. A burden strap is then secured to the frame at two points where the upper [?] strip of bark crosses from side to side, and in such a way as to leave the band part of the burden strap in the center. The strings are then carried down to the bottom of the frame and passed under and around the articles which are to be carried. When the frame is empty the strings are carried up again to the top of the frame and tied as in the figure. The frame when loaded is placed upon the back and the burden strap passed over the head and placed across the chest. To rest one, the strap is put against the forehead for a change. If the load be very heavy, then two straps are attached, one to place against the forehead, and the other against the shoulder and chest.

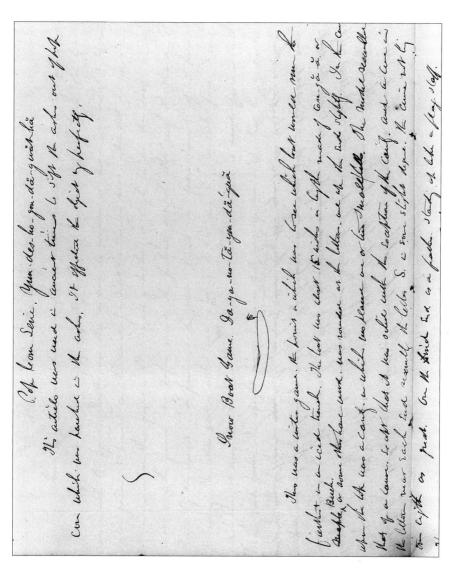

Figure 44. Page from Morgan's 1850 Tonawanda field notes containing sketch of snow boat. (Courtesy of the Department of Rare Books and Special Collections, University of Rochester Library.)

Corn Sieve. Yun-des-ho-gon-dá-gwät-hä.

This article was used in ancient times to sift the ashes out of pop corn which was parched in the ashes. It effected the object very perfectly.

Boat Game. Da-ya-no-tä-yen-dä'-qua.

[*teyenotayętáhkwa*', literally, 'they use it for putting down a reed or flute']

[*For sketch here, see fig. 44.*]

This was a winter game, the point in which was to see which boat would run the farthest in an iced trench. The boat was about 15 inches in length, made of Ose-gă-gă, or beech [*'oskę'ę* 'seed, pit' also 'beech, beechnut'], or some other hardwood, was rounded at the bottom and up the ends slightly. In the center upon the top was a cavity in which was placed one or two small bells. The model resembled that of a canoe, except that it was solid with the exception of the cavity, and a curve in the bottom near each end resembling the letter S in some slight degree, the curve not being one eighth as great. On the hind end is a feather, standing up like a flagstaff. The race is downhill and upon the level below. Each one who enters into the game makes a track or path or trench from the top of some hill to the bottom, and for some distance beyond, as near straight as may be. It is made by treading down the snow the width of the feet. After this water is poured in the trench, and as it runs down the hill leaves behind a track of ice. In this way an ice road is made down the hill and for some distance be-yond. As many as play the game have an iced road of their own. To make the speed still greater water is poured over the bottom of the boat, and made to freeze, until the bottom is covered with ice. At the time appointed the parties meet, and bet, and divide off as in other games. The boat which runs the farthest wins as in the snow snake game. They have six or eight on a side and bets [?], but each one has a road of his own. The people are gen-erally at the bottom of the hill. In ancient times this was a favorite game in the coldest winter months. All the boats must be of a len[g]th. All need not be started together, usually about half are set down at a time, and the remainder when the first get at the bottom of the hill. The game was from 15 to 20, and the one who first made that number won the game. If the bet-ting was unusually great the number of the game was greater. The people divided by tribes as in other games.

Finis. Dec. 30, 1850.

[For list of articles and prices here, see fig. 36.]

8

. . . . .

Morgan's Reports

Second Regents Report

. . . . .
. . .
.

II.

To the Honorable the Board of Regents of the University of the State of New-York.

THE undersigned submits, with the specimens of Indian Art, herewith presented to the State " Historical and Antiquarian Collection," the following Report upon their names and localities:

But few remains of the skill and industry of our predecessors have come down to us, to illustrate the era of Indian occupation. The low state of the most useful arts among them detracts greatly from the interest with which the scanty vestiges of their civilization would otherwise be invested. Such specimens as we discover are rude to the last degree in their construction, and bespeak a social condition of extreme simplicity. Still there is no condition of man, however rude, in which he is not surrounded by mementoes of his handy-work. The possession of the thinking principle, and of the human form, render existence without work impossible. Artificial contrivances are inseparable from the social state; and when these specimens of human ingenuity are brought together, they unlock the social history of the people from whom they come. In this view especially, the artificial remains of our Indian predecessors, inconsiderable as they are in every ordinary sense, possess an intrinsic value, and should be sought out and preserved as the unwritten history of their social existence.

The establishment of an Indian Cabinet, under the shadow of the State Geological Collection, is by no means a barren or unpromising enterprise. There is not in our Republic an Indian Collection which fully and fairly illustrates the condition of the arts among our Indian races. It is much clearer that there should be such a Cabinet, than that it can be collected; and as to the feasibility of the enterprise, it is at least worthy of the effort. The fugitive specimens are sufficiently numerous for a respectable foundation, and new relics will be constantly exhumed for centuries to come.

The remains of Indian art which are found scattered over, and entombed within, the soil of New-York, are of two distinct kinds, and to be ascribed to widely different periods. The first class belong to the Ante-Columbian period, as it is denominated by Indian scholars;

No. 20.] 85

or the era of the " Mound Builders," whose defensive works, mounds, and sacred enclosures are scattered so profusely throughout the West, especially in the State of Ohio, in which they have their fullest development. The remains of this period indicate a semi-civilization of the most imposing character, and also a considerable development of the art of agriculture. Exclusive of the mounds and enclosures, they have left implements of copper and chert, of stone, porphyry and earthen, some of which are elaborately and ingeniously wrought. We have in various parts of our State many trench enclosures, or Fort Hills, as they are popularly called, which belong to the same era, and to the same system of works as those constructed by the " Mound Builders" of Ohio and the Mississippi valley. Within these enclosures, and in their immediate vicinity, artificial remains are always discovered.

With the second period, we may in our State connect the name of the Iroquois. It will also include the remains of the fugitive races, who, since the extermination of the " Mound Builders," have displaced each other in succession until the period of the Iroquois commenced. The remains of this last period are extremely rude, and in themselves barren of interest; but as they stand connected with the Iroquois, and illustrate their social condition, they become more attractive. We have reason to regard the Iroquois as the highest exemplification of the Red Man upon the Continent (except the Aztec race of Mexico), so far as we have positive knowledge. We stand with them in many interesting relations. With them terminated the jurisdiction of the Indian over New-York. They were our immediate predecessors in the territory, throughout its entire extent from the Hudson to Niagara, and from the St. Lawrence to the Chemung. We still speak their dialects in our geographical names. Their government and institutions were more accurately defined and systematic than those of any other Indian race. Under the League, they acquired a supremacy over cotemporary nations, and produced a class of chiefs and warriors, which together have lifted the Iroquois into a renown which no other Indian race in our Republic ever attained. What memento of this race, whose " Long House" was overthrown to make room for our own political structure, has the State preserved? Where are the visible memorials of their existence and of their occupation?

The present time which the Regents of the University have selected to lay the foundation of such an Indian Collection, is a most fortunate one. Within the past few years the Cabinet of Natural History has been founded, and has grown by natural enlargement into a great public attraction. An Indian Collection would be an interesting wing to the former; and in process of time, the two together may not be unworthy of comparison with the more universal collections of the National Government at the Patent Office. Governments owe it to themselves, and to succeeding generations, to make these collections; and there is no good reason why our own favored State should fail in her duty in this respect.

Without any further observations, which had perhaps better have been omitted, a few explanations will be made upon the names and localities of the specimens which accompany this report.

The " Stone Mortar," called in the dialect of the Senecas, a *Ga-ne-ga-ta*, is an Iroquois vessel; and was used for pounding corn, for pulverizing roots, barks, etc. for medicines, and for grinding mineral paint or red clay. Such are the uses for which, the Senecas affirm, the Stone Mortar was employed. It was found near Allen's Hill in the county of Ontario, upon the farm of John C. Mather. The entire stone, which would weigh over 200 pounds, was buried in the ground even with the upper surface, and upon the shady side of an oak. On raising it from the ground, four cavities were found upon the lower surface, much deeper than those upon the upper face, and worn into each other on the sides. As it was impossible to transport so large a stone, it was broken into two parts horizontally, and the upper part selected for preservation, it being the one last in use, and just as it was abandoned by the Senecas. This is the part which is presented. That it had been used for many years, is evident from the fact that it was literally worn out upon the lower face. The stone is the red and green sandstone of the Genesee.

The " Stone Pestle" was found on the Seneca river in the county of Onondaga, at a place called the Reef. Pestles of this description are found very frequently in various parts of the State; from which it is probable that wooden mortars were generally used for the same purposes, the stone mortar rarely ever being found. It may be well to add that the wooden mortar is still in use for pounding corn, among the Senecas and Cayugas, in the western part of the State. They never resort to the mills of the white people, but each family has its wooden mortar. It is simply a cylinder of wood about a foot and a half in diameter, and three feet in length. In one end is formed a cavity of sufficient capacity to hold a peck of corn, in which, after being hulled, the corn is reduced to flour by wooden pounders about five feet in length.

There is also a smaller stone pestle, octagonal in shape, which was found in the county of Wyoming. It was in the use of a wagon-maker, for grinding paint.

The Stone Chisel, *Uh-ga-o-gwat-ha*, is an Iroquois implement,

No. 20.] 87

and was used for cutting trees. Fire was applied at the foot of the tree, and the Stone Chisel was then used to cut out the coal. By a repetition of this process, trees were felled and cut to pieces. Wooden vessels were also hollowed out by the same means, as the fire and the chisel were together their only substitute for the axe. The Stone Chisel is found in all parts of the State, and in great numbers. It will be noticed that among the specimens furnished there are two kinds, one of which have plane faces, but this peculiarity affords no indication of the special uses for which they were designed. This implement was probably unknown to the " Mound Builders," as it is not found in their works.

The Stone Gouge is a different implement from the Chisel, but appears to have been designed for similar uses. Being convex upon one side, concave upon the other, and of greater length than the chisel, it is better adapted for hollowing out wooden vessels, and for giving to the basin thus formed a regular concavity. This specimen was found near Leroy, in the county of Genesee.

Arrow Heads are so common from Maine to Oregon, that it is scarcely necessary to refer to the specimens furnished. One of them is fashioned to revolve, on the same principle as the *twist* in the rifle barrel. It is well known that Indian arrows are feathered at the small end for the same purpose. It is not uncommon in Western New-York to find the places where these arrow heads were manufactured, which is indicated by the fragments of chert which lay about in heaps. As the arrow heads are made by cleavage, it could easily be done without metallic instruments. They are found in the mounds of the west in large quantities, which sufficiently establishes the great antiquity of the art.

If we did not know that the Iroquois never used the Spear (they have no word in their dialects for spear), it would be reasonable to infer that the large specimen was a Spear Head. Its size and weight preclude the idea that it was designed for an arrow. In the Ohio mounds, rows of similar chert heads have been found lying side by side like teeth, the row being about two feet long. This has suggested the idea that they were set in a frame, and fastened with thongs, thus making a species of sword or war club.

Knives of chert were also used by the Iroquois for skinning deer and other animals. The accompanying specimen was found near the site of *De-o-nun-da-ga-a*, or Little Beards Town, in the valley of Genesee, Livingston county.

Among the Iroquois, as all other Indian races, the custom of burying with the dead certain articles which their mythology prescribed, has been the means of preserving nearly all that remains of

Indian art. The mythology of the Iroquois taught that it was a journey of ten days from earth to heaven after death. They consequently buried with the dead, guns, tomahawks, bows and arrows, pipes, brass and earthen vessels containing corn, venison, etc.; and in general all the valuables of the deceased, as they would be needed for the journey. Similar customs appear to have prevailed throughout the whole Indian Family. Among the specimens furnished are several which were found beside the skeletons of Indians. Three of the four iron tomahawks were found buried in this manner. The brass kettle was taken from an Indian grave at the site of the old Indian village of *Ga-nun-da-sa-ga*, near Geneva, which was destroyed by General Sullivan in September 1779. It was thrown out by the ploughshare five years since, after having lain in the earth at least half a century. The gun lock, and portion of a rifle barrel, were also found beside the skeleton of an Indian in Mendon, Monroe county; the skeleton being in a sitting posture, with the gun barrel against the shoulder.

One specimen of an oval stone, with a groove around its greatest length, is furnished. Stones of this description were set in the heads of war-clubs by means of thongs, and thus made formidable weapons.

Perhaps the most singular relic in this little collection is the Moccason Needle. It was found at Fort Hill near Leroy in the county of Genesee, beside a skeleton very much decayed. The bone is from the deer, and taken near the fort. Similar bones are found in the Ohio mounds. The Iroquois used the same bone of the deer, and for the same purpose. In fact it is from the known use to which the Iroquois put this bone, that we infer that the Mound Builders used it for similar purposes, and we thus establish an identity of art between them in moccason making. Of the people who constructed the trench enclosures upon the hill tops in our State, we know nothing. Their works, although inferior in magnitude and different in style from the embankments and enclosures of the West, are nevertheless possessed of the same general features; and there is every reason to believe that they are the remains of the same people who built the mounds. The Iroquois know nothing of these trench enclosures. They disdain all connection with them, and all knowledge of their objects. Not even a tradition have they preserved concerning them. When the area within these enclosures is turned with the plow, fragments of pottery, of shells, and of human bones are found mingled with the soil; and not unfrequently stone pipes of singular design, implements, and ornaments are thus brought again into light. The Moccason Needle in question was found in this way. When this Fort Hill was first visited by the white man, trees

No. 20.] 89

were found growing on the embankment, the grains of which indicated from three to four hundred years. If, then, this bone needle was buried by those who made the work, it would give to it an antiquity of several hundred years.

The " Stone Tube" of variegated limestone is also a singular relic, and belongs likewise to the Ante-Columbian period. Similar tubes, and of the same limestone, some of which are twelve or fourteen inches in length, have been found in the mounds of the West. The bore lessening in diameter, until it became at the neck about an eighth of an inch; the neck itself being flattened down into a sort of mouth piece. In what manner these tubes were bored, becomes an interesting inquiry. Specimens have been found partially bored, the work having been left unfinished; in which cases the end of the bore terminated with a cone having its apex towards the mouth. This has led to the supposition that it was done with sand, and a reed made to revolve. To what use this singular implement was applied, it is impossible to say. It may have been a mere personal ornament. The specimen in question was found in the town of Springport, Cayuga county.

Of the same character, in some respects, is the Amulet of Stone, or whatever it may be called. It was evidently bored in the same manner, and belongs to the same period. This was found at Tonawanda, Genesee county, and was given to the writer by an Indian.

The Necklace of teeth was discovered by the side of a skeleton near Avon, Livingston county, in excavating for the Genesee Valley Canal. It is doubtless an Iroquois ornament.

There is a great difference in the pottery, fragments of which are found in all parts of the State. Some of it is coarse, and rudely manufactured like the clay pipe from Aurora, Cayuga county; while other specimens are not only of a harder and firmer texture, but are worked with considerable taste and skill, like the fragment of the bowl of a pipe, painted with a wolf's head. This last was found near Lima, Livingston county. Whether this black pottery belongs to the Iroquois period, is a matter of great doubt. It seems to be superior to any pottery, which we can with certainty ascribe to them. One of the two other specimens from Fort Hill near Leroy, is probably spurious; but this is not certain.

In connection with these specimens are furnished a head dress, a light war club used in the dance, and a Calumet. The *Gus-to-weh*, or Head Dress, is a simple frame of splint, surmounted with a revolving feather, inclining backward from the head. This revolving feather is the peculiar feature, and the characteristic of the Iroquois head dress. The specimen presented is not well preserved, or a fair representative, but it has done service in the Council House of the Senecas at Tonawanda. To this belongs the *Ga-neah*, or War Club, which is a light article, fashioned after modern notions, and designed to use in the war dance. This is also from Tonawanda. As to the part of a calumet, it is from the West. The bowl was of a soft red stone called Calimite, and inlaid with lead. It is lost.

It would be an easy matter to obtain full Iroquois costumes, male and female, together with the implements, weapons and utensils in common use among them. When collected, they would richly repay the cost and trouble. The birch bark canoe, the bow and arrow, tomahawk, belt, turtle-shell rattle, drum, wampum, war club, ball club, snow snake, and all other articles of this description should have a place in the " Historical and Antiquarian Collection" of the State.

This concludes all that need be said concerning the few specimens which are now placed at the disposal of the Board. The number is large enough to awaken a little curiosity, but too small to be of much importance by themselves.

While reflecting upon the project of the Regents of the University to found an Indian Cabinet for the State — an enterprise which no State in the Union has ever undertaken — the importance and seasonableness of the measure become more and more apparent. If a vigorous movement is now made to secure a small foundation to build upon, the collection would soon come into notice, and acquire sufficient vitality to secure to it a natural growth. It may not be improper to suggest, with reference to this project, that Doctor BEAUREAU, of Gallipolis in Ohio, is understood to have an Indian Collection consisting of about 1500 specimens, many of which, however, are duplicates, which can be purchased for $200 or $300. They belong principally to the period of the " Mound Builders," and would therefore furnish a very appropriate commencement to an Indian Collection in our own State, as our own aboriginal remains reach back to that period, or have their commencement in it. With that collection, and such scattering specimens as can be brought together from various parts of our State by private contribution, our State Collection would at once be placed in advance of all others in the country.

It occurred to the writer, when he received the resolutions of the Regents, to make a brief report on the Trench Enclosures, or Fort Hills in Western New-York; for the purpose of calling their attention to the importance of having them surveyed, before the residue are effaced by the plow. Several drawings or ground plans were accordingly prepared from surveys made personally a few years since;

No. 20.] 91

and five or six are sent herewith, to show the general character of these works. A singular coincidence has made it unnecessary to say much upon the subject. But ten days since, and after these drawings were prepared, Mr. E. G. Squier passed though our city, for the express purpose of surveying these mounds and enclosures under the auspices of the New-York Historical Society. When it is remembered that Mr. S. is one of the authors of the work on the Ancient Monuments of the Mississippi valley, &c., published by the Smithsonian Institute, we may rest satisfied that the long neglected subject will be thoroughly explored; and we may also expect that a new interest will be awakened throughout the State, in the subject of our aboriginal remains.

It is only necessary to add, with reference to these drawings, that the first of them, the Palisade Fortification of which a ground plan is given, is a Seneca work. The bastions indicate that it was made with the aid of the English or French. This work was destroyed by General Sullivan in 1779, during his destructive inroad into the Seneca country. The stub of the palisade at the gate or opening was still above ground at the end of the trench. It was preserved by the writer when he made the survey, and accompanies the other specimens. The remaining drawings are of works which reach beyond the Iroquois period, and testify to the ancient occupation of a race, whose name we know not : neither know we the era of their departure. But this report is increasing beyond its intended, as well as its proper limits, and must be abruptly concluded.

All which is respectfully submitted.

L. H. MORGAN.

Rochester, November 13, 1848.

Third Regents Report

. . . . .
. . .
.

(F.)

REPORT

TO THE

REGENTS OF THE UNIVERSITY,

UPON THE ARTICLES FURNISHED THE

THE INDIAN COLLECTION:

BY L. H. MORGAN. DECEMBER 31, 1849.

REPORT.

The Regents of the University having made an appropriation for the enlargement of the Indian Collection, and having entrusted the execution of their resolution with the undersigned, he asks leave to submit the following report.

Within the past century great changes have been wrought among the descendants of the ancient Iroquois. Their primitive fabrics have mostly passed away, and with them many of their original inventions. The substitution of the fabrics of more skillful hands, has led to the gradual disuse of many of their simple arts. At the present moment, therefore, much of the fruit of their inventive capacity is entirely lost. Fragments, indeed, are frequently disentombed from the resting places to which they had been consigned by filial or parental affection; but they are mere vestiges of the past, and afford but a slight indication of their social condition, or of the range of their artisan intellect. It is impossible, therefore, at the present day, to make a full collection of the implements, domestic utensils, and miscellaneous fabrics of our Indian predecessors. Many of their inventions are still preserved among their descendants, who yet reside within our limits; but that portion of them which would especially serve to illustrate the condition of the hunter life, have passed beyond our reach.

In the present advanced condition of our Indian population, a large proportion of their articles are of a mixed character. They rather exhibit the application of Indian ingenuity to fabrics of foreign manufacture, as shown in their reduction into use, than originality of invention. But this class of articles are not without a peculiar interest. They furnish no slight indication of artisan capacity, and will make a species of substitute for those articles which they have displaced, and those inventions which they have hurried into forgetfulness.

68   [SENATE

The specimens collected, are as diversified as the shortness of the time and the means appropriated would permit. In the accompanying schedule they are classified, under their aboriginal names, into eighty-three distinct classes, and number in all about three hundred. They were obtained among the Senecas, in the western part of the State. It is hoped that they will prove an acceptable addition to the State Collection, and will induce its further enlargement. After the lapse of a few more years, it will be impossible to bring together these silent memorials of our primitive inhabitants. Their social condition has changed greatly, and is changing from day to day; while their simple arts are dropping from their hands one after the other, as they gradually take up agricultural pursuits. It is but just to them, to save from oblivion the fruits of their inventive intellect, however rude and simple they may be, that they themselves may be at least correctly judged. Succeeding generations, also, have a right to require of us these memorials of a departed race; of that race who christened our rivers, lakes, and hills; who maintained them against hostile bands, with a patriotism as glowing as such a fair domain could inspire in the heart of man, but to surrender them at last, and without an equivalent, to a more fortunate possessor.

It is not deemed necessary to describe the articles in detail. A few of the leading specimens will be selected, and some notice given of their origin, manufacture, and uses. Their names are in the Seneca dialect. In their pronunciation the following signs will indicate the several sounds of the vowel a, upon which the greatest variations are made.

(ä, as in arm — ă, as in at — a, as in ale.)

Ah-tä-quä-o-weh, or MOCCASIN, (for male.) See plate 1.

MOCCASIN, (for female.) See plate 2.

The moccasin is preëminently an Indian invention, and one of the highest antiquity. It is true to nature in its adjustment to the foot, beautiful in its materials and finish, and durable as an article of apparel. It will compare favorably with the best single article for the protection and adornment of the foot ever invented, either in ancient or modern times. With the sanction of fashion, it would supersede among us a long list of similar inventions. Other nations have fallen behind the Indian, in this one particular at least. The masses of the Romans wore the Calceus Ligneus, or wooden shoe; the masses of Germany and Ireland, and many of the nations of Europe, formerly wore the same.

No. 75.]　　　　　　69

With the cothurnus, and sandal of the ancients, and the boot of the moderns, the perfection of pedal inventions, the moccasin admits of no unfavorable comparison. It deserves to be classed among the highest articles of apparel ever invented, both in usefulness, durability and beauty.

The mocassin is made of one piece of deerskin. It is seamed up at the heel, and also in front, above the foot, leaving the bottom of the moccasin without a seam. In front the deerskin is gathered, in place of being crimped ; over this part porcupine quills or beads are worked, in various patterns. The plain moccasin rises several inches above the ankle, like the Roman cothurnus, and is fastened above the ankle with deer strings ; but usually this part is turned down, so as to expose a part of the instep, and is ornamented with bead work, as represented in the plate. A small bone near the ankle joint of the deer, has furnished the moccasin needle from time immemorial ; and the sinews of the animal, the thread. These bone needles are found in the mounds of the West, and beside the skeletons of the Iroquois, where they were deposited with religious care. This isolated fact would seem to indicate an affinity, in one act at least, between the Iroquois and the mound builders, whose name, and era of occupation and destiny, are entirely lost.

In ancient times the Iroquois used another shoe, made of the skin of the elk. They cut the skin above and below the *gambrel* joint, and then took it off entire. As the hind leg of the elk inclines at this joint nearly at a right angle, it was naturally adapted to the foot. The lower end was sewed firmly with sinew, and the upper part secured above the ankle with deer strings.

In connection with this subject is the art of tanning deer skins, as they still tan them after the ancient method. It is done with the brain of the deer, the tanning properties of which, according to a tradition, were discovered by accident. The brain is mingled with moss, to make it adhere sufficiently to be formed into a cake, after which it is hung up by the fire to dry. It is thus preserved for years. When the deerskin is fresh, the hair, and also the grain of the skin are taken off, over a cylindrical beam, with a wooden blade or stone scraper. A solution is then made by boiling a cake of the brain in water, and the moss, which is of no use, being removed, the skin is soaked a few hours in the solution. It is then wrung out and stretched, until it becomes dry and pliable. Should it be a thick one, it would be necessary to repeat the process until it becomes thoroughly penetrated by the solution. The skin is still porous and easily torn. To correct both, a smoke is made, and the skin placed over it in such a manner as to enclose it entirely. Each side is smoked in this way until the pores are closed, and the skin has become thoroughly toughened, with its color changed from white to a kind of brown. It is then ready for use.

They also use the brain of other animals, and sometimes the back bone of the eel, which, pounded up and boiled, possesses nearly the same properties for tanning. Bear skins were never tanned. They were scraped until softened, after which they were dried, and used without removing the hair, either as an article of apparel, or as a mattress to sleep upon.

Gä-je-wä, or WAR CLUB.

2 feet 2 inches.

WAR CLUB, smaller size.

Before the tomahawk came into use among the Iroquois, their principal weapons were the bow, the stone tomahawk, and the war club. The Gä-je-wä was a heavy weapon, usually made of ironwood, with a large ball of knot at the head. It was usually about two feet in length, and the base five or six inches in diameter. In close combat it would prove a formidable weapon. They wore it in the belt, in front.

No. 75   71

Gä-ne-u-ga-o-dus-ha, or DEER-HORN WAR CLUB.

2 feet 4 inches.

This species of war club was also much used. It was made of hard wood, elaborately carved, painted, and ornamented with feathers at the ends. In the lower edge, a sharp-pointed deer's horn, about four inches in length, was inserted. It was thus rendered a dangerous weapon in close combat, and would inflict a deeper wound than the former. They wore it in the girdle. In the collection are six war clubs, of the two kinds above described. One of them is a light article, designed for the war dance.

O-sque-sont, or TOMAHAWK.

The tomahawk succeeded the war club, as the rifle did the bow. With the invention of this terrible implement of warfare the Red man had nothing to do, except in having it so fashioned as to be adapted to his taste and usage. The tomahawk is known as widely as the Indian, and the two names have become apparently inseparable. They are made of steel, brass, or iron. The choicer articles are surmounted by a pipe-bowl, and have a perforated handle, that they may answer the double purpose of ornament and use. In such the handle, and often the blade itself, are richly inlaid with silver. It is worn in the girdle, and behind the back, except when in actual battle. They used it in close combat with terrible effect, and also threw it with unerring certainty at distant objects, making it revolve in the air in its flight. With the Indian, the tomahawk is the emblem of war itself. To bury it, is peace ; to raise, is to declare the most deadly warfare.

Wä-a-no, or Bow.

4 feet.

Gä-no, or ARROW.

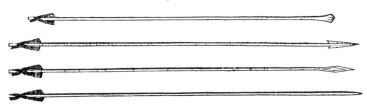

3 feet.

In archery, the Indian has scarcely been excelled. With a quick eye and a powerful muscle, he could send the arrow as unerringly as the archers of Robin Hood. It may be claimed as an Indian invention, although the bow and the arrow have been used by all nations in their primitive state. The Indian bow is usually from three and a half to four and a half feet in length, and so difficult to spring, that an inexperienced person could scarcely bend it sufficiently to set the string. To draw the string back an arrow's length when set, could only be done by practice, superadded to the most powerful muscular strength. An arrow thus sent would strike its object with fearful velocity. The arrow is feathered at the small end with a twist, to make it revolve in its flight. It gives to its motion uniformity and quickness, and, doubtless, suggested the idea of the twist in the rifle barrel, by which the ball is made to revolve in the same manner. The English and Scottish archer feathered his arrow, but without this peculiarity. Three feathers were also used, which were set parallel with each other, and with the arrow, but upon one side. Originally the Indian arrow was pointed with a flint or chert head, which would make it penetrate deeply any object at which it was directed. With such an arrow it was an easy matter to bring down the deer, the wild fowl, or the warrior himself. Skeletons have been disentombed having the skull penetrated by an arrowhead of this description, with the flint head itself still in the fracture, or entirely within the skull. In Oregon, and on the upper Mississippi, the Indian arrow is still pointed with flint. Thus it was with the Iroquois, until the bow was laid aside for the rifle. Arrow heads of this description are still scattered over the whole surface of the State. Six bows, of different sizes, and some bundles of feathered arrows, will be found in the collection. With Indian youth, the bow and arrow is still a favorite source of amusement.

Gus-hä-ah, or BURDEN STRAP.

Rope-making, from filaments of bark, is also an Indian art. The deer string answers a multitude of purposes in their domestic economy; but it could not supply all necessities. The bark rope (Gä-sken dä) has been fabricated among them from time immemorial. In its manufacture they use the bark of the slippery elm and the basswood. Having removed the outer surface of the bark, they divide it into narrow strips, and then boil it in ashes and water. After it is dried it is easily separated into small filaments, the strings running with the grain several feet without breaking. These filaments are then put up in skeins (specimens of which are furnished) and laid aside for use. Basswood makes the most pliable rope; it is soft to the touch, can be closely braided, and is very durable. The burden strap is worn around the forehead and lashed to a litter, which is borne by Indian women on their back. It is usually about fifteen feet in length, and braided into a belt in the centre, three or four inches wide. Several specimens are furnished, one of which is new, and neatly manufactured. A clothes line, of three-strands bark rope, about forty-feet in length, is also among the articles. This art, like many others, is falling into disuse. But few Indian families now provide themselves with skeins of bark thread, or make any use of ropes of this description.

74   [SENATE

A bark barrel, (Gä-na-quă) which has been used about thirty years, will also be found with the other specimens. It is stitched up the side, has a bottom and lid, and shows no signs of decay. Such barrels are used to store dried corn, fruit, beans, &c.

Gä-o-wä, or BARK TRAY.

Trays of this description are found in every Indian family. They serve a variety of purposes, but are chiefly used for kneading, or rather preparing corn bread. A strip of elm bark, of the requisite dimensions, is rounded and turned up on the sides and at the ends, so as to form a shallow concavity; around the rim, both outside and in, splints of hickory are adjusted, and stitched through and through with the bark. It thus makes a durable and convenient article for holding corn meal, for preparing corn bread, and for many other purposes.

Gä-oo-wä, or BARK SAP TUB.

Our Indian population have been long in the habit of manufacturing sugar from the maple. Whether they learned the art from us, or we received it from them, is uncertain. One evidence, at least, of its antiquity among them, is to be found in one of their ancient religious

No. 75.] 75

festivals, instituted to the maple. It is called the Maple Dance, (O-tä-de-none-neo-wa-tä) which signifies "Thanks to the Maple." In the spring season, when the sap begins to flow, it is still regularly observed by the present Iroquois. The sap tub is a very neat contrivance, and surpasses all articles of this description. Our farmers may safely borrow, in this one particular, and with profit substitute this Indian invention for the rough and wasteful trough of their own contrivance.

A strip of bark about three feet in length, by two in width, makes the tub. The rough bark is left upon the bottom and sides. At the point where the bark is to be turned up to form the ends, the outer bark is removed; the inner rind is then turned up, gathered together in small folds at the top, and tied around with a splint. It is then ready for use, and will last several seasons. Aside from the natural fact that the sap would be quite at home in the bark tub, and its flavor preserved untainted, it is more durable and capacious than the wooden one, and more readily made.

Gä-ne-gä-tä, Gä-nih-gä-dä, or CORN MORTAR and POUNDER.

The Senecas use three varieties of corn: the White, (O-na-o-ga-ant) the Red, (Tic-ne) and the White Flint, (Ha-go-wä.) Corn is, and always has been, their staple article of food. When ready to be harvested, they pick the ears, strip down the husks, and braid them together in bunches, with about twenty ears in each. They are then hung up ready for use. The white flint ripens first, and is the favorite corn for hominy; the red next, and is used principally for charring and drying; the white last, and is the favorite corn of the Indians; it is used for bread, and supplies the same place with them that wheat does with us. They shell their corn by hand, and pound it into flour in wooden mortars. In two hours from the time the corn is taken from the ear it is ready to eat, in the form of unleavened bread. It is hulled in the first instance, by boiling in ashes and water; after the outer skin is thus removed from each kernel, it is thoroughly washed, and pounded into flour or meal in a mortar, of which a representation will be found on the next page, (76.) Having been passed through a sieve basket, to remove the chit and coarser grains, it is made into loaves or cakes about an inch in thickness, and six inches in diameter; after which they are cooked by boiling them in water. Upon bread of this description, and upon the fruits of the chase, the Indian has principally subsisted from time immemorial.

76   [SENATE

MORTAR AND POUNDER.

Mortar, 2 feet. Pounder, 4 feet.

The practice of charring corn is of great antiquity among the Red race. In this condition it is preserved for years without injury. Caches or pits of charred corn, have been found in the vicinity of ancient

No. 75.] 77

works and deserted settlements, in various parts of the country. Many of these are supposed to reach back to the period of the Mound builders. How far this custom prevailed among the Iroquois, cannot with certainty be determined ; neither do we know whether those caches, which are still discovered in various parts of the State, are to be ascribed to them. It is certain, however, that they were in the habit of charring corn, to preserve it for domestic use. The Senecas still do the same. For this use the red corn is preferred. When green the corn is picked, and roasted in the field before a long fire, the ears being set up on end in a row. It is not charred or blackened entirely, but roasted sufficiently to dry up the moisture in each kernel. The corn is then shelled, and dried in the sun. In this state it is chiefly used by hunting parties, and for subsistence on distant excursions. Its bulk and weight having been diminished about half by the two processes, its transportation became less burdensome. The Red races seldom formed magazines of grain, to guard against distant wants. It is probable, therefore, that these pits of charred corn owe their origin to the sudden flight of the inhabitants, who buried their dried corn because they could not remove it, rather than to a desire to provide against a failure of the harvest.

There is another method of curing corn in its green state, quite as prevalent as the former. The corn is shaved off into small particles, and having been baked over the fire in pans or earthen dishes, it is then dried in the sun. In this condition it is preserved for winter use.

A favorite article of subsistence is prepared from the charred corn. It is parched a second time, after which, having been mixed with about a third part of maple sugar, it is pounded into a fine flour. This is carried in the bearskin pocket of the hunter, and upon it alone he subsists for days together. It was also the principal subsistence of the war party on distant expeditions. Its bulk is reduced to the smallest possible compass, and it is so light that the Indian could carry, without inconvenience, sufficient for a long adventure. When we consider the rapidity of their journeys, and their powers of enduring abstinence, it becomes easy to understand how the war party could leave the valley of the Genesee, make an inroad upon the Cherokees of the south, and return, relying almost entirely upon this species of subsistence. A basket of each of the three varieties of corn, of the two species of dried corn, and of this flour, will be found among the specimens.

This noble grain, one of the gifts of the Indian to the world, is destined eventually to become one of the staple articles of human consumption. Over half of our republic lies within the embrace of the tributaries of the Mississippi. Upon their banks are the corn-growing districts of the country ; and there, also, at no distant day, will be seated the millions of our race. Experience demonstrates that no people can rely wholly upon exchanges for the substance of their breadstuffs, but that they must look chiefly to the soil they cultivate. This law of production and consumption, is destined to introduce the gradual use of corn flour, as a partial substitute at least, for its superior rival, in those districts where it is the natural product of the soil. In the southern portions of the country this principle is already attested, by the fact that corn bread enters as largely into human consumption as wheaten. Next to wheat, this grain, perhaps, contains the largest amount of nutriment. It is the cheapest and surest of all the grains to cultivate ; and is, also, the cheapest article of subsistence known among men. Although wheat can be cultivated in nearly all sections of the country ; although its production can be increased to an unlimited degree by a higher agriculture ; we have yet great reason to be thankful for this secondary grain, whose reproductive energy is so unmeasured as to secure the millions of our race, through all coming time, against the dangers of scarcity or the pressure of want.

O-yeh-quä-ä-weh, or INDIAN TOBACCO.

Tobacco is another gift of the Indian to the world ; but a gift, it must be admitted, of questionable utility. We call both corn and tobacco the legacy of the Red man ; as these indigenous plants, but for his nurture and culture through so many ages, might have perished, like other varieties of the fruits of the earth. Many of our choicest fruits owe their origin to vegetable combinations entirely fortuitous. They spring up spontaneously, flourish for a season and become extinct, but for the watchful care of man. Nature literally pours forth her vegetable wealth, and buries beneath her advancing exuberance the products of the past. But few of the fruits and plants, and flowers of the ancient world, have come down to us unchanged ; and still other plants, perhaps, have perished unknown in the openings of the past, which contained within their shrivelled and stinted foliage, the germ of some fruit, or grain, or plant, which might have nourished or clothed the whole human family. We may therefore, perchance, owe a debt to the Indian, in these particulars, beyond our utmost acknowledgments.

The Senecas still cultivate tobacco. Their name signifies " *The only Tobacco,*" because they considered this variety superior to all others. A specimen is furnished. It is raised from the seed, which is sown or planted in the spring, and requires but little cultivation. The leaves are picked early in the fall, when their color first begins to change, and when dried are ready for use. After the first year it grows spontaneously, from the seed shed by the plant when fully ripened. If the plants become too thick, which is frequently the case, from their vigorous growth, it becomes necessary to thin them out, as the leaves diminish in size with their increase in number. This tobacco is used exclusively for smoking. The custom of chewing the cud, appears to have been derived from us. Although this tobacco is exceedingly mild, they mingle with it the leaves of the sumac, to diminish its stimulating properties. The sumac has been used by the Indian to temper tobacco from time immemorial.

Until within a few years, the Iroquois used the wild potato as an article of food. It still grows spontaneously upon the western reservations, and is usually about the size of a hen's egg. They never cultivated this potato, but gathered it in its wild state.

Six varieties of the bean, and four of the squash, are also furnished. Which varieties were of original cultivation and indigenous, the writer cannot state.

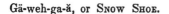

Gä-weh-ga-ă, or Snow Shoe.

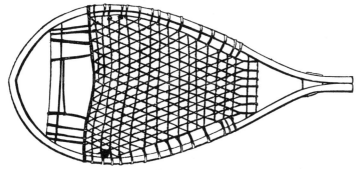

2 feet 10 inches.

The snow shoe is an Indian invention. Upon the deep snows which accumulate in the forest, it would be nearly impossible to travel without them. They were used in the hunt, and in warlike expeditions undertaken in the season of winter.

The snow shoe is nearly three feet in length, by about sixteen inches in width. A rim of hickory, bent round with an arching front, and brought to a point at the heel, constitutes the frame, with the addi of cross pieces to determine its spread. Within the area, with the exception of an opening for the toe, is woven a net work of deer strings, with interstices about an inch square. The base of the foot is lashed at the edge of this opening with thongs, which pass around the heel for the support of the foot. The heel is left free to work up and down, and the opening is designed to allow the toe of the boot to descend below the surface of the shoe, as the heel is raised in the act of walking. It is a very simple invention, but exactly adapted for its uses. A person familiar with the snow shoe can walk as rapidly upon the snow, as without it upon the ground. The Senecas affirm that they can walk fifty miles per day upon the snow shoe, and with much greater rapidity than without it, in consequence of the length and uniformity of the step. In the bear hunt, especially, it is of the greatest service, as the hunter can speedily overtake the bear, who, breaking through the crust, is enabled to move but slowly.

Gä-wä-sä, or SNOW SNAKE.

Side section 6 feet, ¼ inch in thickness; bottom section ⅜ to ½ inch in width.

Among the amusements of the winter season, in Indian life, is the game with Snow Snakes. The snakes are made of hickory, and with the most perfect precision and finish. They are from five to seven feet in length, about a fourth of an inch in thickness, and gradually diminishing from about an inch in width at the head, to about half an inch at the foot. The head is round, turned up slightly, and pointed with lead. They are thrown with the hand, by placing the fore finger against the foot, and skim along upon the snow crust nearly with the speed of an arrow, and to a much greater distance. The game itself is rendered exciting by the numbers engaged, and the amount wagered upon the result. As in all Indian games, the people divide by tribes, certain tribes playing against the others. A limited number are chosen to play the game from each side. The snake which runs the farthest wins, and a count is made by each snake which leads all upon the opposite side. A minute description is necessary, to a full understanding of the game, but enough has been said to designate the uses of the article. Specimens are furnished.

Gä-geh-dä, or JAVELIN.

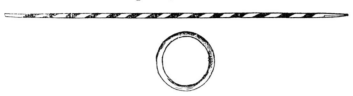

Javelin 5¼ feet, ¼ inch in diameter.   Ring 6 inches in diameter.

The game of Javelins, or shooting sticks, is also of Indian invention. It is a simple game, depending upon the dexterity with which the javelin is thrown at the ring, as it rolls upon the ground.   The javelin itself is the forfeit, and the game is lost when all the javelins upon one side are won.   As in other Indian games, the people array themselves according to their tribal divisions ; the Wolf, Bear, Turtle, and Beaver tribes, playing against the Deer, Snipe, Heron, and Hawk.   From fifteen to thirty on a side are chosen, each taking from three to six javelins.   The parties having stationed themselves several rods apart, upon opposite sides of a given line, a hoop or ring is rolled by one party in front of the other, who throw their javelins at the ring as it passes. If the hoop is struck by one of them, the other party are required to stand in the place of the successful person and throw all their javelins in succession at the ring.   Those which hit are saved, and those which fail are handed over to the other party, who in turn throw them at the ring.   Of this number, those which hit the hoop are won finally, and laid out of the play ; the balance are returned to their original owners. The successful party then rolls back the ring, and the game is thus continued until all the javelins upon one side are forfeited.

Gä-ne-ä, or BALL BAT.

5¼ feet.

This is the great game of the Indians.   It is also of the highest antiquity, universal among the Red races, and played with a zeal and enthusiasm which would scarcely be credited.   In playing it they denude themselves entirely, with the exception of the Gä-kä, or waist cloth, each one holding a bat, of the species represented in the figure. Gates are erected about sixty rods apart, upon opposite sides of a field, and the point in the game is, for each party to carry the ball through their own gate. Usually they have from six to eight on a side to play the game, who are surrounded by a concourse of spectators. Commencing at the centre, each party strives to direct the ball towards their own gate, knocking it upon the ground or through the air; but more frequently taking it up upon the deerskin net-work of the ball bat, and carrying it in a race towards the gate. When an opposite player strikes it ahead of the runner, the latter throws the ball over the head of the former towards the gate. Oftentimes the play is contested with so much animation, that the ball is recovered at the edge of the gate; and finally, after many shifts in the tide of success, is carried to the opposite side. The game is usually from five to seven, and requires from noon until evening to determine it, each trial is conducted with so much ardor and diversity of success. Specimens of the ball bat are furnished.

Gus-ga-e-sa-tä, or DEER BUTTONS.

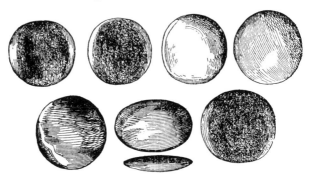

A set of deer buttons will also be found among the articles. This is a fireside game. Eight buttons, an inch in diameter, are made of deer bone, and blackened upon one side. They are thrown with the hand, the count depending upon the number of faces which turn up of one color. If they all come up white, for instance, it counts twenty; if seven of the eight, it counts four; if six, two. These are the only counts. Fifty beans make the bank, and the game continues until one party has won them.

No 75.]   83

Gus-ka-eh, or PEACH STONES.

Gä-jih, or BOWL.

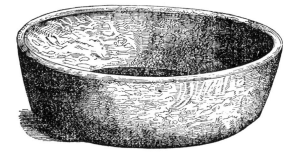

Another favorite game of the Iroquois is played with a bowl and peach
stones. A dish, about a foot in diameter, is carved out of a knot, or
made of earthen. Six peach stones are then filed or cut down into an
oval form, reducing them about half in size ; after which they are burned
slightly upon one side, to blacken them. These are shook in the bowl,
and the count depends upon the number which turn up of the same color.
This game is one of their amusements after holding a council. They
divide by tribes, as in other games, and bet largely upon the result. It
is played by persons selected on each side, who are skilled in the game.
The Iroquois ascribe its invention to To-do-dä-ho, the renowned sachem of
the Onondagas, who flourished at the time of the formation of the league.

Betting upon all Indian games, when played by tribe against tribe,
was as common among the Iroquois, as betting at races by the whites.
No restraint whatever was laid upon this practice, and from their fondness for excitement, it frequently led to the most reckless indulgence.
It not unfrequently happened that the Indian gambled away every
hing which he possessed, his rifle, his tomahawk, and even his blanket.

84 [Senate

Ah-da-dä-quä, or Indian Saddle.

This is an Indian invention, but came originally from the west. It closely resembles the saddle of the native Mexicans in its general plan, but its pommel is not as high, and its side pieces are longer. It is still used among the Iroquois, and among the Indian tribes of the west. The frame is made of four pieces of wood, firmly set together, over which is a covering of raw hide. The side pieces are about eighteen inches in length, six in width, and about an inch in thickness at the centre, but terminating in a sharp edge above and below. In front the pommel rises about five inches above the side pieces. It is made of a stick having a natural fork, which is so adjusted as to embrace the side pieces, and determine the spread of the saddle. Another piece, in the same manner, embraced the side pieces at the opposite end, rising several inches above, and descending nearly to their lower edges. These side pieces at the top, are about three inches apart, leaving a space for the back-bone of the horse. The fastenings of the saddle, including those of the stirrup, were originally of ropes, made of Buffalo's hair. Triangular stirrups, of wood, completed the trappings of the saddle. As the Iroquois seldom made use of the Indian horse, the saddle with them was rather an accidental, than a usual article. A specimen, of Seneca manufacture, will be found among the articles.

Gä-ga-an-dä, or Air Gun; and Gä-no, or Arrow.

Air gun, 6 feet.   Arrow, 2¼ feet.

The air gun is claimed as an Indian invention, but with what correctness the writer cannot state. It is a simple tube or barrel, about six feet in length, above an inch in diameter, and having a uniform bore, about half an inch in diameter. It is made of alder, and also of other wood, which is bored by some artificial contrivance. A very slender arrow, about two and a half feet in length, with a sharp point, is the missile. Upon the foot of the arrow, the down or floss of the thistle is fastened on entire, with sinew. This down is soft and yielding, and when the arrow is placed in the barrel, it fills it air tight. The arrow is then discharged by the lungs. It is used for bird shooting.

Ya-o-dä-was-tä, or Indian Flute.

1¼ feet.

This instrument is unlike any known among us, but it clearly resembles the clarionet. Its name signifies " a blow pipe." It is usually made of red cedar, is about eighteen inches in length, and above an inch in diameter. The finger holes, six in number, are equidistant. Between them and the mouth-piece, which is at the end, is the whistle, contrived much upon the same principle as the common whistle. It makes six consecutive notes, from the lowest, on a rising scale. The seventh note is wanting, but the three or four next above are regularly made. This is the whole compass of the instrument. As played by the Indians, it affords a species of wild and plaintive music. It is claimed as an Indian invention.

86   [SENATE

Gus-dä-wa-să, or RATTLE.

Turtle-shell Rattle.

The turtle-shell rattle is used in the dance, both as an accompaniment to the singing, and to mark the time. In all of their dances, except the war dance, the singers are seated in the centre of the room, and the dancers pass around them in an elliptical line. They strike the rattle upon the bench, in beating time, as frequently as thrice in a second, and accompany it with singing. After removing the animal from the shell, a handful of flint corn is placed within it, and the skin sewed up. The neck of the turtle is stretched over a wooden handle.

Squash-shell Rattle.

As an accompaniment for singing, the squash-shell rattle is also used. Corn is placed within the hollow shell, and the sound of the rattle varies with its size. In their songs for the dead, it is chiefly used. Frequently twenty of these rattles are heard in one song, each one giving a different note, and the whole together making a very strange substitute for music.

The Iroquois have about twenty distinct dances, a few of them, as the war dance, are performed by select dancers, who dress in full costume and paint for the occasion. A few, also, are exclusively for the females, but in the most of them all participate. The thanksgiving, or religious dance, (O-sto-weh-go-wä) is the most spirited and striking in the list; but the war dance (Wä-säs-seh) is the greatest favorite. In this dance the drum is chiefly used.

No. 75.] 87

Gä-no-jo-o, or INDIAN DRUM.

1 foot.

Over one head of the drum the skin of some animal is stretched to its utmost tension, and held firmly by a hoop. Vocal music is essential to every Indian dance; the drum being used to mark time, and as an accompaniment. These primitive amusements are still maintained by a certain portion of the present Iroquois, with undiminished interest. Their social intercourse still takes on this form, and scarcely a week passes, in the winter season, without a dance. They are eminently calculated to keep alive their Indian sympathies and notions; and for this reason, the first efforts of their missionaries are, with great propriety, directed to their suppression. There is a wildness in the music and excitement of the dance, exactly attuned to the nature of the Indian; and when he loses his relish for the dance, he has ceased to be an Indian.

Yun-ga-sa, or TOBACCO POUCH.

The tobacco pouch is made of the skin of some small animal, which s taken off entire. It was anciently an indispensable article, and was worn in the girdle. Four specimens are furnished, one of white weasel, one of squirrel, one of mink, and one of fisher skin. The latter was worn many years by Johnson, (Sose-ha-wä) a nephew of Red Jacket, and now one of the most distinguished living chiefs of the Senecas.

Dä-ya-yä-dă-gä-ne-at-hä, or Bow AND SHAFT, for striking fire.

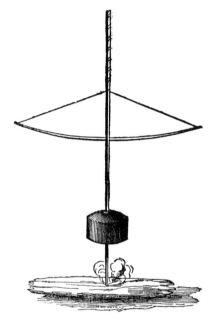

This is an Indian invention, and of great antiquity. Its rudeness may excite a smile, in this day of lucifer matches, but yet the step backward to the steel and flint is about the same, as from the latter to the contrivance in question. Not knowing the use of metals or of chemicals, it was the only method of creating fire known to the Red man. It consisted of an upright shaft, about four feet in length and an inch in diameter, with a small wheel set upon the lower part, to give it momentum. In a notch at the top of the shaft was set a string, attached to a bow about three feet in length. The lower point rested upon a block of dry wood, near which are placed small pieces of punk. When ready to use, the string is first coiled around the shaft, by turning it with the hand. The bow is then pulled downward, thus uncoiling the string, and revolving the shaft towards the left. By the momentum given to the wheel, the string is again coiled up in a reverse manner

No. 75.] 89

and the bow again drawn up. The bow is again pulled downward, and the revolution of the shaft reversed, uncoiling the string, and recoiling it in reverse as before. This alternate revolution of the shaft is continued, until sparks are emitted from the point where it rests upon the piece of dry wood below. In a moment's time sparks are produced by the intensity of the friction, and ignite the punk, which speedily furnishes a fire.

O-no-ne-ä Gos-ha-dä, or Corn-husk Salt Bottle.

Several varieties of basket work will be found among the articles. In this useful art the Indian women excel. They are made with a neatness, ingenuity and simplicity, which deserve the highest praise. Among the number are two sieve baskets, used for sifting corn meal. Another variety is made of corn-husks and flags, an ingeniously manufactured basket, which is seldom met with. Two corn-husk bottles for salt, are also furnished.

Gä-de-us-ha, or Necklace. See plate 3, fig. 2.

This necklace is made of silver and wampum beads. The latter are of a dark color, and are cut from a species of sea shell. Beads of this description are held in the highest estimation. In strings of wampum beads, the laws of the ancient confederacy of the Iroquois were recorded. According to their method of expressing the idea, the law was " talked into the string of wampum," and it became ever afterwards the visible record of the law itself. By an original law of the league, a sachem of the Onondagas (Ho-no-we-nă-to) was made the hereditary keeper and interpreter of these strings; and to this day, the Onondaga sachem who holds this title, performs this duty.

A silver cross is also attached to this necklace. The Indian women wear a profusion of silver ornaments, and among them the cross is frequently conspicuous.

In their costumes for the war dance, the Iroquois indulged their taste for finery and ornament to its fullest extent. Some of them would excite admiration by the exactness of their finish and adjustment, the neatness of the materials, and the striking appearance of the whole, as seen in the graceful movements of the dance. They are diversified in their materials and ornaments, but yet consist of the same articles of apparel. Two costumes are furnished. One is that of a warrior, and was designed for the dance. The other is the ordinary dress of the Indian female. If the fabrics of which they are composed were of their own manufacture exclusively, it would add much to their interest; but since the intercourse of the Iroquois commenced with the whites, they have laid aside their deerskin apparel, and substituted materials, in fact, of our own manufacture. Since we have known them, however, their costumes have been of this description. No change has been made of the articles of apparel themselves, but the deerskin has been laid aside for the broadcloth, the bearskin blanket for the woolen, and the porcupine quill for the bead.

Much taste is exhibited in the bead work, which is so conspicuous in the female costume. The colors are blended harmoniously, and the patterns are ingeniously devised and skilfully executed. It sufficiently appears, from the furnished specimens of their handywork, that the Indian female can be taught to excel with the needle. It remains to notice briefly the several articles of apparel, of which these costumes are composed; and first, of the female.

Ah-tä-quä-o-weh, or MOCCASIN.

This has been sufficiently described elsewhere in this report.

Gise-hä, or PANTALETTE. Plate 4.

The Gise-hä is usually made of red broadcloth, and ornamented with a border of bead work around the lower edge, and also up the side. It is secured above the knee, and falls down upon the moccasin. The one furnished is beautifully made, and a fine specimen of bead work.

No. 75.]   91

Gä-kä-ah, or Skirt.   Plate 5.

The skirt is secured around the waist, and descends about half way to the bottom of the pantalette. It is usually of blue broadcloth, and is more elaborately embroidered with bead work than any other portion of the dress. A heavy border is worked around the lower edge. Up the centre, in front, it is also embroidered. At the angle upon the right side, a figure is worked representing a tree or flower. This part of the costume furnished, is a rare specimen of Indian needle work.

Ah-de-a-dä-we-sä, or Over Dress.   Plate 6, and 6 a.

The over dress is generally of calico, of the highest colors. It is loosely adjusted to the person, and falls below the waist. Around the lower edge is a narrow border of bead work. In front they wear a profusion of silver broaches, of various sizes and patterns, and arranged agreeably to the taste of the wearer.

E-yose, or Blanket.

This indispensable and graceful garment is of blue or green broadcloth, of which it requires two yards. It falls from the head or neck in natural folds, the width of the cloth, and is gathered around the person like a shawl. It is worn very gracefully, and makes a becoming article of apparel. Other ornaments are worn, but the costume has been described with sufficient minuteness to give a general idea of its character.

Gus-to-weh, or Head Dress.   Plate 3, fig. 1.

Upon the head dress, the most conspicuous part of the male costume, much attention was bestowed. The frame consists of a band of splint, adjusted around the head, with a cross band arching over the top, from side to side. A cap of net work, or silk, is then made to enclose the frame. Around the splint a silver band is fastened, which completes the lower part. From the top, a cluster of white feathers depends. Besides this a single feather, of the largest size, is set in the crown of the head dress, inclining backwards from the head. It is secured in a small tube, which is fastened to the cross splint, and in such a manner as to allow the feather to revolve in the tube. This feather, which is usually the plume of the Eagle, is the characteristic of the Iroquois

92 [SENATE

head dress. The feather, in the specimen furnished, has been worn for many years by Sose-ha-wä, (above referred to) and has been conspicuous at many of the councils of the Senecas.

Gä-kä-ah, or KILT. Plate 7.

The kilt is secured around the waist by a belt, and descends nearly to the knee. It is fringed around the lower edge, and covered with various ornaments. This article of Indian apparel is not much unlike the kilt of the Highlander.

Gise-hă, or LEGGIN. Plate 8.

The leggin is usually made of red broadcloth. It is embroidered around the lower edge and up the side, with bead work. Two narrow bands depend from the knee in front. It is secured above the knee, and descends to the moccasin.

Gus-da-wä-să Yen-che-no-hos-ta, or KNEE RATTLE OF DEER'S HOOFS.

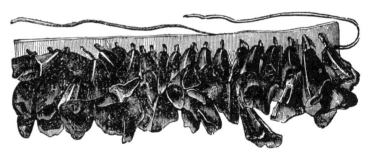

In the dance, rattles were worn around the knee. They are usually made of the hoofs of the deer, which are strung in two or three rows upon a belt, and the belt itself then tied around the knee.

Gä-geh-tä, or BELT. Plate 9.

The belt is of Indian manufacture. It is braided by hand, the beads being interwoven in the process of braiding. They are worn around the waist, and over the left shoulder. No part of the costume is prized so highly as the belt.

Gä-nuh-sä, or SEA-SHELL MEDAL.

The government have long been in the habit of presenting silver medals to the chiefs of the various Indian tribes, at the formation of treaties, and on the occasion of their visit to the seat of government. These medals are held in the highest estimation. Red Jacket received one from Washington, in 1792, which is now worn by the Seneca chief Sose-ha-wä. It is an elliptical plate of silver, surrounded by a rim, and is about six inches in its greatest diameter. On each side it is engraved with various devices. Medals of sea shell, inlaid with silver, are also worn suspended from the neck, as personal ornaments. A specimen of the latter description is furnished.

Tuesh-tä-ga-tas-tä, or TIN BREAST-PLATE.

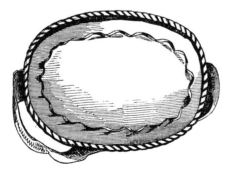

The above is a representation of a species of tin breast-plate, worn by the Seneca Indians.

ARM BANDS, KNEE BANDS, AND WRIST BANDS. Plate 10.

These, also, form a part of the costume. They are usually of bead work, but often of silver. The war club, tomahawk, and moccasin, complete the costume.

Gä-yä-ah, or WORK POCKET. Plate 11.

Ya-wa-o-dä-quä, or NEEDLE BOOK. Plate 12.

Ya-wa-o-dä-qua, or PIN CUSHION. Plate 13.

Got-gwen-dä, or POCKET BOOK. Plate 14.

These are furnished as further specimens of the handiwork of the Indian female in bead work. The figures themselves will dispense with the necessity of any description. The patient industry of the Indian female is quite remarkable, when seen in contrast with the impatience of labor in the Indian himself. In the work of their reclamation and gradual induction into industrial pursuits, this fact furnishes no small degree of encouragement.

Gä-kä, or BREECH CLOTH. Plate 15.

In the ball game the players denude themselves entirely, with the exception of a belt, which is secured below the waist, and the Gä-kä, which passes under it before and behind. It is usually of broadcloth, and ornamented with bead work.

Several articles of silver ware will also be found in the collection. They consist of hat bands, arm and wrist bands, ear rings and broaches, of various patterns and sizes. They are principally of Indian manufacture. The following cuts represent a pair of ear rings worn by Ho-ho-e-yu, in 1849.

Ah-was-hă, or EAR RING.

Plate No. 17 is an engraving of Pipes, in use among the Indians.

No. 75.]   95

Ga-on-seh, or BABY FRAME. Plate 16.

This is likewise an Indian invention. It appears to have been designed rather as a convenience to the Indian mother, for the transportation
of her infant, than, as has generally been supposed, to secure an erect
figure. The frame is about two feet in length, by about fourteen inches
in width, with a carved foot-board at the small end, and a hoop or bow
at the head, arching over at right angles. After being enclosed in a
blanket, the infant is lashed upon the frame with belts of bead work,
which firmly secure and cover its person, with the exception of the
face. A separate article for covering the face, is then drawn over the
bow, and the child is wholly protected. When carried, the burden
strap attached to the frame is placed around the forehead of the mother,
and the Ga-on-seh upon her back. This frame is often elaborately
carved, and its ornaments are of the choicest description. When cultivating the maize, or engaged in any out-door occupation, the Ga-on-
seh is hung upon a limb of the nearest tree, and left to swing in the
breeze. The patience and quiet of the Indian child, in this close con-
finement, are quite remarkable. It will hang thus suspended for hours,
without uttering a complaint.

With the Ga-on-seh, closes the enumeration of articles. Several
have been necessarily omitted, and others noticed but slightly. Sufficient, however, has been written, to illustrate the general character of
our Indian fabrics, implements and utensils. Some of them have been
noticed minutely, as they appeared calculated to exhibit the artisan
intellect of our primitive inhabitants. It is in this view that they are
chiefly interesting. Some general observations naturally present themselves upon this branch of the subject, but the prescribed limits of this
report will not permit their introduction.

Such is the diffusion of Indian arts and Indian inventions among the
Red races, that it is impossible to ascertain with what nation or tribe
they in fact originated. Many of them were common to all, from
Maine to Oregon, and from the St. Lawrence to the peninsula of Flo-
rida. To this day Indian life is about the same over the whole republic.
If we wished to discover the inventions of the Iroquois, we might expect to find them as well among the Sioux of the upper Mississippi, as
among the descendants of the Iroquois themselves. It is for this reason,
that in forming an Indian collection, we should take in the whole range
of Indian life, from the wild tribes dwelling in the seclusions of Oregon,
to the semi-agricultural Cherokees of the south, and the present Iroquois

who reside among ourselves. They have passed through all the intermediate stages, from extreme rudeness to comparative civilization. If
we wished to connect the fabrics of the former with those of our own
primitive inhabitants, we may find that connection in the fact, that
similar implements and similar fabrics, at no remote period, were in
the hands, and of the manufacture, of the Iroquois themselves. Many
of the relics disentombed from the soil of New-York, relate back to the
period of the Mound builders of the west; and belong to a race of men
and an age which have passed beyond the ken of even Indian tradition.
Our first Indian epoch is thus connected with that of the Mound builders.
In the same manner, the fabrics of the Iroquois are intimately connected
with those of all the tribes now resident within the republic. One system of trails belted the whole face of the territory, from the Atlantic to
the Pacific; and the intercourse between the multitude of nations who
dwelt within these boundless domains was constant, and much more
extensive than has ever been supposed. If any one, therefore, desired
a picture of Iroquois life before Hendrick Hudson sailed up the river
upon whose banks rested the eastern end of their "Long House,"* he
should look for it in Catlin's Scenes at the skirts of the Rocky Moun-
tains. There are diversities, it is true, but Indian life is essentially the
same.

A collection, therefore, which embraced within its range the utensils,
implements, and miscellaneous fabrics of the whole Indian family,
would best illustrate the era of Indian occupation within our own State.
Such a collection can, and ought to be made. It would be doing, in
our republic, what European nations have taken unwearied pains to ac-
complish within their own territories. They have treasured up, with
watchful care, the memorials of their own territorial history. These
memorials unlock the social history of the past; and although silent,
they speak more eloquently than all human description. Our own are
essentially Indian. An Indian collection is all that we can offer to the
European, in acknowledgment of the gratification and instruction we
have derived from theirs. While every petty State abroad has its Historical Cabinet, the visitation of which furnishes the chief pleasure of
the traveler, our own States, one of which numbers three millions of
people, have nothing of the kind for the entertainment of the foreign
traveler. The custom among all civilized nations, of making such col-

* Ho-de-no-sau-ne, the name of the Iroquois as one people, signifies " The
People of the Long House." They symbolized the League by a house, which
reached from the Hudson to the Genesee; and afterwards to Niagara, on the ex-
pulsion of the Eries and Neuter Nation, about the year 1650.

lections, rests upon sound considerations of public utility; and the reasons which induce them are just as applicable here, as elewhere; and just as appropriate to each single State, as to the National Government.

This enterprise has been fairly entered upon, under the fostering care of the Regents of the University. The foundation, at least, of an Indian Collection, has been established. Were it enlarged, upon the principles suggested in this report, it would soon become one of the most interesting of all Historical Cabinets. It would grow in public value, as the people whose social condition it reveals, recede from public observation; and in after years it would become inestimable. But such are the changes, and causes of change at work among our Indian races, that the present moment should be improved with diligence. Time buries every thing in a common tomb.

The Red races are passing away before the silent, but irresistible spread of civilization. The tenure of Indian sovereignty is as precarious as the habitation of the deer, his co-tenant of the forest. Their gradual displacement is as inevitable as the progress of events. A portion, indeed, of the Indian family, if present indications are to be trusted, is destined eventually to be reclaimed, and raised to a citizenship among ourselves. But this can only be accomplished by their adoption of agricultural pursuits, and the diffusion of knowledge among them. When this change is effected, they will cease to be Indians. A different destiny awaits the residue. At no distant day the war shout of the Red man will fall away into eternal silence, upon the shores of the distant Pacific. Industry will then have taken up her abode in the seclusions of the forest, the church will rise upon the ruins of the council-house, the railway pursue the distant trail, the ploughshare turn the sod of the hunting ground; and the pursuits of peace having diffused themselves over the whole republic, one universal and continuous hum of industry will rise from ocean to ocean. When the destiny of the Indian is thus fulfilled, the words of the great Seneca orator will rise up in perpetual remembrance:

"Who then lives to mourn us? None. What marks our extermination? Nothing."

All which is respectfully submitted.

LEWIS H. MORGAN.

Pl. 1.

AH-TA-QUA-O-WEH, or MOCCASON.

FOR   MALE.

Pl. 2.

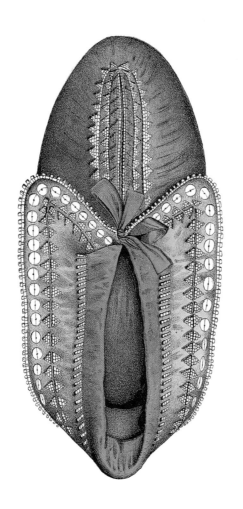

AH-TÄ-QUÄ-O-WEH, OR MOCCASON.
FOR FEMALE.

GUS-TO-WEH or HEAD DRESS.

GÄ-DE-US-HA or NECKLACE.

Pl. 5.

GÄ-KÄ-AH or SKIRT.

Pl.6.

AH-DE-A-DÄ-WE-SÄ or OVER-DRESS.
FRONT

Pl. 6 ͣ.

AH-DE-A-DĂ-WE-SĂ ᴏʀ OVER DRESS.

BACK

Pl. 7.

GÄ-KÄ-AH or KILT.

Pl. 8.

Gise,hă, or Male Leggin.

Pl. 10.

GÄ-GEH-TÄ, YEN-CHE-NO-HOS-TA-TÄ,
OR KNEE BAND

YEN-NIS-HO-QUÄ-HOS-TÄ,
OR WRIST BAND

GA-GEH-TA, YEU-NIS-HÄ-HOS-TA,
OR ARM BAND

Pl. 11.

GÄ-YÄ-AH or WORK BAG.

Pl. 12.

YA-WA-O-DÄ-QUÄ or NEEDLE BOOK.

Pl. 13.

YA-WA-O-DÄ-QUÄ or PIN CUSHION.

Pl.14.

GOT-GWEN-DÄ or POCKETBOOK.

Pl. 15.

GÄ-KÄ or BREECH CLOTH.

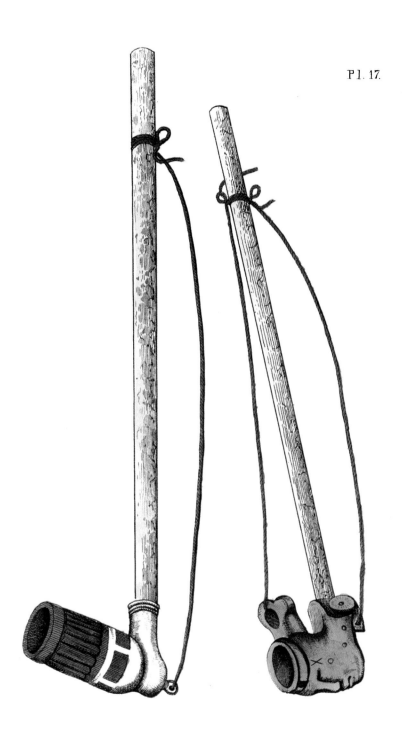

Pl. 17.

AH - SO - QUÄ - TÄ.
PIPES

Fifth Regents Report

· · · · ·
· · ·
·

APPENDIX.

REPORT

ON THE

FABRICS, INVENTIONS, IMPLEMENTS AND UTENSILS

OF THE

IROQUOIS,

MADE TO THE REGENTS OF THE UNIVERSITY, JAN. 22, 1851,

BY LEWIS H. MORGAN.

ILLUSTRATIVE OF THE COLLECTION ANNEXED

TO THE

State Cabinet of Natural History,

With Illustrations

BY RICHARD H. PEASE, ALBANY.

ORDERED TO BE PRINTED, BY THE ASSEMBLY, 1852.

REPORT.

The Regents of the University having renewed their appropriation for the further enlargement of the Indian collection, and again committed its expenditure to the undersigned, he asks leave to submit the following

REPORT:

It is an easy matter to bring together the fabrics and inventions of the modern Iroquois in sufficient completeness to illustrate the present condition of Indian society within the limits of the State. Their range and diversity are neither so wide, or so complicated, as to preclude the possibility of a minute exhibition of the articles, of every name, which are either of original or secondary manufacture. If the effort for their collection is continued for a few successive years, it will not only result in exhausting the subject, so far as their present fabrics are concerned, but, acting backwards upon the past, it will draw forth many ancient inventions which are now held in the memory of the aged, or in the grasp of tradition.

When every thing which the Iroquois can furnish of their present manufacture, or recall through tradition from the past, is brought into one collection, it is but a commencement of the interesting work of gathering together whatever will illustrate the inventive intellect of the Indian family. In a general, but correct view of this subject, it is unnecessary to discriminate, except for classification, between the fabrics and inventions of the Iroquois, and those of the Indian family at large. They are united in one harmonious and connected system, sprang from a common mind, and all together are necessary to exhibit the artizan capacity and social condition of the Indian from the era of aboriginal occupation down to the present period, when Indian life, in some parts of the republic, is merged in comparative civilization.

While the attention of the Regents, and of the people of the State, is very naturally directed, in the first instance, to the fabrics of the Iroquois, a people with whom we stand in many interesting relations, it should not, and cannot properly be limited to them alone. A collection, worthy of the State, must necessarily take a wider range, and aim at a general and universal collection of the fabrics, inventions, implements and utensils of the whole Indian family: from the stone tomahawk of the Pequod, and the rude pottery of the Mobilian tribes, to the beautiful bark and moose hair basket-work of the Chippeway, and the delicate, bead-work embroidery of the modern Iroquois. A few years of well directed effort, with a small expenditure of money, would secure such a collection; one which would not only become as widely known as the Indian whose social history it proclaims, but would form an enduring monument to the enlightened munificence of the State.

By a reference to the schedule which accompanies this report, it will be perceived that the additions the present year are, at least, equal in variety and interest with those of the preceding. Some of them are of the same name and general character; but in such cases the article itself will be found to be either a more perfect specimen, different in some essential particular, or from some other locality. A minute description of each article will not be attempted. It will be proper, however, to introduce the most prominent among them with a brief explanation of their objects and uses. A portion of these articles were obtained of the Mohawks, Onondagas, Cayugas, Senecas and Tuscaroras, who, to the number of two thousand four hundred and fifty, now reside upon a large reserve secured to them by the British government, on Grand river, in the Niagara peninsula in Upper Canada. But the residue, and the chief portion, were obtained from the Sene-

No. 122.]   71

cas in the western part of the State. They number in all two
hundred and twenty, and the articles themselves are of one hundred and fifteen distinct species.

Gä-sweh-tä Ote-ko-ă,[1] or BELT OF WAMPUM.
No. 3. Plate 1, figure 1.

Ote-ko-ă, or STRING OF WAMPUM.
No. 4. Plate 2, figure 2.

The use of Wampum reaches back to a remote period upon
this continent.   It was an original Indian notion which prevailed among the Iroquois as early, at least, as the formation of the
League.   The primitive wampum of the Iroquois consisted of
strings of a small fresh water spiral shell, called in the Seneca
dialect *Ote-ko-ă*, the name of which has been bestowed upon the
modern wampum.   When *Da-gä-no-we-dä*, the founder of the
League, had perfected its organic provisions, he produced several strings of this ancient wampum of his own arranging, and
taught them its use in recording the provisions of the compact
by which the several nations were united into one people.   At a
subsequent day the wampum in present use was introduced
among them by the Dutch, who in the manufactured shell bead
offered an acceptable substitute for the less convenient one of
the spiral shell.   These beads, as shown in the plate, are purple
and white, about a quarter of an inch in length, an eighth in diameter, and perforated lengthwise so as to be strung on sinew or
bark thread.   The white bead was manufactured from the great
conch sea shell, and the purple from the muscle shell.   They
are woven into belts, or used in strings simply, in both of which
conditions they are employed to record treaty stipulations, to
convey messages, and to subserve many religious and social purposes.   The word *wampum* is not of Iroquois origin.   Baylie, in his
History of New Plymouth, informs us that it was first known in
New-England as *Wampumpeag*, from which its Algonquin deri-
vation is to be inferred; and Hutchinson says that the art of
making it was obtained from the Dutch about the year 1627.

1. NOTE.—The reader should note the characters by which the different sounds of
the vowel *a*, the letter upon which the greatest variations are made, is indicated:—
ä is sounded as in arm; ă as in at; a as in ale. All of the Indian words used are in
the Seneca dialect of the Iroquois language.

In making a belt no particular pattern was followed: sometimes they are of the width of three fingers and three feet long, in other instances as wide as the hand, and over three feet in length; sometimes they are all of one color, in others variegated, and in still others woven with the figures of men to symbolize, by their attitudes, the objects or events they were designed to commemorate. The most common width was three fingers, or the width of seven beads, the length ranging from two to six feet. In belt making, which is a simple process, eight strands or cords of bark thread are first twisted, from filaments of slippery elm, of the requisite length and size; after which they are passed through a strip of deer skin to separate them at equal distances from each other in parallel lines. A piece of splint is then sprung in the form of a bow, to which each end of the several strings is secured, and by which all of them are held in tension, like warp threads in a weaving machine. Seven beads, these making the intended width of the belt, are then run upon a thread by means of a needle, and are passed under the cords at right angles, so as to bring one bead lengthwise between each cord, and the one next in position. The thread is then passed back again along the upper side of the cords and again through each of the beads; so that each bead is held firmly in its place by means of two threads, one passing under and one above the cords. This process is continued until the belt reaches its intended length, when the ends of the cords are tied, the end of the belt covered, and afterwards trimmed with ribbons. In ancient times both the cords and the thread were of sinew.

The belt possesses an additional interest from the fact, that the beads of which it is composed, formerly belonged to the celebrated Mohawk Chief, Joseph Brant *Tä-yen-dä-ná-ga*. They were purchased, by the writer, of his youngest daughter Catharine in October last, at the reservation on Grand river in Upper Canada before referred to; and were afterwards taken to Tonawanda in this State and made into the present belt. In this form it will be most convenient to preserve them as a relic of the distinguished war captain of the Mohawks.

Wampum was also put up in strings, from two to three and sometimes four feet in length, several of which were joined together into

No. 122]   73

one. The string represented in the plate was obtained of an Onondaga on Grand river.

Both in strings and belts, wampum was put to a great variety
of uses. Its office was to record treaties, and preserve such transactions as were worthy of particular remembrance. Whatever
was to be entrusted to its keeping was " talked into". the belt or
string which ever afterwards could tell, by means of an interpreter, the exact transaction of which it was made at the time the
sole evidence. Operating upon the principle of association, the
belt or string gave fidelity to the memory. As the laws and usages
of the League were entrusted to the guardianship of such belts
and strings, one of the Onondaga sachems, *Ho-no-we-nä-to*, was
made hereditary keeper of the Wampum, and he, and his succes-
sors, were required to be versed in its interpretation. These belts
and strings were the only visible records of the Iroquois, and
were of no use except by the aid of those special personages who
could draw forth the secret records locked up in their remembrance.

White wampum was the Iroquois emblem of purity and of faith,
It was hung around the neck of the White Dog before it was burned; it was used before the periodical religious festivals for the
confession of sins, no confession being regarded as sincere unless
recorded with white wampum ; further than this, it was the
customary offering in condonation of murder, although the purple
was sometimes employed. Six strings was the value of a life, or
the quantity sent in condonation, for the wampum was rather
sent as the evidence of a regretful confession of the crime, with a
petition for forgiveness, than as the actual price of blood.

Wampum has frequently been called the money of the Indian ;
but there is no sufficient reason for supposing that they ever made
it an exclusive currency, or a currency in any sense, more than
silver or other ornaments. All personal ornaments, and most
other articles of personal property passed from hand to hand
at a fixed value; but they appear to have had no common stand-
ard of value until they found it in our currency. If wampum had
been their currency it would have had a settled value to which
all other articles would have been referred. There is no doubt

that it came nearer to a currency than any other species of property among them, because its uses were so general, and its transit from hand to hand so easy, that every one could be said to need it. The ancient value of wampum was half a cent per bead, according to the statement of Catharine, the daughter of Brant. It is now very scarce and difficult to procure, as the manufacture of it ceased many years ago, and the quantity has been gradually diminishing with the lapse of time. It bids fair to rise again to its primitive value, at the period when it was exchanged for furs.

Gä-däs-hă or SHEAF.

No. 1.

2 feet.

The sheaf is an Indian invention of great antiquity, and universal among Indian races. It was sometimes made of the skin of a small animal, like the wolf, which was taken off entire, dressed with the hair on, and hung upon the back, the arrows being placed within it. But the choicer articles were made of dressed unhaired deer skin, and embroidered with porcupine quills as represented in the figure. It was made of two strips of deer skin about two feet in length and of unequal width; one of these was narrow for the back side; the other about three times its width so as to make a convex front, thus forming a species of sac in which the arrows were deposited. The ordinary sheaf, as used by the Iroquois in ancient times, would hold from fifteen to twenty-five arrows; but those used by the western Indians were generally large enough for forty or fifty. It was worn on the back inclining from the left shoulder down towards the belt on the right side of the body, crossing the back diagonally. There are deer string fastenings at each end, the lower ones being attached to the waist belt, and the upper ones passing around the neck and under the left arm. To draw forth an arrow and place it in the bow, it was necessary to raise the right hand to the left shoulder when it came at once in contact with the feathered end, which projected from the sheaf; so that it was but the work of a sec-

No. 112.]   75

ond to set an arrow in its place. Originally the Indian bow was about three feet in length, and the arrow two; and it is said to have been an easy matter for an Iroquois hunter, with a bow of this description, to send an arrow, pointed with flint or horn, entirely through a deer. But in later days, when this weapon came to be used merely for amusement, and the muscular strength acquired, by its use, had abated, the bow was lengthened to four feet and the arrow to three.

Gä-ne-ko-wä-ah, BURDEN FRAME, or LITTER.

No. 113.

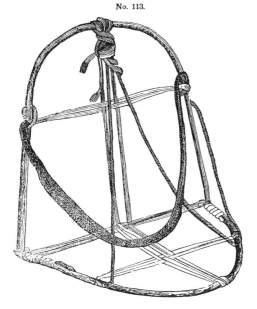

This is an ancient contrivance to assist in carrying burdens. Game, cooking utensils, wood, bark, in fact everything which could be transported by hand could be borne upon this frame. They were a necessary appendage to every house, to the traveller, and to the hunter. Sometimes they were elaborately carved and finished, but more frequently were of a plain piece of hickory, like the one represented in the figure, and made with the quickest dispatch. The frame consists of two bows of Hickory, brought together at right angles, and fastened to each other by means of an eye and head. The upright part of the frame is the same as the horizontal in all particulars, except its greater length. Strips

76   [ASSEMBLY

from the inner rind of bass wood bark were then passed between
the bows both length and crosswise, and fastened to the rim
pieces. A burden strap was then attached to the frame at the
point where the strip of bark passed across the upright bow from
side to side; and from thence it passed diagonally across to the
horizontal part of the frame, to the point where the lower strip
of bark crossed that part of the frame. There were several feet
of rope at each end, reserved to lash around whatever burden
was placed upon the frame; but when the frame was empty, as
it is shown above, these ropes were passed up to the top of the
frame and there secured. After being loaded the frame was
placed upon the back, and the burden strap passed over the head
and placed across the chest. If the burden was very heavy it
was customary to use two straps, one across the chest, and the
other against the forehead. At the present day the burden frame
is still in use.

Gä-ose-hä, or BABY FRAME.

No. 19.

In the collection will be found two specimens, one of which was
procured of a Tuscarora woman on Grand river, and the other of
a Seneca at Tonawanda. This figure is introduced to show the
frame divested of the belts and drapery by which, when in actual
use, it is entirely concealed. It consists of but three principal
pieces of wood, the bow, bottom board and foot board, upon the
first and last of which the most labor was bestowed. They are

always carved, and frequently inlaid with silver, or with wood of different colors and in various figures. The bow, which arches over, is held to the bottom board by means of a cross piece, passing under it, into which the ends of the bow are inserted. It is further secured in its perpendicular position by means of side pieces in which the bow is embedded. The foot board at the small end of the frame is also carved, and often inlaid, it being the only part of it which is exposed when the infant is lashed upon the frame. Deer strings are run along the outer edges of the bottom board under which the belts are passed from side to side passing over the body of the child. As a whole the Gä-ose-hä, with its embroidered belts, and other decorations, is one of the most conspicuous articles pertaining to their social life.

Gä-swä-hose-hä, or BABY FRAME BELT: }
Gä-nose-gä, or BABY FRAME BELT. }
Plate 2.

Gä-nose-gä, or BABY FRAME BELT.

The covering of the frame consists of a spread to draw over the bow, and these belts. The largest belt (*Gä swä-hose-hä*, Fig. 1,) is of red broad cloth, beautifully embroidered with bead work. This is attached to the frame next to the bow, and passed over the frame from side to side, under the deer strings and above the child, finally bringing that part of it, which is most embroidered in the centre of the frame. In like manner the second belt, (*Gä-nose-gä*, Fig. 2,) which is made of broad cloth, is adjusted at the foot of the frame. Between the two the short belts (fig. 3,) is inserted. Over the bow is drawn the spread (*Yen-dus-ho-dä-quä*) usually of red merino, embroidered with beads, and often decorated with silver ornaments. Rattles were attached to the bow for the amusement of the child; but as its arms were confined beneath the belts, this gratification was only afforded when the frame was rocked by the Indian mother, or waved by the breeze while depending from the branch of a tree.

Gät-go-ne-as-heh, or HOMMONY BLADE.
No. 35.

4 feet.

Many of the domestic utensils of the Iroquois were of wood.
Figures of animals, of birds, and sometimes of reptiles were carved upon them in the most ingenious manner. The hommony
blade or soup stick is one of this description; an article used in
every Indian household for making hommony, succotash, or soup,
and for many other purposes. It is usually from three to four
feet in length, and made of hard maple, or other tough wood, in
the general form of the one represented in the figure. This hommony blade is made out of one piece of wood, although the end
piece is attached to the blade by a link. In the end piece are
two wooden balls, also cut out of the solid wood within the frame
in which they are confined. For a wooden utensil it is beautifully made.

No. 36.

This specimen is made in a different fashion, although much
the same as the former. In the handle are two balls cut out, like
the above, of the solid wood within the frame in which they are

No. 122.]   79

seen, while the end of the utensil terminates in two human figures facing each other. Sometimes several links are cut out at the end of the handle, of which kind two specimens will be found in the collection. Those figured above are of Seneca manufacture.

Ya-ä-go-gen-tä-quä, or BREAD TURNER.

No. 38.

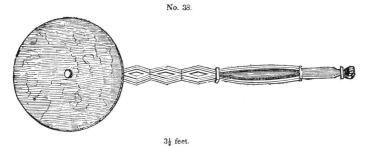

3½ feet.

The corn bread of the Indian is unleavened, and cooked by boiling in water. After hulling the corn and pounding it into flour, it is made into loaves about six inches in diameter and two in thickness. These loaves or cakes are then boiled until they are hard, which is the general mode of cooking; but they are sometimes baked. The bread turner is used, as its name indicates, to handle these loaves while under the process of cooking. The specimen given above was obtained from a Tuscarora woman on Grand river.

80　　　　　[ASSEMBLY

Ah-do-gwä-seh, or LADLE.

No. 40.

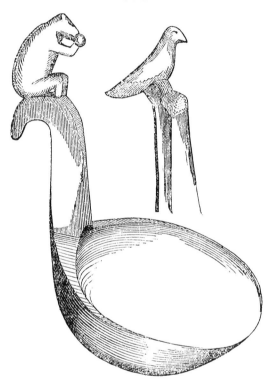

In ancient times the ladle not only answered as a substitute for the spoon among the Iroquois, but supplied the place of every other contrivance for taking food from the dish. They are made of hard wood, of different sizes and patterns, and very perfectly finished. The end of the handle is often surmounted with the figure of an animal or bird, so carved as to form a species of hook upon the back of the ladle with which to hang it upon the side

No. 122.]   81

of the dish.   These figures were often carved with surpassing
skill, the proportions, and attitude of the animal being accurately
preserved and studied.   Of the two figured above, the one surmounted with a squirrel was made at Tonawanda by a Seneca;
and the other, with a hawk, upon Grand river, by a Cayuga.
They are both finished specimens of the Indian ladle.

LADLE, WITH WRESTLERS.

No. 39.

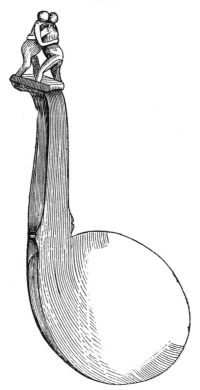

82

LADLE WITH SITTING FIGURES.
No. 41.

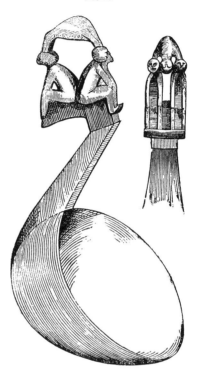

In other instances the human form was introduced in various attitudes. The figure of the wrestlers is quite spirited, and a good specimen of wood carving. Upon the others it will be seen there are five figures; four of them in a stooping posture, and the fifth bending over backwards, with his hands and feet each upon the head of one of the sitting figures. Other specimens are surmounted with a turtle, or a swan, or a wolf, at the fancy of the maker. These ladles are found in large numbers in every Indian family, at least one for every member of the household, in which to the present day they are the substitute for the spoon, and in most families, for the knife and fork. In minuteness, delicacy, and beauty of carving the ladle surpasses all the other wooden utensils of the Iroquois. In the collection will be found four specimens carved with human figures, seven with those of animals, and two plain; part of them were obtained among the Senecas, and the residue of the Iroquois in Canada.

No. 122.]   **83**

BARK LADLE.
No. 42.

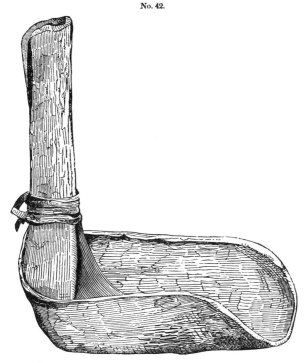

The original ladle was of bark and a very simple contrivance, as will appear from the above representation. It was made of red elm bark, and would hold but little more than the common spoon. In ancient times ladles of this description only were used; but they were laid aside when the possession of metalic implements enabled them to substitute the present one of wood. The ladle is, without doubt, an original Indian utensil, and in all probability the origin of the common wooden ladle still in general use among our own people.

O-sä, or BASSWOOD BARK.
No. 88.

In the former report the subject of rope making from filaments of bark was adverted to, but not particularly explained. As fabrics of bark occupy a conspicuous place in their domestic economy, as well as form an interesting department of Indian manufacture, some further notice of the art will be made. The Iro-

84   [ASSEMBLY

quois used but two kinds of bark, the slippery elm and the basswood, the former for thread, twine, and burden straps; and the
latter, which is a coarser bark, for ropes and heavy belts. At
the proper season the inner rind of the bark was peeled off in
narrow strips six or eight feet in length and tied up in bunches,
as represented in the figure above, this being the first stage in
the process of manufacture.

O-să, or SKEIN OF BASSWOOD FILAMENTS.

No. 87.

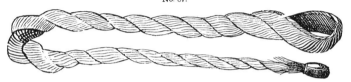

Before it would run off into filaments or small threads, it was
boiled in ashes and water, washed thoroughly, and dried in the
sun. It could then be separated into natural threads or filaments
of any size, which, unless too fine, would run the length of the
strips of bark. It was then put up in skeins, as shown in the
figure, ready for use.

Gä-a-sken-dä, or BARK ROPE.

No. 81.

Basswood filaments were usually run off coarse, and, in that
condition, braided into ropes, as represented above. Three
strands only were used, and in the process of braiding, which
was done by hand, these strands were not twisted, as their
strength would not thereby be increased. A specimen of this
bark rope fifty feet in length is furnished, and two others about
thirty feet each. In some instances burden straps of a coarser
kind were made of basswood, which was braided into an open

No. 122   85

work belt, with interstices between the strands. Upon the burden frame mentioned above is a strap of this description.

The inner rind of the slippery elm bark is peeled off, in the first instance, in narrow strips about four feet in length, and tied up in bundles. It is sometimes preserved for months in this form before it is made into threads. After being boiled in ashes and water, and washed and dried in the same manner as basswood bark, it is run off into filaments, which can be made as fine as small thread, if desired.

Ose-gă, or SKEIN OF SLIPPERY ELM FILAMENTS.
No. 83.

These threads are then tied up in skeins, as represented above, and laid aside for use. For burden straps of the best quality, this thread alone is used, it being stronger, more pliable, and of a finer texture than the basswood. The skeins themselves have a reddish tinge usually, but the first quality has a grayish color. They are sometimes dyed black or some fancy color, to give variety to the belts into which they are woven. A specimen of the gray and of the colored bark thread is also furnished.

In the manufacture of the several species of burden strap, more skill, ingenuity and patient industry are exhibited, perhaps, than in any other single article fabricated by the Iroquois. The strap consists of a belt in the centre about two feet in length by two and a half inches in width, with ropes at each end about seven feet each; thus making its entire length from fifteen to twenty feet. It is used attached to the litter or burden frame, to the baby frame, and to the basket, when these burdens are to be borne on the back; in which cases the belt is passed around the forehead. Fifteen or twenty small cords are first made, about three feet in length, by twisting the filaments of bark by hand. These cords, which make the warp, or substance of the belt, are then placed parallel with each other, and side by side; after which finer threads of the same material, usually colored, are prepared for the filling, to be passed across the cords over and under each alternately from side to side and back again. The fine thread, or filling, is twisted in the first instance, and also again as it is braided or woven in with the warp while being passed across from side to side. As the work is all done by hand, it is a slow and laborious process, but the specimen will show how successfully it is accomplished. After the filling has thus been braided in with the warp, each of the main cords, although covered on both sides, literally wound with the finer threads in crossing and returning, is still distinctly visible, giving to the belt the appearance of being ribbed. The whole process is exactly the same as the modern process of weaving, the main difference consisting in this, that in the latter the warp and filling are nearly equal in the size of the threads, while in the Indian art the warp is several times larger than the filling.

Towards the ends the belt is narrowed gradually by joining two of the cords in one, until its width is diminished about one-third. The cords are then lengthened out by adding new filaments, and braided into an open-work band or bark rope about an inch wide, and flat; the band consisting of as many strands as there were cords at the end of the belt. The surface of these belts is generally smooth and even, and the belt itself so closely braided as to leave no interstices through which the eye could penetrate. When threads of different colors were used, the belt was variegated simply, or small figures were woven in it for ornament.

Another species of burden strap, of more expeditious manufacture, was made by placing the warp cords side by side, and stitching them through and through with bark thread, in which case the cords themselves were made larger than in the ordinary burden strap. For stitching, a hickory or bone needle, without an eye, was used in ancient times. As the cords consisted of two strong threads twisted into one, the stitching thread was passed through each cord, between its two parts, from one side to the

No. 122.]　　　　　　　**87**

other and back again. Ropes were then attached to the ends of the belt and the work was completed.

O-ä-ta-ose-kä, or MOOSE HAIR BURDEN STRAP, ⎫
Gus-hä-ah,　　or DEER HAIR　　　do　　⎬
⎭

No. 74　Plate 3.

Near the rump of the Moose (*Yen-dä-ne,*) and near the neck between the shoulders, there are small tufts of white hair, about four inches in length, each yielding a small handful. These hairs were carefully preserved, dyed red, blue and yellow, and used in the manufacture of the finest varieties of burden straps. Similar tufts of hair, but inferior in quality, are found upon the Elk, (*Jo-rä-dä,*) and in the tail of the deer (*Na-o-geh.*) The Moose hair burden strap is made in all respects as above described, except that the thread, which serves as the filling, is wound with this hair upon one side of the belt, in such a way, as either to cover the whole face of the belt, or to sprinkle it through with small figures at the pleasure of the maker. The one represented in the plate (fig. 1.) is a very perfect and beautiful piece of work, nearly the whole upper surface of the belt being covered with Moose hair, white, yellow, red and blue, which is woven into the belt in a regular figure. It was made by an Onondaga woman on Grand river in·Upper Canada, where it was purchased in October last. Although it has been used many years, and the colors have lost some portion of their original brilliancy, it is yet wholly unimpaired, and a remarkable specimen of finger weaving, as well as of artizan skill. It is not only woven compactly, but with such evenness of thread as to present a smooth surface and uniform texture. It is difficult to believe, upon an examination of the under side of the belt, that it is manufactured with bark threads; and perhaps still more incredible, that in the mechanism of this belt, can be found the primary elements of the art of weaving.

In figure 2 of the plate is a representation of a burden strap in which deer's hair is used. It is made in the same general fashion as the preceding, and is the work of a Seneca woman at Tonawanda.

1. Among the Chippeways a great variety of fancy work in the nature of baskets, &c., is made of birch bark, upon which various figures are worked with moose hair of the kind above described.

88   [ASSEMBLY

Da-gä-yä-sont, or SILVER CROSS.
No. 6. Plate 4.

The passion of the Iroquois for silver ornaments in ancient
times was very extravagant; and down to the present day it has
suffered but little abatement. This inclination was seized upon
by the trader, who purchased the richest furs with articles of this
description of small comparative value. Among the number is
found the silver cross, which doubtless owed its introduction
among them, in the first instance, to the pious ministrations of the
Jesuits; but at the present day it is regarded merely as a personal ornament, and is without significance to them as a religious emblem. When worn they were attached to a necklace, or perhaps
fastened to the hat, or hung upon the hair. The one figured in
the plate is of unusual dimensions, the longest part being about
ten inches, and the transverse about six, and made of solid silver.
It was purchased of a Cayuga on Grand river. They are frequently found with two transverse pieces of silver, as shown in
the two small crosses, figures 2 and 3. Sometimes they are engraved with figures of animals or birds, as a swan. The name
"Montreal" is stamped upon two out of the three other crosses in
the collection, thus indicating the place of manufacture.

An-ne-as-gä, or SILVER BROACH.
No. 9. Plate 5.

Ah-was-hä, or EAR RING.
No. 15. Plate 5.

Au-ne-ä-hus-hä, or FINGER RING.
No. 11. Plate 5.

Broaches of silver are worn by every female. They are of all
sizes and patterns, from six inches in diameter, and worth as many dollars, to half an inch and worth a half dime; answering
upon the female dress the double purpose of ornament and use.
At a fixed value they pass from hand to hand, thus forming a
species of currency among them. Every Indian female, however
humble, has some silver broaches, while occasionally those can
be found who count them by hundreds. The larger ones are
usually worn upon the *Ah-de-a-dä-we-sä*, or over dress, in front,
as a button or pin, the largest being placed at the bottom. Some-

No. 122.]   89

times the smaller ones are strung together and worn as a hat
band, or as a necklace.

Finger and ear rings of the same material, specimens of
which may be seen in the plate, were also very common. The
most of these silver ornaments in later years have been made
by Indian silversmiths, one of whom may be found in nearly every Indian village. They are either made of brass, of silver, or
from silver coins pounded out, and then cut into patterns with
metalic instruments. The ear rings figured in the plate were
made out of bar silver, by an Onondaga silversmith on Grand
river, under the direction of the writer.

Ont-wis-tä-ne-un-dä-qua, or SILVER BEADS.

No. 17. Plate 6.

The long silver beads, represented in the plate, were very common in former times, but are now rarely to be met with. They
are simply tubes of silver, varying from one to two inches in
length, and strung upon deer string, with round silver beads between them part of the way from the lower end of the string.
In this string there are seven strands, all of which are banded together by the deer strings which issue from the small ends of the
several strings; but at the larger ends, they are disunited. It
was purchased of the wife of a distinguished Cayuga sachem,
John Jacobs, (*Jote-ho-weh-ko*) on Grand river. Beads of this description are worn around the neck, or in the hair, or perhaps as
a hat band, to which use they were devoted at the time of their
purchase. They bear evidence of long usage.

O-wìs-tä-no-o, or ROUND SILVER BEADS.

No 18. Plate 7. Fig. 2.

Gä-te-as-hä, or GLASS BEADS.

No. 47. Plate 7. Fig. 1.

The round silver beads figured in the plate, which were obtained of a Seneca female at Tonawanda, were evidently made in
imitation of the old fashioned gold beads, as there is a close resemblance in size and workmanship. At an early day these
beads were in great favor with the Indian female, but now they

are seldom to be met with.   Every fifth bead upon the string is
of an opaque blue glass, introduced for contrast.

The common glass beads (fig. 1) have always been and still
continue to be in high favor.   From the period of their discovery to the present time, glass trinkets of this description have continued to dazzle the eye of the Indian maiden, and to be seized
upon with the greatest avidity.   The brilliancy of their colors,
the neatness of their finish, and their conspicuous appearance as
personal ornaments, have ever given to necklaces of this description a peculiar charm; a charm sufficiently potent to draw forth
the richest furs from the depths of the wilderness, to be freely
exchanged, although a thousand fold more valuable, for these
glittering baubles.   The specimen figured in the plate was procured of a Mohawk girl in Canada.

Gä-te-äs-hä Gä-a-o-tä-ges, or GRASS SHOULDER ORNAMENT.
No. 78.   Plate 8.

This article of dress is in the nature of a necklace.   It is made
of a fragrant marsh grass called by the Senecas Gä-a-ó-tä-ges,
which is first braided into small three strand cords, after which
several of them are united in one chain.   At intervals of three
or four inches small discs, made of the same material, but sometimes covered upon the upper face with bead work, are attached,
together with some other ornaments.   On the specimen represented may be seen a small and delicately made basket of the
size of a thimble, made of the same grass.   This is more particularly a female ornament, although in ancient times it appears to
have been worn by both sexes.   The grass of which it is made
constantly emits an agreeable odor, the fragrance of which made
a species of substitute for artificial perfumery.   It was obtained
of an Oneida female on Grand river

No. 122] 91

Gä-gä-ne-as-heh, or KNIFE AND BELT.

No. 54.

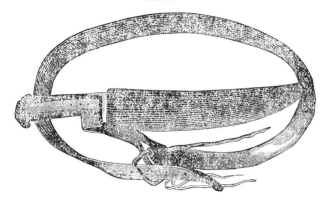

Among the Senecas in this State, and the Iroquois in Canada, the knife and belt are very frequently to be seen as a part of their daily apparel. To the leather belt a plain sheath is attached, in which the knife is worn, the handle appearing partly above it. Formerly the tomahawk was worn in the belt, and behind the back, from which circumstance doubtless originated the habit of wearing the knife in the same manner; for it is as frequently seen behind the back as upon the side. The blade, which is usually from six to ten inches in length, is that of a common knife; and it is used as a substitute for the pocket knife, as well as for a great variety of purposes. The one figured above was procured of a Seneca on Grand river.

Yun-des-ho-yon-dä-gwat-hä, or POP CORN SEIVE.

No. 98.

Corn was charred by roasting it before a long fire in the field while in its green state. Before reducing it to charred corn flour

it was parched over in the ashes to reduce its weight still more
by drying. The splint seive represented in the figure was used
to sift out the fine ashes which might adhere to the kernel. After
the corn was thus purified it was pounded into flour and mixed
with a portion of maple sugar; in which condition it not only
made a very palatable and nutritious food, but was so light that
sufficient could be carried in the bear or deer skin pocket of the
hunter or warrior for many days subsistence.

Gıs-tät-he-o Gä-yä-ah, or FAWN SKIN BAG.
No. 62.

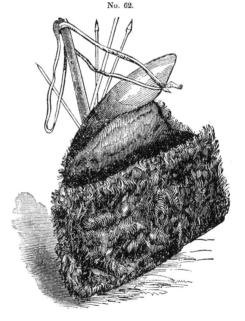

Bags or pockets of this description, made of the skins of animals, were in constant use among the Iroquois in ancient times.
They were hung to the girdle of the warrior and the hunter, and
would contain within their narrow folds sufficient subsistence for
a long expedition, thus answering very perfectly the purposes of
the knapsack. At home they were used as repositories for the
safe keeping of choice articles. Occasionally these pockets were
made of the skin of the speckled fawn, a fine specimen of which
is given on plate 7.

No. 122.] 93

BIRD TRAP.

No. 89 1-2.

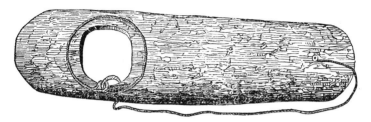

Trapping game of all kinds, from the bear and deer to the quail and snipe, was a common practice. For deer, a young tree was bent over and held in this position by the mechanism of the trap. When sprung a noose was fastened around the hind leg of the deer, and he was drawn up in the air by the unsprung tree. Bear traps were constructed in such a way as to let down a heavy timber upon the back of the animal, when sprung, and thus pin him to the earth. Nets of bark twine were also spread for pigeons and quails. An attempt was made to procure models of these traps, but the project failed for the present year. A simple bird trap, however, for small birds, will be found in the collection. It consists of a rounding strip of elm bark about eight inches long by four wide, with an eye cut in one end and a piece of bark twine with a noose at the end of it, attached to the other. After the bark is secured upon the ground, a few kernels of corn are dropped through the eye upon the ground, and the noose adjusted around it. When a bird attempts to pick up the corn the ruffled plumage of the neck takes up the string, and brings the noose around the neck, which is tightened the moment the bird attempts to fly, and either strangles or holds it in captivity. The trap is said to be very successful.

Gä-wä. or MOCCASIN AWL.

No. 59.

In ancient times the moccasin awl was a small bone about five inches in length taken near the ankle joint of the deer. But in

later days· they have substituted a metalic point, inserting it however in a bone handle. These handles are often carved with
such care and labor as to make them tasteful implements. In
sewing deer skin either with sinew, or deer strings, or bark thread,
the Iroquois women are very expert.

Ah-tä-quä-o-weh, or MOCCASIN.

No. 33.

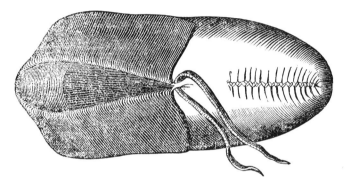

In the common moccasin the side pieces instead of folding down
rise above the ankle, and are secured with strings. Many of the
Iroquois both male and female, and especially the elders, still
cling to the moccasin as the most acceptable protection for the
foot; and wear it plain, as represented in the figure, as a part of
their daily apparel. The bottom and sides are without seams,
the only ones being on the instep in front, and up the heel behind.
In the figure the moccasin is thrown out of shape by being flattened on the side. When in actual use the thickness of the moccasin would be the thickness of the foot. Two specimens of the
plain moccasin are furnished, one from Canada and the other
from Tonawanda.

No. 122.]   95

Gus-to-weh, or HEAD DRESS.
No. 58.

This figure is introduce to show the skeleton or frame of the Iroquois head dress, which, when completed, is the most striking feature of their costume. It is made of splint in the manner represented, except that in some instances another band arches over from side to side. The large feather revolves in the tube in which it is inserted. It was obtained of a Seneca on Grand river.

Gä-kä-ah, or KILT.
No. 27.   Plate 9.

The ancient male costume of the Iroquois consisted, in its principal parts, of the moccasin made plain ; deer skin leggins made plain, setting tight to the legs, and rising considerably above the knees ; the Gä-kä, or breech cloth also of deer skin, worn about the loins ; and a bear or deer skin blanket. This is especially the present daily costume of the wild tribes, which roam over the plains in and beyond the Indian territory, and west of the Mississippi States ; and was, doubtless, the primitive costume of the whole Indian family. The first innovation among the Iroquois was the introduction of cotton shirts, after their intercourse commenced with the Dutch and English. With the use of the

96   [ASSEMBLY

shirt the *Gä-kä* was laid aside ; and soon afterwards blankets of
skin gave place to those of woolen, which were supplied by the
traders. At a later period the pantaloon was substituted for the
leggin, and the woolen blanket was made into a frock coat. The
ancient Iroquois male costume is now retained only as an apparel
for the dance. The kilt is of modern introduction among them,
and never was used except in the dance. At an early day, when
the *Gä-kä* was in universal use, the kilt was not even worn for this
purpose. It is difficult to determine from whom it came, but it
has become the favorite part of their dancing costume. The kilt
shown in the plate, is a superb specimen made of white buckskin
embroidered with bead work. It is secured around the waist by
a belt, and falls down to the knees. The plate itself will supersede the necessity of any description ; making it only necessary
to add, that this article is of Seneca manufacture.

Got-ko-on-dä Gise-hä, or DEER SKIN LEGGIN.
No. 23. Plate 10.

This leggin is a pure Indian article made after the antique fashion. It is made of brown colored deer skin tanned in the Indian
manner, designed to set tight to the skin, and to rise above the
knee. Upon the projecting edge, which is worn in front, a porcupine quill border is worked in the ancient style. This leggin
is a reproduction of that worn before the kilt came into use, when
the leggin rose higher than at present.

Ah-tä-quä-o-weh, or MOCCASIN.
No. 31. Plate 11.

O-ha-dä, or PORCUPINE QUILL.
No. 109. Plate 14. No. 1.

Both the male and female moccasin were introduced in the last
report ; but they were chiefly embroidered with bead work. The
moccasin represented in the plate is such a beautiful specimen of
porcupine quill work, that it will justify an equal illustration.
The porcupine (*Gä-ha-dä*) is covered with a species of quill perfectly round, without down or feather, and terminating in a sharp
point. The small quills are from one to four inches in length, and
are white with the exception of the tip ends or about one fifth of
the quills, which are of a dark brown color, and give to the ani-

No. 122.]   97

mal its dark appearance. After being picked and seasoned they
are colored red, blue and yellow by artificial dyes, (see fig. 24,
plate 12,) and then used in connection with the white ones.
For heavy border work the quills are moistened and flattened down, and in that form are used, as will be seen in
the plate; but for vine or figure work, a thread is stitched
through the deer skin and around the quill, and drawn down
so as to compress it. This process is repeated at intervals,
the quill being bent between the stitches. No patterns are used
to work from, the eye and the taste being the principal guides.
In combining colors much taste is displayed.

Yunt-ka-to-dä-tä, or DEER SKIN SHOULDER BELT.
No. 30. Plate 12.

Da-yunt-wä-hos-tä, OR DEER SKIN WAIST BELT.
No. 29. Plate 13.

Whether the practice of wearing a belt over the left shoulder
was a primitive custom of the Iroquois, or an imitation of the
corresponding article in our own military costume is uncertain ;
but the latter seems to be probable. At an early day these belts
were worn, made of deer skin worked with porcupine quills like
the one represented in the plate. Having been passed over the
left shoulder and across the chest diagonally to the waist belt on
the right side it was there secured. The waist belt was a narrow
strip of deer skin embroidered in the same manner. It was put
on like the bead and worsted belt, with the centre in front, the
belt being passed around the body from before back, and the ends
brought around in front again to be tied, in order that the ornamented part might occupy a conspicuous place.

[Assembly, No. 122.]   7

98   [ASSEMBLY

Gä-go-sä, or FALSE FACE.

No. 73.

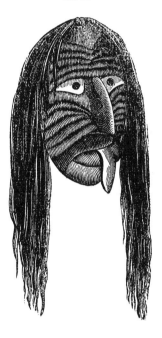

The tendency of the Iroquois to superstitious beliefs is especially exemplified in their notion of the existence of a race of supernatural beings whom they call Falsefaces. This belief has prevailed among them from the most remote period, and still continues its hold upon the Indian mind. The Falsefaces are believed to be evil spirits or demons without bodies, arms or limbs, simply faces, and those, of the most hideous description. It is pretended that when seen they are usually in the most retired places, darting from point to point, and perhaps from tree to tree, by some mysterious power; and possessed of a look so frightful and demoniacal as to paralyze all who behold them. They are supposed also to have power to send plagues and pestilence among men, as well as to devour their bodies when found, for which reasons they were held in the highest terror. To this day there are large numbers of the Iroquois who believe implicitly in the personal existence of these demons.

No. 122.]   99

Upon this belief was founded a regular secret organization called the Falseface band, members of which can now be found in
every Iroquois village both in this State and Canada, where the
old modes of life are still preserved.   This society has a species
of initiation, and regular forms, ceremonies and dances.   In ac-
quiring or relinquishing a membership their superstitious notions
were still further illustrated, for it depended entirely upon the
omen of a dream.   If any one dreamed he was a Falseface, it was
only necessary to signify his dream to the proper person, and give
a feast, to be at once initiated ; and so any one dreaming that he
had ceased to be a False face, had but to make known his dream
and give a similar entertainment to effect his exodus.   In no other way could a membership be acquired or surrendered.   Upon
all occasions on which the members appeared in character they
wore False-faces of the kind represented in the figure, the masks
being diversified in color, style and configuration, but all agreeing in their equally hideous appearance.   The members were all
males save one, who was a female, and the Mistress of the Band.
She was called *Gā-go-sā Ho-nun-nas-tase-tā*, or the keeper of the
Falsefaces; and not only had charge of the regalia of the band,
but was the only organ of communication with the members, for
their names continued unknown.

The prime motive in the establishment of this organization
was to propitiate those demons called Falsefaces, and among other good results to arrest pestilence and disease.   In course of
time the band itself was believed to have a species of control over
diseases, and over the healing art ; and they are often invoked
for the cure of simple diseases, and to drive away, or exorcise the
plague, if it had actually broken out in their midst.   As recently
as the summer of 1849, when the cholera prevailed through the
State, the Falsefaces, in appropriate costume, went from house to
house at Tonawanda, through the old school portion of the village, and performed the usual ceremonies prescribed for the ex-
pulsion of the pestilence.

When any one was sick with a complaint within the range of
their healing powers, and dreamed that he saw a Falseface, this
was interpreted to signify that through their instrumentality he

was to be cured. Having informed the mistress of the band, and prepared the customary feast, the Falsefaces at once appeared, preceded by their female leader, and marching in Indian file. Each one wore a mask or falseface, a tattered blanket over his shoulders, and carried a turtle shell rattle in his hand. On entering the house of the invalid they first stirred the ashes upon the hearth, and then sprinkled the patient over with hot ashes until his head and hair were covered ; after which they performed some manipulations over him in turn, and finally lead him around with them in the falseface dance (*Gä-go-sä*), with which their ceremonies concluded. When these performances were over, the entertainment prepared for the occasion was distributed to the band, and by them carried away for their private feasting, as they never unmasked themselves before the people. Among the simple complaints which the Falsefaces could cure infallibly, were nose bleed, toothache, swellings, and inflammation of the eyes. The falseface shown in the figure was purchased of an Onondaga on Grand river; the other one in the collection came from Tonawanda.

Da-ya-no-tä-yen-dä-quä, or SNOW BOAT.

No. 111.

Top view.

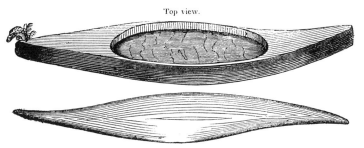

Bottom view.

With the snow boat was played one of the winter games of the Iroquois, in which the strife was to discover which boat would run the farthest in an iced trench or path. The boat was about fifteen inches in length, and made of beech, or other hard wood, something in the fashion of a canoe. It was solid, with the exception of an oblong cavity in the centre, over which arched a hickory bow, designed to suspend bells or other rattles upon.

No. 122.]   101

In the stern of this little vessel a white feather was inserted for a flag, by which to follow it in its descent. On the bottom the boat was rounded, but with a slight wind lengthwise, as shown in the figure, to give it a true direction.

A side hill with an open plain below was the kind of place selected to try the speed of the boats. Trenches in a straight line down the hill, and about a foot wide, were made by treading down the snow ; after which water was poured into them that it might freeze and line the trenches throughout their whole extent with ice. These trenches to the number of a dozen, side by side, if as many individuals intended to play, were finished with the greatest care and exactness, not only down the hill side, but to a considerable distance across the plain below. At the same time the boats themselves were dipped in water that they might also be coated with ice.

The people divided by tribes in playing this, as in all other Iroquois games; the Wolf, Bear, Beaver and Turtle tribes playing against the Deer, Snipe, Heron and Hawk. At the time appointed the people assembled at the base of the hill and divided off by tribes, and then commenced betting upon the result, a custom universally practised on such occasions. The game was played by select players who were stationed at the top of the hill, each with two or three boats, and standing at the head of his own trench. When all was in readiness the boats were started off together at the appointed moment, and their rapid descent was watched with eager interest by the people below. It is not necessary to describe the scene. If the game was twenty it would be continued until one side had made that number of points. A count of one was made for every boat which led all upon the adverse side, so that if there were six players on a side it was possible for that number to be made at one trial. On the contrary, if all the boats but one upon one side were in advance of all on the adverse side but one, and the latter was in advance of all, this head boat would win and count one. The principles of the game are precisely the same as in the Snow Snake game described in the last report. All of these Indian games were played with great zeal and enthusiasm. To us they appear to be puerile amusements for men in the prime of manhood; but yet they were adapted to the ways and habits of a people living without arts, and without the intellectual employments which pertain to civilized life. Such games mark the infancy of the human mind, but they often beget a generous emulation and a ready skill which lead to future improvement and elevation.

Gä-no-sä, or CONCH SHELL BREAST PLATE.
No. 48. Plate 14. Fig. 2.

Breast plates of this description were much worn in ancient times. The leading chiefs of the Iroquois wore medals either of silver or sea shell on public occasions. This medal is in the common form, and is chiefly interesting as the personal ornament of Peter Fish Carrier, (So-ace) a Cayuga Chief about 60 years of age, now residing on Grand river. He is the only surviving son of the distinguished Cayuga chief (*Ho-jä-ga-ta*,) who bore the name of Fish Carrier, and who resided at Cannoga on the Cayuga lake during the period of the revolution. A reservation was set apart for his special benefit at this place, by the treaty of 1795, made at the Cayuga bridge. He died near Buffalo about the year 1800, after which his family removed to Grand river.

Ah-dä-dis-hä, or CANE.
No. 49.

This cane is also chiefly interesting as a memento of the most distinguished living sachem of the Cayugas, John Jacobs, (*Jote-ho-weh-ko*,) now about eighty years of age, and residing upon Grand river. He was born about the year 1770, at the chief village of the Cayugas *Gä-yä-gä-an-ha*, which was situated upon the north side of Utts creek, about one and a half miles from the Cayuga lake, and about four miles north east from Aurora. When General Sullivan was on his return from the invasion of the Seneca territory in 1779, he sent a detachment into Cayuga county to destroy the villages of the Cayugas. The people fled to Niagara, and *Jote-ho-weh-ko*, then a small lad, was carried by his family. At a subsequent day he returned to his former home and resided

No. 122.]   103

there until the Cayugas finally disposed of all their lands to the State and emigrated. His family removed to Grand river where at a subsequent day he was made one of the ten Cayuga sachems, as his name indicates. The cane itself is curious as a specimen of Indian carving, it being wreathed with serpents. It has been used by *Jote-ho-weh-ko* for many years, and was obtained of him for the collection in October last on Grand river.

Ah-so-quā-tā, or PIPE.
No. 50.

The pipe represented in the figure is made of a soft red stone, called Catlinite, or the Missouri pipe stone, that State being the chief, if not the only place, in which it is found. It is in common use among the western Indians for making the calumet, and also for common pipes. Like soap stone, which was much used by the Iroquois for the same purpose, it can be fashioned into pipes without the aid of metalic instruments. There is a tradition in relation to this pipe that it was taken from a Sioux many years ago by a Seneca, in one of the many inroads of the Senecas into the territories of the former people. It bears decisive marks of its antiquity, and also of severe usage, for the original orifice in which the stone piece was inserted has been taken away, and a new one made above in which the present stone is fastened. It was obtained of a Seneca.

104   [ASSEMBLY

Ah-so-quā-tā, or PIPE.
No 50.

This pipe is made of stone ; but without the stem piece it is in
the exact fashion of the ancient earthen pipe of the Iroquois. As
the stone is intensely hard it is difficult to say how it was drilled
out. Stone implements are often found of Indian manufacture,
some of which are bored with great regularity. It has been supposed that the boring was done by means of a reed made to revolve back and forth by hand, and sand employed to do the cutting. Nothing is known of the origin or manufacture of this pipe;
it was purchased of a Mohawk on Grand river.

STONE PIPE MADE OF NODULE.
No. 52.

1 feet

Among the western Indians large pipe bowls with long stems,
ornamented in various ways, and called calumets, are very common ; but among the Iroquois the pipe was usually short, and
without a stem piece. Fancy pipes are occasionally to be met
with, like the one represented in the figure, having a long stem
piece and a huge bowl. In this case the bowl is a nodule of stone,
with a rough exterior, weighing about a pound ; and has been
drilled out by artificial means. The handle is of wood colored
black and perforated by means of wire. A cluster of feathers
depends from the centre of the handle. It was procured from a
Seneca at Tonawanda.

No. 122.| 105

Gä-re-gwä, or SPEAR.

No. 64.

5 feet.

The spear is not an Iroquois weapon; although in later years articles of this description of American manufacture have sometimes been found among them. They had no name in their language for spear, until it became necessary to give one to the foreign weapon. The one figured above was purchased of an Onondaga on Grand river, and is said to have been used in the last war between the United States and Great Britain.

Gä-ne-a-ga-o-dus-ha, or WAR CLUB.

No. 65.

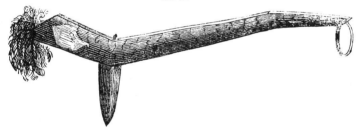

The deer horn war club was one of the ancient weapons of the Iroquois at the period of their discovery. In some instances in later times a steel blade was substituted for the deer horn, as in the above specimen, thus rendering it a more deadly weapon than formerly.

Gä-snä Gä-o-wo, or BARK CANOE.

Plate 15.

In the construction of the bark canoe, the Iroquois exercised considerable taste and skill. The art appears to have been common to all the Indian races within the limits of the republic, and the mode of construction much the same. Birch bark was the best material; but as this birch did not grow within the home territories of the Iroquois, they generally used the red elm and bitternut hickory. The canoe figured in the plate is made of the bark of the red elm, and consists of but one piece. Having taken off a bark of the requisite length and width, and removed the rough outside, it was shaped in the canoe form. Rim pieces of white ash, or other elastic wood, of the width of the hand, were then run around the edge outside and in, and stitched through and through with the bark itself. In stitching they used bark thread or twine, and splints. The ribs consisted of narrow strips of ash, which were set about a foot apart along the bottom of the canoe, and having been turned up the sides, were secured under the rim. Each end of the canoe was fashioned alike, the two side pieces inclining towards each other until they united, and formed a sharp and vertical prow. In size, these canoes varied from twelve feet, with sufficient capacity to carry two men, to forty feet, with sufficient capacity for thirty. The one figured is about twenty-five feet in length, and its tonnage estimated at two tons, about half that of the bateau or river boat in use upon our inland waters before the construction of the canal. Birch bark retained its place without warping, but the elm and hickory bark canoes were exposed to this objection. After being used, they were drawn out of the water to dry. One of the chief advantages of these canoes, especially the birch bark, was their extreme lightness, which often became a matter of some moment, from the flood-wood and water-falls which obstructed the navigation of the inland rivers. Two men could easily transport these light vessels around these obstacles, and even from one river to another, when the portage was but a few miles.

For short excursions one person usually paddled the canoe, standing up in the stern; if more than two, and on a long expedition, they were seated at equal distances upon each side alternately. In the fur trade these canoes were extensively used. They coasted lakes Erie and Ontario, and turning up the Oswego river into the Oneida lake, they went up Wood Creek, and from thence over the carrying place at Rome into the Mohawk, which they descended to Schenectady. The Iroquois thus possessed a connected water route from the Hudson to Lake Superior. Their canoes would usually carry about twelve hundred pounds of fur. At the periods of the invasions of the Iroquois territories by the French, large fleets of these canoes, sometimes numbering two hundred, were formed for the conveyance of troops and provisions. With careful usage they would last several years.

Gä-snä Gä-ose-hă, or BARK BARREL.

No. 44.

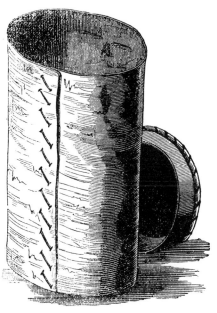

The bark barrel was used to store charred and dried shell corn, beans, fruit, cured venison and other meats, and a variety of other articles. When corn was buried in pits or caches, it was usually put in bark barrels of this description. During the war of 1812, when the British forces were expected over the frontier, the Senecas at Tonawanda, who had enlisted in the American army, buried their corn in bark barrels, after the ancient custom. These barrels were made of all sizes, from those of sufficient capacity to hold three bushels, to those large enough for a peck. They are made of black ash bark, the grain being run around the barrel. Such barrels were found in every family in ancient times, and among other purposes to which they were devoted, they were made repositories for articles of apparel and personal ornaments. With proper care they would outlast the longest life.

Several specimens of bark trays and bark sap tubs will be found in the collection. These vessels are always made of red elm bark.

Gä-no, or ARROW.

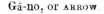

No. 69.

3 feet.

In ancient times arrows were pointed with horn or bone as well as with flint, and made even more dangerous missiles in the former cases. The above is a representation of an arrow of this description, which, with several others, was purchased of an Oneida on Grand river. It is about three feet in length and pointed with deer's horn.

O-no-gä Gus-dä-weh-sä, or HORN RATTLE.

No. 57.

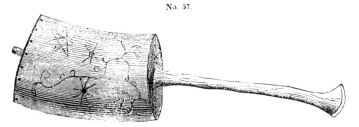

Various kinds of rattles were used by the Iroquois in their dances, of which, the turtle shell rattle was the most common; but occasionally, in later days, one is to be met with of this description. It was obtained of a Cayuga lad on Grand river.

No. 122.]   109

Yont-kā-do-quā, or BASKET FISH NET.

No. 79

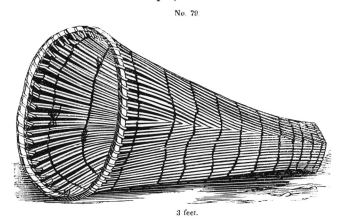

3 feet.

The basket net was made of splint in a conical form, about three feet in length, fifteen inches in diameter at the mouth, and six at the small end. In using it, the fisherman stood in the rapids of the creek or river, where the water rippled over the stony bottom, and with a stick or rod managed to direct the fish into the partly submerged basket, as they attempted to shoot down the rapid. When one was heard to flutter in the basket, it was at once raised from the water, and the fish was found secure within it. In those forest days, when fish abounded in every stream, it was an easy matter thus to capture them in large numbers.

Basket-making is preëminently an Indian art. It was the intention of the writer to enter into this subject somewhat minutely, and for that purpose a collection of splints in their various stages, from their condition when first taken from the tree, to those ready to be made into the most delicate baskets, was put up and arranged. But the unexpected length of this report will prevent any thing more than a passing notice. Black ash furnishes the only splint used by the Iroquois, and perhaps the same may be said of all other Indians. They choose a tree about a foot in diameter and free from limbs, after which they cut off a stick about six feet in length. After removing the bark they pound the stick with some heavy implement to start the splints, which can thus be made to run off with the utmost regularity and uniformity of thickness. This process is continued until the log is stripped down to the heart. These splints, which are about three inches wide and an eighth of an inch thick, are afterwards subdivided both ways until reduced to the required width and thickness. When resplit into thinner strips the splints have a white and smooth surface. If the baskets are to be variegated, the splints are dyed upon one side before they are woven, and are also moistened to make them pliable before they are used. The patient industry of the Indian female while engaged in this manual labor, and her skill and taste are alike exemplified in this interesting manufacture.

E-yose, or BLANKET.
No. 103 1-2. Plate 16.

In ancient times the Iroquois female costume consisted of moccasins, leggins, a deer skin skirt, and a deer or bear skin blanket dressed with the hair upon it. Since then they have adhered to the ancient costume with great fidelity so far as the articles of apparel are concerned, although they have changed the materials of which they were made. They still wear the moccasin, the leggin, the skirt and the blanket as a part of their ordinary dress; but the deer skin has been laid aside for the broadcloth and the woolen; and the porcupine quill in a great measure for the bead. We can yet discover in the broadcloth blanket, however tastefully embroidered or ribboned, the legitimate descendant of the ancient deer skin blanket. As now worn by the Indian female, the blanket is a very graceful and becoming article of apparel. It is either passed over the head and falls down around the person in natural folds, or rests upon the shoulders and is gathered like a shawl. The one shown in the plate is of the latter description. It is bordered with ribbon, the colors of which are tastefully combined, and also with beadwork, which will be more fully appreciated from the plate than from any description.

Gä-ka ah, or SKIRT.
No. 101. Plate 17.

This is without question the finest specimen of Indian beadwork ever exhibited. Next to the article itself the plate will

No. 122.]   111

furnish the best description. It was made by Miss Caroline G. Parker (*Gā-hā-no*), a Seneca Indian girl, now being educated in the State Normal School, to whose finished taste, and patient industry the State is indebted for most of the many beautiful specimens of beadwork embroidery now in the Indian collection.

In doing this work, the eye and the taste are the chief reliances, as they use no patterns except as they may have seen them in the works of others. In combining colors certain general rules, the result of experience and observation, are followed, but beyond them each one pursued her own fancy. They never seek for strong contrasts, but break the force of it by interposing white, that the colors may blend harmoniously. Thus light blue and pink beads, with white beads between them, is a favorable combination; dark blue and yellow, with white between, is another; red and light blue, with white between, is another; and light purple and dark purple, with white between, is a fourth. Others might be added were it necessary. If this beadwork is critically examined it will be found that these general rules are strictly observed; and in so far beadwork embroidery may be called a systematic art. The art of flowering, as they term it, is the most difficult part of beadwork, as it requires an accurate knowledge of the appearance of the flower, and the structure and condition of the plant at the stage in which it is represented. These imitations are frequently made with great delicacy, of which a very favorable exhibition may be seen in the plate, in the flower introduced at the angle of the skirt.

Gā-yā-ah, or satchel.

No. 24.   Plate 18.

This beautiful article is also of Seneca manufacture. Upon the lowest part of the front side (fig. 1) there is an ingenious imitation of a rose bush, with its flowers at different stages of maturity, from the one just opening its bud, to the full blown rose. The success of the imitation, considering the nature of the materials, and the artist, is quite commendable. It is easy to recognize the opening rose in the bud at the left, which, with its envelope and stem, is very accurately delineated. In flowering, dark green beads are used for the stalk of the shrub, and glass beads of various colors and tints, for the flowers.

On the reverse side of the Satchel are two stars, which as specimens of fancy beadwork are tastefully and ingeniously made. This is not an original Indian article, but a naturalized invention.

Yä-wä-o-dä-quä, or PIN CUSHION.
Plate 19.

The plate is intended merely as a further illustration of the general character of bead work embroidery. It is of Seneca manufacture and requires no description beyond the plate itself.

Gä-nó-sote, or BARK HOUSE.
No. 114. Plate 29.

The bark house of the Iroquois has long since given place to a more substantial structure; but occasionally in some secluded corner a *Gä-nó-sote*, may yet be seen, constructed by some one whose age or fondness for the ancient mode of life led him to prefer the light, but convenient lodge of his forefathers. The single *Gä-nó-sote* was usually about twenty feet by fifteen upon the ground, and from ten to twenty feet high. The frame consisted of upright poles firmly set in the ground, usually five upon the sides and four at the ends, including those at the corners. Upon the forks of these poles, about ten feet from the ground, cross poles were secured horizontally, to which the rafters, also poles, but more numerous and slender, were adjusted. The rafters were strengthened with transverse poles, and the whole was usually so arranged as to form an arching roof. After the frame was thus completed, it was sided up and shingled with black ash bark, the rough side out. The bark was flattened and dried, and then split in the form of boards. To hold these bark boards firmly in their places another set of poles, corresponding with those in the frame, were placed on the outside, and by means of splint and bark rope fastenings the boards were secured horizontally between them. It usually required four lengths of boards, and four courses from the ground to the rafters to cover a side, as they were lapped at the ends, as well as clapboarded; and also in the same proportions for the ends. In like manner the roof was cov-

No. 122.]   113

ered with bark boards, smaller in size, with the rough side out,
and the grain running up and down; the boards being stitched
through and through with fastenings, and thus held between the
frames of poles, as on the sides. In the centre of the roof was an
opening for the smoke, the fire being upon the ground in the centre of the house, and the smoke ascending without the guidance
of a chimney. At the two ends of the house were doors, either
of bark hung upon hinges of wood, or of deer or bear skin suspended before the opening; and however long the house, or
whatever the number of fires, these were the only entrances.
Over one of these doors was usually cut or painted the tribal de-
vice of the head of the family. Within upon the two sides were
arranged wide seats, also of bark boards, about two feet from the
ground, well supported underneath, and reaching the entire
length of the house. Upon these they spread their mats of skins,
and also their blankets, using them as seats by day and couches
by night. Similar berths were constructed on each side about
five feet above these and secured to the frame of the house, thus
furnishing accommodations for the family. An interior view of
the house is given in the plate. Upon cross poles near the roof
was hung in bunches, braided together by the husks, the winter
supply of corn. Charred and dried corn, and beans were generally stowed in bark barrels, and laid away in corners. Their
implements for the chase, weapons, articles of apparel, and miscellaneous notions were stowed away, and hung up, wherever an
unoccupied corner was discovered. A house of this description
would accommodate a family of eight, with the limited wants of
the Indian, and afford shelter for their necessary stores, making a
not uncomfortable residence.

The Iroquois resided in permanent villages. About the period
of the formation of the League, when they were exposed to the
inroads of hostile nations, their villages were compact and stock-
aded. Having run a trench several feet deep around five or ten
acres of land, and thrown up the ground upon the inside, they
set a continuous row of stakes or palisades in this bank of earth,

fixing them at such an angle that they inclined over the trench.[1]
Sometimes a village was surrounded by a double or even treble
row of palisades. Within this enclosure they constructed their
bark houses, which were very large and designed for several families, and in them secured their stores. Around it was the village field, consisting oftentimes of several hundred acres of cultivated land, which was subdivided into planting lots; those belonging to different families being bounded by uncultivated
ridges.

But at the commencement of the seventeenth century, when
their power had become consolidated, and most of the adjacent
nations had been brought under subjection, the necessity of stock-
ading their villages in a measure ceased, and with it the practice.
At the period of the discovery of the inland Iroquois, about the
year 1640, few, if any of the villages of the Senecas, Cayugas, or
Onondagas were surrounded with palisades; but the Oneidas and
Mohawks continued to stockade their villages for many years afterwards in consequence of the inroads of the French. From
being compact, their villages afterwards came to be scattered over
a large area, and their houses were planted, like the trees of the
forest, at irregular intervals. No attempt in the modern village
was made at a street, or at an arrangement of their houses in a
row; two houses seldom fronting the same line. They are merely
grouped together sufficiently near for a neighborhood.

As their villages at an early day were reckoned by the number
of houses, it is important to notice the difference between the
bark house of the ancient and of the modern period, to arrive at
any estimation of the number of inhabitants in former times.
When the village was scattered over a large area, the houses
were single, and usually designed for one family; but when
compact, as in early times, they were very large, and subdivided
so as to accommodate a number of families. The long house was
often over an hundred feet in length, by about sixteen in width,

1. Herein is doubtless the origin of many if not all of the Trench Enclosures which
are found in various parts of the State. Not all of them necessarily made by the
Iroquois, but by them and the nations who preceded them in the occupancy of New-
York.

with partitions at intervals of about ten or twelve feet, or two lengths of the body. Each apartment was in many respects a separate house, accommodating two families, one upon each side of the fire. Sometimes there was a fire in every apartment, but more frequently for every other partition, so that one fire would answer for four families. Not unfrequently one of these houses contained from ten to twenty families, all bound together by the nearer ties of relationship, and constituting in effect one family. They carried the principle of " living in common" to its full extent. Whatever was taken in the chase, or raised in the fields, or gathered in its natural state by any member of the united families, enured to the benefit of all, for their stores of every description were common. They had regular hours for cooking through the whole establishment, and whatever was prepared was free to all. After the morning repast the Iroquois had no regular meal, but they satisfied their appetites whenever it was convenient. As they used no tables in ancient times they took their food separately, and whenever it could be done with the least trouble, the males first, and the females afterwards. There were no side doors to the long house, and as a necessary consequence there was a species of hall or avenue through the house from end to end. In constructing one of these houses, spaces were left at intervals through it for store rooms, which were open to those who were contiguous. Other peculiarities of these patriarchal households of the Iroquois might be pointed out; but sufficient has been said to give a general idea of both the single and the long house of our primitive inhabitants.

A Mr. Greenhalgh, in 1677, visited the Seneca village of *Dă-yo-de-hok-to*, signifying a " bended creek," situated upon a bend of the Honeoye outlet west of Mendon, in the county of Monroe. Under the name of " Tiotohatton," he thus speaks of it :—(Doc. Hist., N. Y., vol. 1, p. 13) " Tiotohatton lies on the brink or edge of a hill; has not much cleared ground; is near the river Tiotohatton, which signifies bending. It lies to the westward of Canagorah, about thirty miles, containing about 120 houses, being the largest of all we saw, (the ordinary being from fifty to sixty feet long,) with from twelve to thirteen fires in one house. They have good store of corn growing about a mile to the northward of the town." He further states (ib. 12, 13) that Canagorah contained 150 houses, Onondaga 140, and Oneida 100. It is not improbable that the largest of the Iroquois villages in ancient times, or about the period of their discovery, contained from two to three thousand inhabitants.

It is difficult to form a correct estimate of the total number of the Iroquois at any particular period, the opinions of those, having the best opportunity of judging, have been so various. They have been rated from ten, to seventy thousand. An opinion may perhaps be indulged, without giving the statistics upon which it is founded. The period of their greatest prosperity, and of their highest military supremacy was about the year 1650 ; and their total population at that period may be safely placed at 25,000. A higher estimate would be better supported by such data as the case affords, than a lesser one ; although the impression of later writers seems to be the contrary. An approximation to the relative strength of the several nations of the League upon this basis may be made by the following apportionment : To the Senecas 10,000 ; to the Cayugas 3,000 ; to the Onondagas 4,000 ; to the Oneidas 3,000 ; and to the Mohawks 5,000. A century later or about 1750, their total population was probably about half this number, the Mohawks having wasted away the most rapidly.

To return from this digression to the bark house from which it proceeded, it is proper to observe that among the articles furnished is the model of the original Gä-no-sote of the Iroquois, some six feet by four, in its ground plan, and made as large as it could be conveniently transported. The model shows very perfectly the mechanism of the bark house throughout ; but it is defective in its proportions. It was designed for two fires, or four families, and therefore should be either longer or narrower, and not as high. With this criticism in mind the plate gives a faithful impression of the primitive house of the Iroquois.

The great length of this report forbids those suggestions upon the further enlargement of the Indian collection, and those reflections upon its importance, which the subject is calculated to inspire. With a fair portion of the fabrics, implements and utensils of the most gifted race of Indian lineage within the limits of our Republic, as the nucleus of a general Indian collection, the way is fairly opened by the State for successfully accomplishing an enterprise, which is both full of historical interest and worthy of its enlarged munificence. It is greatly to be hoped that the time is not distant when one collection, at least, may exist in the country, which is sufficiently general, and sufficiently minute, to illustrate the social life and the artizan intellect of the whole Indian family.

There is also a collateral consideration which cannot be overlooked. In the fabrics of the modern Iroquois there is much to inspire confidence in their teachableness in the useful arts. When their minds are unfolded by education, and their attention is attracted by habit to agricultural pursuits, as has become the case to some extent, there is great promise that a portion, at least, of this gifted race will be reclaimed, and raised, eventually, to a citizenship among ourselves. In that great work, the people of the State have a part to perform. It would be a grateful spectacle yet to behold the children of our primeval forests cultivating the fields over which their fathers roamed in sylvan independence ; and worshiping that God, in the fullness of light, and knowledge, whom, in the Great Spirit, however imperfect their conceptions, they most distinctly discerned.

All which is respectfully submitted.

LEWIS H. MORGAN.

Rochester, January 22, 1851.

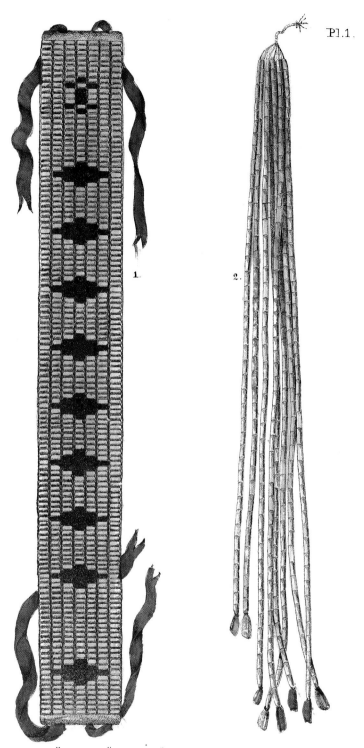

Pl.1.

1.

2.

1. GÄ-SWEH-TA OTE-KO-Ä or BELT OF WAMPUM.

2. OTE-KO-Ä or STRING of WAMPUM

GÄ-SWÄ-HOS-HÄ ᴏʀ BABY FRAME BELT

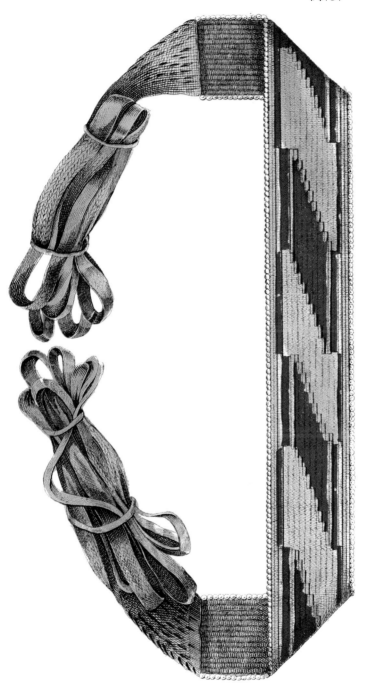

Pl. 3.

O-Ă-TA-OSE-KÄ or MOOSE HAIR BURDEN STRAP.

Pl. 4.

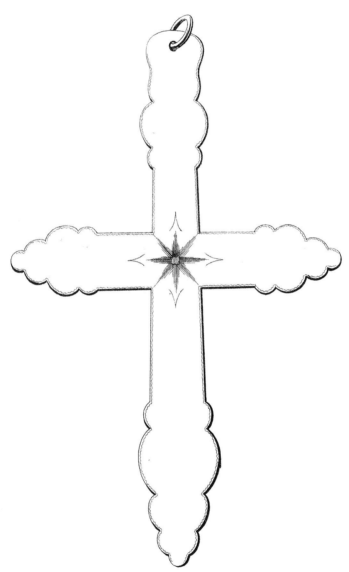

DÄ-GÄ-YÄ-SONT or SILVER CROSS

Ten Inches long.

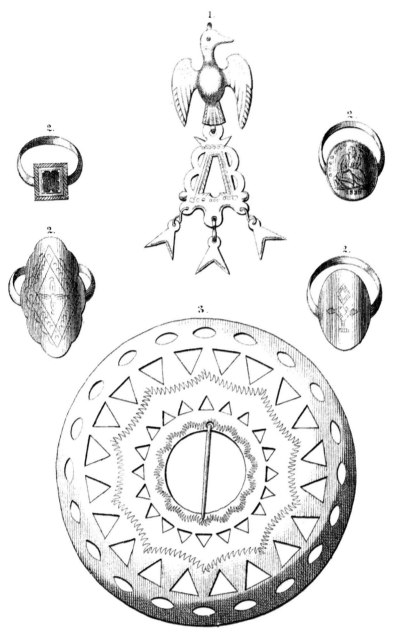

Pl. 5.

1. AH-WAS-HÄ or SILVER EAR RING

2. AH-NE-A-HUS-HA SILVER FINGER RINGS

3. AN-NE-ÄS-GA or SILVER BROACH

Pl. 6.

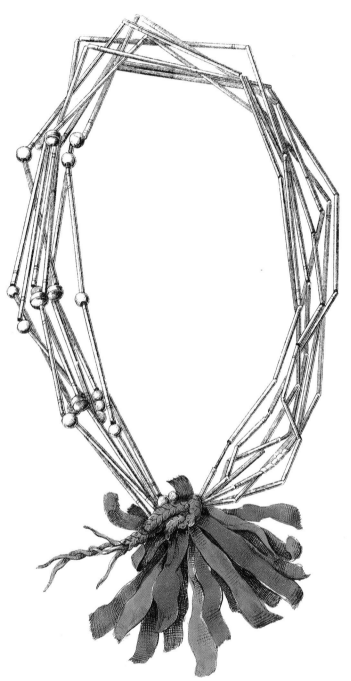

OUT-WIS-TÄ-NE-UN-DÄ-QUÄ or SILVER BEADS

1.

2.

1 GÄ-TE-AS-HĂ or GLASS BEADS.

2 O-WIS-TÄ-NO-O O-STÄ-O-QUÄ or SILVER BEADS.

Pl. 8.

GĂ-TE-ÄS-HĂ GÄ-A-O-TÄ-GES
OR
GRASS SHOULDER ORNAMENT.

GÄ-KÄ-AH or DEER SKIN KILT

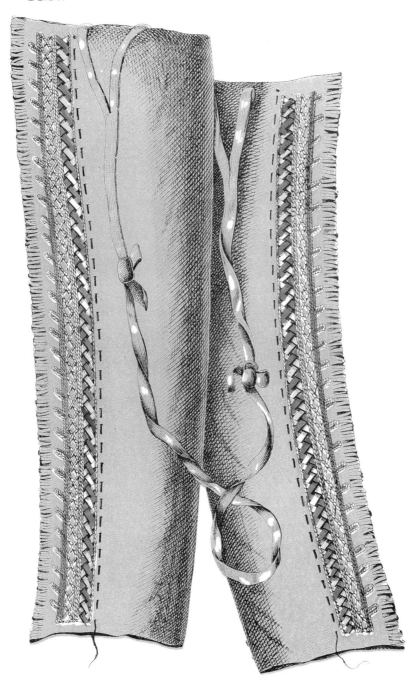

Pl. 10.

GISE-HA or DEER SKIN LEGGIN.

Pl.11.

AH-TÄ-QUÄ-O-WEH or **MOCCASON**
Embroidered with porcupine quills

Pl.12.

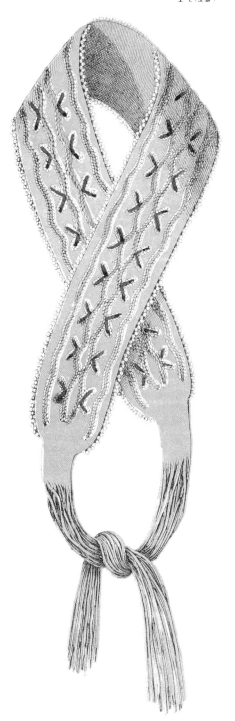

YUNT-KA-TO-DA-TA or DEER SKIN SHOULDER BELT

Pl. 13.

DA-YUNT-WA-HOS-TÄ or DEER SKIN WAIST BELT

Pl. 14.

1.

2.

1. O·HA·DA or PORCUPINE QUILL
2. GÄ·NO·SÄ or CONCH SHELL BREAST PLATE

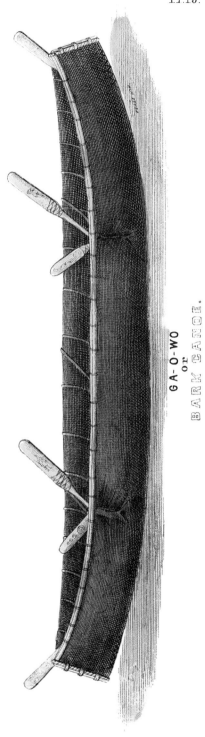

Pl.15.

GA-O-WO
or
BARK CANOE.

E YOSE or BLANKET

Pl.17.

GÄ-KÄ-AH or SKIRT

Pl. 18.

GÄ-YÄ-AH . or SATCHEL.

YÄ-WÄ-O-DÄ-QUÄ OR PIN CUSHION

Pl. 20.

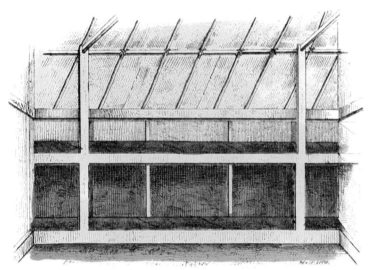

Interior View of

BARK HOUSE.

GÄ-NÓ-SOTE
or
BARK HOUSE.

APPENDIX I

Articles Donated to the State in November 1848

· · · · ·
· · ·
·

74　　　　　　　　　　　　　　　[Senate

FROM LEWIS H. MORGAN, OF ROCHESTER.

1. *Ga-né-ga-tah* (Stone mortar), used by the Senecas for pounding corn, pulverizing roots, etc. Sandstone. Found near Allen's Hill, Ontario county, May 9, 1843.

2. Stone pestle, found at Jack's Reef, Onondaga county.

3. Stone pestle, found in the town of Middlebury, Wyoming co.

4. Stone chisel, from Groveland Livingston county.

5. Stone chisel. Fort Hill, town of Seneca, Ontario county.

6. Stone chisel. Town of Coventry, Genesee county.

7. Stone chisel. Ontario county.

8. Stone chisel, used for chipping out coal. Fort Hill, town of Seneca, Ontario county.

9. Stone chisel, from Auburn, Ontario county.

10. Stone chisel. Used by the Iroquois in felling trees. Fire was applied near the root of the tree, and the chisel was used to cut out the coal; after which, fire was again applied. The chisel and fire were also used to hollow out wooden vessels. From Tonawanda, Genesee county.

11. Stone chisel. From the town of Coventry, Genesee county.

12. Stone chisel. From Mendon, Monroe county.

13. Stone chisel. From Allen's Hill, Ontario county.

14. Stone chisel. From Mendon, Monroe county.

15. Stone chisel. From Coventry, Genesee county.

16. Stone gouge. Found near Leroy, Genesee county.

17. Spear-head (chert). Found at Fort Hill, Seneca, Ontario county.

18. Arrow-head. Town of Seneca, Ontario county.

19. Arrow-head. Town of Chili, Monroe county.

20. Arrow-head. Fort Hill, Ontario county.

21. Indian knife (chert), used for skinning deer. Found near Avon at the site of Little Beard's town, Livingston county.

22. Tomahawk, found by the skeleton of an Indian, near Lima, Livingston county.

23. Tomahawk, found by the skeleton of an Indian at Mendon, Monroe county.

24. Tomahawk. Town of Lima, Livingston county.

25. Tomahawk. Town of Ledyard, Cayuga county.

No. 20.]   75

26. BRASS KETTLE, taken from an Indian grave at the site of the old Indian village of Gá-nun-da-sa-ga, near Geneva, 1840.

27. PART of a GUN LOCK and RIFLE BARREL found by the skeleton of an Indian, in the town of Mendon, Monroe county.

28. HEAD of a *Ga-ne-ah* or WAR CLUB, fastened into the head of a club by a thong or withe. Ledyard, Cayuga county.

29. *Yuh-tah-gun-he-a-tah*. *Geh-weh*, or MOCCASIN NEEDLE (bone of the deer). Used by the "Mound Builders," and also by the Iroquois. Found at Fort Hill, near Leroy, N. Y.

30. STONE TUBE (of variegated limestone). Town of Springpor', Cayuga county. A relic of the "Mound Builders," and not of the Iroquois. Similar tubes, some of which are fifteen inches in length, are found in the Ohio mounds.

31. STONE AMULET. Tonawanda, Genesee county.

32. INDIAN NECKLACE of TEETH, found near the skeleton of an Indian. Genesee valley, near Avon, Livingston county.

33. *A-so-gwa-ta*, or CLAY PIPE, from Aurora, Cayuga county.

34. FRONT PART of the BOWL of a PIPE (similar to those found in the Ohio mounds). Lima, Livingston county.

35. FRAGMENT of *Ga-jeh*, or EARTHEN BASIN. Fort Hill, near Leroy, Genesee county; with a tooth found in the same place.

36. POTTERY, affected by water. Fort Hill.

37. *Gus-to-weh*. HEAD DRESS. Seneca — Iroquois.

38. *Ga-neah*, or WAR CLUB. A species used in the War Dance. Seneca — Iroquois.

39. INDIAN CALUMET. From the West (imperfect).

40. LEADEN CROSS. Found near the Tonawanda Council House, Genesee county, October, 1845.

41. FRAGMENT of the TOMBSTONE of REDJACKET, found upon his grave, four miles from Buffalo. The stone is mutilated by travellers.

42. FRAGMENT (slag?) taken from the fireplace of the old picket enclosure of Kon-non-da-sa-sa, at the foot of the Genesee lake, in 1845. This picket was destroyed by General Sullivan.

43. STUB of the palisade at the gate or opening of the above picket enclosure. Found November 21, 1845.

Articles Donated to the State in December 1848

· · · · ·
· · ·
·

ADDITIONAL DONATIONS RECEIVED FROM MR. MORGAN,
DECEMBER 8, 1848.

44. FRAGMENT of an INDIAN PIPE. Monroe county.

45. *A-se-qua-tah*, or CLAY PIPE, taken from a Seneca burial place near
Lima, Livingston county, 1848.

46. ARROW-HEAD. Mendon, Monroe county.

47. ARROW-HEAD. Mendon, Monroe county.

48. ARROW-HEAD of COPPER. Bend of the Honeoye creek, Monroe co.

49. PART of a GUN-BARREL, from an Indian burying ground, Ball farm,
Monroe county.

BY PURCHASE OF WILLIAM H. C. HOSMER, OF AVON (LIVINGS-
TON COUNTY).

1. INDIAN ARROW-HEADS (6), picked up in ploughed fields in the vicinity
of Avon.

2. INDIAN ARROW-HEADS of small size, used by Indian boys in killing
birds and inferior game (9). These arrows were inserted
into the split end of tough wooden shafts, and fastened at
the notches with ligatures of sinew or string bark.

3. INDIAN ARROW-HEADS (4), found on a plain near Fort Niagara, and
of greater antiquity than those of flint formation.

4. INDIAN ARROW-HEADS (2), found on the farm of Timothy Hosmer, in
the town of Porter, Niagara county, near the Lake shore ;
one of them curiously twisted.

5. A HATCHET-SHAPED FLINT, obtained from Col. Jewett of Lockport.

6. BROKEN ARROW-HEADS.

7. STONE DEERSKIN-DRESSERS, found on the farm of Mr. Hurlburt, in
the northeast part of the town of Avon.

8. STONE DEERSKIN-DRESSER, found on the farm of Jeptha Wilber, Avon.

9. STONE DEERSKIN-DRESSER, found on the farm of James Wadsworth,
near Borley's mill in the bend of the Conesus outlet, town
of Livonia, Livingston county. The place where they were
found was called "Fort Hill" by the early settlers ; and
mound, trench and gateway were visible in the memory of
men now living.

10. STONE PESTLE, used in pounding maize ; found on the farm of J.
Wilber, Avon.

Articles Donated to the State in 1849

· · · · ·
· · ·
·

52 [Senate

From William J. McAlpine, *Engineer.*

1. A Plaster model of the United States Dry Dock, at Brooklyn.
2. Fourteen specimens of granite, viz: 6 from Staten Island quarry, New-York ; 6 from Quincy quarry, Massachusetts ; and 2 from Blue Hill quarry, Maine ; being samples of the granite used in the construction of the Dry Dock.
3. A glass tube, hermetically sealed, containing specimens of the various soils through which the excavations were made, stratigraphically arranged ; with figures on the tube, indicating the aggregate depth of the excavations, and the proportional thickness of the different strata of earth excavated.
4. A vial, containing earth, excavated at the depth of sixty-eight and a half feet.

The Dry Dock at Brooklyn, taking into consideration the strength, accuracy and beauty of workmanship, has been pronounced, by competent judges, to be the finest piece of masonry in the world. And the Engineers, not only of this country, but of Europe, have justly denominated it the great work of the age.

Additional donations from Lewis H. Morgan, *Esq., of Rochester.*

50. Stone skull cracker. From Aurora, Cayuga county. This is the vulgar name. It was fastened in the head of a club, and thus made a formidable weapon.
51. Necklace bead. From Scipio, Cayuga county.
52. Unfinished arrowhead. From Cayuga county.
53. White chert arrowhead. From Ledyard, Cayuga county.
54. Fragment of the bowl of an Ah-so-quä-tä, or pipe. From Scipio, Cayuga county.
55. Six arrowheads, or Gä-nuh-yä. From Ledyard and Scipio, Cayuga county.
56. Fragment of a white chert arrowhead.
57. Two twist arrowheads. From Ontario county.
58. Fragment of a Ga jih, or earthen basin. From Cayuga county.
59. Gä-ne-gä-tä, seneca mortar, for pounding corn.
60. Gä-nih-gä-dä, pounder. (Same name as mortar.) Two specimens.
61. Gä-ne-ah, ball bat. Two specimens.
62. Wä-a-no, Indian bow. Two specimens.
63. Gä-no, feathered arrow. Six specimens.
64. Gä-wä-sä, Snow snake. Two specimens.
65. Bark tray, or platter.

No. 75.]   53

66. SPLINT BASKET. Two varieties.

67. A quantity of WHITE CORN. The New-York Indians cultivate this
         variety of corn principally; which is known, I believe, as
         the Tuscarora. They put it up and preserve it in bunches.

From the Rev. DUNCAN KENNEDY, D. D., *Albany.*

1. PEQUOD STONE HATCHET. From New-England.

2. PEQUOD STONE HATCHET. From New-England. This relic differs
         from No. 1 in its form, and in the material from which it is
         constructed.

3. STONE AXE. From Westmoreland, Oneida county, New-York.

4. STONE CHISEL. From Westmoreland, Oneida county, New-York.

*Additional articles constituting the Collection of Indian Relics purchased
from* WILLIAM H. C. HOSMER, *of Avon, Livingston county, and as
described by him.*

34. STONE, of octagonal shape, hollowed out. Supposed to have been
         used by Indian jugglers. Paint stone ? Found on the Street
         farm, (so called) which is situated three miles from Avon,
         in a northwest direction, on the west side of the river, in
         Livingston county.

35. STONE CHISEL, (in two pieces) used in excavating canoes. Found
         near Spanish hill, a few miles from Athens, in Tioga county,
         New-York. The place has been occupied, for purposes of
         fortification, and Indian traces abound.

36. STONE DEERSKIN DRESSER ; and

37. A FRAGMENT of a PIPE, (so supposed by Squire.) These imple-
         ments were found near Fowlerville bridge, in the town of
         Avon, on a farm of W. W. Wadsworth, (leased by Hamil-
         ton, a Scotchman) after the first plowing of a new field, about
         one mile from the river bed, and three and a half miles, in
         a southwestern direction, from Avon Springs. They refute
         the position of O. H. Marshall, that the valley was more
         recently occupied by the Red man, than the higher ground,
         or upper terrace.

38. A BONE FISH SPEAR. Found on the Hurlburt farm, in Avon, four
         miles from the springs, in a northeast direction. The place
         where it was found, is known to the inhabitants as Fort
         Hill. It was unquestionably a Jesuit station. Corn, in a
         charred state, is found commingled with the subsoil. This
         place was destroyed by De Nonville, in 1687. Bone crosses
         have been discovered, and rosaries; also many articles used
         by the French traders in Indian traffic.

Articles Sent to the State in 1849

. . . . .
. . .
.

SCHEDULE OF ARTICLES

Obtained from Indians residing in western New-York, being the product of their own handicraft and manufacture, for the New-York Historical and Antiquarian Collection, under the direction of LEWIS H. MORGAN, *of Rochester.*

Mr. Morgan has furnished the following, and adds, that the name of each article is in the Seneca dialect of the Iroquois language.

(ä, is sounded as in arm — ă, as in at — a, as in ale.)

1. Gä-no-jo-o. Indian drum, used in dances. 3 varieties.
2. Gus-dä-wa-să. Turtle-shell Rattle, used in dances. 2 specimens.
3. Gus-dä-wa-să. Squash-shell Rattle, used in dances. 4 varieties.
4. Gus-dä-wa-să Yen-che-no-hos-ta. Knee Rattle, of deer hoofs. Used in dances. 1 pair.
5. Gä-geh-tä Yen-nis-hä-hos-ta. Arm Bands. 1 pair.
6. Yen-nis-ho-quä-hos-ta. Wrist Bands. 1 pair.
7. Gä-geh-tä Yen-che-no-hos-ta-ta. Knee Bands. 1 pair.
8. Gä-geh-tä. Indian Belt. 3 varieties.
9. Ah-tä-quä-o-weh. Moccasin, for male. 1 pair.
10. The same. Mocassin, for female. 1 pair.
11. Gä-kä-ah. Kilt or Skirt, worn in war dance.
12. Gä-kä-ah. Kilt or Skirt, worn by Indian women.
13. Gise-hă. Leggin, for male. 1 pair.
14. Gise-hă. Leggin, female. 1 pair.
15. Gä-swhen-tä. Necklace.
16. Ya-wa-o-dä-qua. Pin Cushion. 3 varieties.
17. Gä-yä-ah. Work Bag. 5 varieties.
18. Got-gwen-dä. Pocket Book. 6 varieties.
19. Gä-kä. Breech cloth. Used in ball game, foot race, &c.
20. Gä-de-us-ha. Wampum Necklace. Da-yu-yä-sont. Name of a cross.
21. Ya-wa-o-dä-quä. Needle Book. 5 varieties.
22. Ga-on-seh. Baby Frame.
23. Gä-o-wä. Bark Tray. 3 specimens.

24. Ah-de-gwas-hä. Hominy Blade, or Soup Stick. 4 specimens.
25. Ah-was-hä. Ear Ring. 1 pair.
26. Gä-jih. Bowl, for a game with peach stones.
27. Gus-ka-eh. Peach Stones. 6 specimens.
28. Gus-ga-e-sa-tä. Deer Buttons, for an Indian game. 8 specimens, or one set.
29. Gä-geh-dä. Javelin or Shooting Stick, for an Indian game. 18 specimens.
30. Yun-ga-sa. Tobacco Pouch. 4 specimens.
31. Gä-ne-gä-tä. Mortar, for pounding corn. 2 specimens.
32. Gä-nih-gä-dä. Mortar Pounder. 2 specimens.
33. Gä-ne-ah. Ball Bat, used in playing an Indian game. 4 specimens.
34. Gä-wä-sä. Snow Snake. 4 specimens.
35. Gä-je-wä. War Club, with ball head. 4 specimens.
36. Gä-ne-u-ga-o-dus-ha. War Club, with deer-horn tooth. 2 specimens
37. O-sque-sont. Tomahawk.
38. Ah-so-quä-tä. Pipe, (made from a *Cyathophyllum*.)
39. Wä-a-no. Indian Bow. 6 specimens.
40. Gä-no. Arrow. 50 specimens.
41. Gä-go-shä. False Face.
42. Gä-weh-ga-ä. Snow Shoe. 3 pairs.
43. O-tä-quä-osh-ha. Snow Shoe, of splint. 1 pair.
44. Gä-sken-dä. Bark Rope, made of Slippery Elm.
45. Gus-hä-ah. Burden Strap, made of Slippery Elm.
46. Gus-hä-ah. Burden Strap, made of Basswood.
47. Ose-gä. Skein of Slippery Elm strings.
48. Ose-hä. Skein of Basswood-bark strings.
49. Ah-da-dä-quä. Indian Saddle.
50. Gä-na-quä. Bark Barrel. Used for beans, dried corn, &c.
51. Gä-oo-wä. Bark Sap Tub. 3 specimens.
52. O-nus-quä Ah-hose-hä. Knot Ball. Used in playing a game 2 specimens.
53. O-no-ne-ä Gos-ha-dä. Husk Salt Bottle. 2 specimens.
54. O-je-she-wä-tä. Cake of deers' brains and moss, for tanning deerskins.
55. Gä-nuh-sä. Breast-plate of sea shells.
56. Got-kase-hä. Axe-helve.
57. Gä-ga-an-dä. Air Gun.
58. Dä-ya-yä-dä-gä-ne-at-hä. Bow and wheel for striking fire.
59. Gä-gis-dä. Steel, Flint and Punk, for striking fire.

No. 76.]　　　　　　　**59**

60. Gis-tak-he-ä.　Skin Bag.　(Speckled **Faun.**)
61. Gis-tak-he-ä.　Skin Bag.　(Bearskin.)
62. Tuesh-tä-ga-tas-tä.　Tin Breast-plate.
63. Skä-wä-ka.　Splint Broom.
64. Ya-o-dä-was-tä.　Indian Flute.
65. Ne-us-tase-ah.　Basket Sieve.　Used for sifting white corn.
66. O-ne-ose-to-wa-nes.　Basket Sieve; coarser.　For White Flint corn.
67. Ta-gase-hä.　Market Basket.
68. Gase-hä.　Covered Basket.
69. O-gä-kä-ah.　Open-work Basket.　3 specimens.
70. Ga-yuh.　Splint Cradle.
71. Gä-nose-hă.　Husk and Flag Basket.　4 specimens.
72. Ya-nuh-ta-dä-quä.　Toilet Basket.
73. O-gus-ha-ote.　Small square Basket.　17 specimens.　These baskets are numbered from 1 to 17, inclusive, and contain specimens of the several varieties of corn, beans, squashes, tobacco, dried corn, &c., raised and prepared by the Senecas, viz :

　　1. O-na-o-ga-ant.　White corn.
　　2. Tic-ne.　Red corn.
　　3. Ha-go-wä.　White Flint corn.
　　4. O-nä-dä.　Charred, or roasted corn.
　　5. O-go-ou-să.　Baked corn.
　　6. O-si-dä.　Long-vine bean.
　　7. Gweh-dä-ä- O-si-dä.　Red bean.
　　8. Te-o-gä-ga-wä O-si-dä.　Speckled bean.
　　9. Ta-gä-gä-hät.　Short-vine bean.
　　10. Ah-wa-own-dä-go.　Red-flower pole-bean.
　　11. Hä-yoke.　Cranberry pole-bean.
　　12. O-gä-gä-ind.　Gray squash.
　　13. Gä-je-ote.　Big-handle squash.
　　14. Sko-ak.　Toad squash.
　　15. O-ne-ä-sä-ä-weh.　Small squash.
　　16. O-yeh-quä-ä-weh.　Indian tobacco.
　　17. O-so-wa.　Parched corn, pounded into flour, with maple sugar.

74. Gä-no.　Arrow for air-gun.　2 specimens.
75. O-sque-sont.　Tomahawk.　Used in the Bear hunt.
76. Da-ya-no-a-quä-tä Gä-ga-neä-sä.　Scalping knife.　2 specimens.
77. O-na-o-ga-ant.　Two ears of White corn.

78. Tic-ne. Two ears of Red corn.
79. Ho-go-wä. Two ears of White Flint corn.
80. Gus-to-weh. Head Dress.
81. Gä-ger-we-sä Dun-daque-quä-do-quä. New Year's Shovel.
82. To-do-war-she-do-wä. Ribbon for hair.
83. Gä-de-us-ha. Necklace.
84. De-con-deä-da-hust-tă. Belt for female costume.
85. Ah-de-a-dä-we-sä. Female upper dress, with silver broaches, &c.
86. Dä-yase-ta-hos-ta. Silver Hat Band.
87. Yen-nis-ho-quä-hos-ta. Silver Wrist Bands. 1 pair.
88. To-an-jer-go-o O-no-no-do. Ground-nuts, (*Apios tuberosa*) from
    Tonawanda.

Articles Sent to the State in 1850

. . . . .
. . .
.

No. 122.]   51

SCHEDULE OF ARTICLES

Obtained from Indians residing in western New-York and on Grand River in Upper Canada, being the product of their own handicraft and manufacture, for the Historical and Antiquarian collection in the State Cabinet of Natural History, by Lewis H. Morgan, Esq., of Rochester.

The following extract is taken from Mr. Morgan's report to the Regents of the University in relation to the Indian articles mentioned in the schedule.

"By a reference to the schedule, it will be perceived that the additions the present year are at least equal in variety and interest with those of the preceding. Some of them are of the same name and general character; but in such cases the article itself will be found to be either a more perfect specimen, different in some essential particular, or from some other locality. A portion of the articles were obtained of the Mohawks, Onondagas, Cayugas, Senecas and Tuscaroras, who, to the number of two thousand four hundred and fifty, now reside upon a large reserve secured to them by the British government on Grand River in the Niagara peninsula, in Upper Canada. But the residue and the chief portion were obtained from the Senecas in the western part of the State."

1. Gä-däs-hä. SHEAF for carrying arrows.
2. Gä-je-wä. WAR CLUB, with ball head.
3. Gä-such-tä Ote-ko-ä. BELT OF WAMPUM.
4. Ote-ko-ä. STRING OF WAMPUM.
5. Ah-so-quä-tä. STONE PIPE.
6. Da-gä-yä-sont. SILVER CROSS, 8 inches by 5.
7.   do.   do.   6 inches by 4.
8.   do.   do.   3 inches by $1\frac{1}{2}$. 2 specimens
9. Au-ne-as-gä. SILVER BROACH, 4 inches diameter.
10.   do.   do.   3 inches diameter.
11.   do.   do $1\frac{1}{2}$ inches diameter. There are in all 13 broaches of various sizes.
12.   do.
13.   do.
14. Au-ne-ä-hus-hä. FINGER RING. 4 specimens.

52 [ASSEMBLY

15. Ah-was-hä. EAR RING. 1 pair.
16. Dä-yase-ta-hos-ta. SILVER HAT BAND.
17. Ont-wìs-tä-ne-un-dä-quä. SILVER BEADS. (Long.)
18. O-wìs-tä-no-o O-sta-o-quä. ROUND SILVER BEADS. (Variety.)
19. Gä-ose-hä. BABY FRAME.
20. Gä-swä-hos hä. BABY FRAME BELT.
21. Gä-nose-gä. BABY FRAME BELT.
22. do do
23. Da-ya-he-gwä-hus-ta. HAT BAND OF BROACHES.
24. Gä-yä-ah. SATCHEL.
25. Gä-ya-äh. WORK BAG.
26. Ya-wa-o-dä-qua. PIN CUSHION. (2 spec.)
27. Gä-kä-ah. KILT. (Made of fawn skin.)
28. Got-ko-on-dä Gise-hä. DEER SKIN LEGGIN.
29. Da-yunt-wä-hos-tä. DEER SKIN WAIST BELT.
30. Yunt-ka.to-dä-tä. DEER SKIN SHOULDER BELT.
31. Ah-tä-quä-o-weh. MOCCASIN.
32. do do
33. do do
34. HAIR ORNAMENT.
35. SHOT POUCH.
36. Gät-go-ne-as-heh. HOMMONY BLADE. (2 spec.)
37. do do (A chain cut on the end of the handle.)
38. Ya-ä-go-jen-ta-quä. BREAD TURNER.
39. Ah-do-gwä-seh. WOODEN LADLE.
40. do do (2 specimens.)
41. do do
42. Ah-do-gwä-seh. BARK LADLE.
43. Ah-do gwä-seh. WOODEN SPOON.
44. Gä-na-quä. BARK BARREL. (3 sizes.)
45. Gä-o-wä. BARK TRAY. (6 sizes.)
46. Gä-oo-wä. BARK SAP TUB.
47. Gä-te-as-hä. GLASS BEADS.
48. Gä no-sä. CONCH SHELL BREAST PLATE.
49. Ah-dä-dis hä. CANE. (2 specimens.)
50. Ah-so-quä-tä. PIPE, made of Missouri stone.
51. do do made of black stone.
52. do do made of Nodule.

No. 122.]   53

53. Ah-so-quä-tä. PIPE, made of wood and lead.
54. Gä-gä, ne-as-heh. BELT AND KNIFE.
55. Gus-dä-wah-sä. TURTLE SHELL RATTLE.
56.   do   do
57. O-no-gä Gus-da-wah-sa. HORN RATTLE.
58. Gus-to-weh. HEAD DRESS.
59. Gä-wä. MOCCASIN AWL.
60.   BUNCH OF SUMAC.
61. O-yeh-quä-ä-weh. INDIAN TOBACCO.
62. Gis-tät-he-o Gä-yä-ah. FAWN SKIN BAG.
63. Gus-dä-wa-sä Yen che-no-hos-ta. KNEE RATTLE, of deer
      hoofs.
64. SPEAR used in the war of 1812.
65. Gä-ne-a-ga-o-dus-ha. WAR CLUB.
66. Ya-o-dä-was-tä. INDIAN FLUTE. (2 specimens.)
67. Wä-a-no. INDIAN BOW.
68. Gä-ne-ah. BALL BAT.
69. Gä-no. ARROW. (Pointed with deer's horn.)
70. Gä-no. FEATHERED ARROWS. (18 specimens in sheaf.)
71. O-dä-da-one-dus-tä. EYE SHOWERER.
72. Yun-ga-sa. TOBACCO POUCH, made of the foot and leg of the
      snapping turtle.
73. Gä-go-sä. FALSE FACE.
74. O-ä-ta-ose kä. MOOSE HAIR BURDEN STRAP.
75. Gus-hä-ah. MOOSE HAIR AND BARK BURDEN STRAP.
76. Gus-hä-ah. BURDEN STRAP, (bark thread and worsted.)
77. Gus-hä-ah.   do   (bark with moose hair figures.)
78. Gä-te-äs hä Gä-a-o-tä-ges. GRASS SHOULDER ORNAMENT.
79. Yout-kä-do-quä. BASKET FISH NET.
80.   HUSK MOCCASINS, (one pair.)
81. Gä-a-sken-dä. BARK ROPE—made of basswood filaments.
82.   do   do   2 specimens from Tonawanda.
83. Ose-gä. SKEIN OF SLIPPERY ELM THREAD.
84. Ose-gä.   do   (colored.)
85.   do   TWISTED INTO STRINGS.
86. Ose-gä. STRIPS OF SLIPPERY ELM BARK.
87. O-sä. SKEIN OF BASSWOOD FILAMENTS.
88. O-sä. STRIPS OF BASSWOOD BARK.
89. Go-yo-ga-ace. FINGER CATCHER.

89½.   BIRD TRAP FOR CATCHING QUAILS.

90. Gus-hä-ah.   DEER HAIR BURDEN STRAP.

90½ Gus-hä-ah.   BASSWOOD BURDEN STRAP.

91. Ne-us-tase-ah.   BASKET SIEVE.

92. Gase-hä.   COVERED BASKET.

93. O-gä-kä-ah.   OPEN-WORK BASKET.

94. Ta-gase-hä.   MARKET BASKET.

95. Gä-geh-dä.   JAVELIN, or SHOOTING STICK.

96. Ah-de-gwas-hä.   HOMINY BLADE.

97.   PADDLES. (6 specimens.)

98. Yun-des-ho-yon-dä-gwat-hä.   POP CORN SIEVE.

99. An-ne-us-gä.   SILVER BROACH. (9 specimens on a card.)

100. An-ne-us-gä.   do   (20 specimens on a card—
        small.)

101. Gä-ka-ah.   SKIRT.

102. Gise-hä.   LEGGIN FOR FEMALE. (1 pair.)

103. Ah-de-a-dä-we-sä.   FEMALE OVER-DRESS.

103½ E-yose.   BROADCLOTH BLANKET.

104. O-sta-o-quä.   BEAD NECKLACE.

105. Gä-ka-ah.   SKIRT FOR FEMALE.

106. Gise-hä.   LEGGIN FOR FEMALE. (1 pair.)

107. Ah-de-a-dä-we-sä.   OVER-DRESS FOR CHILD.

108. Yen-nis-ho-quä-hos-ta.   WRISTBANDS OF BEADS. (1 pair.)

109. O-ha-dä.   PORCUPINE QUILLS.

110. DEER's HAIR, used for making burden straps, &c.

111. Da-ya-no-ti-yen-dä-quä.   SNOW BOAT.

112. Gä-wä-sä.   SNOW SNAKE. (5 specimens.)

113. Gä-ne-ko-wä-ah.   BURDEN FRAME.

114. Gä-no-sote.   BARK HOUSE.

115. Gä-snä Gä-o-no.   BARK CANOE.

APPENDIX 2

The Cornplanter Tomahawk
by Ely S. Parker

. . . . .
. . .
.

(G.)

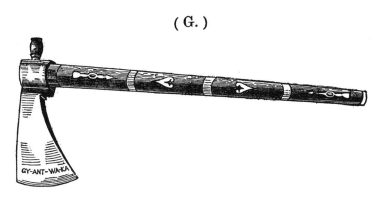

GY-ANT-WA-KA

THE CORNPLANTER TOMAHAWK,

IN THE STATE COLLECTION.

To the Regents of the University :

As the history of Cornplanter is already well known, it is unnecessary for me to relate any of the incidents of his life, except as they may be connected with the tomahawk.

Cornplanter was a Seneca by birth, and resided, after the American Revolution, upon a reserve in Pennsylvania, granted to him by the general government, in consideration, it is said, of his valuable services as a peace-maker between the Indian nations generally, and the people of the United States. During the Revolution, and for a long time subsequent, he enjoyed the rights and exercised the duties of a chief of the Seneca nation, and was for a long time known by the name of Gy-ant-wa-ka, or the Cornplanter, as the name literally signifies. He cultivated a large tract of land and became a considerable farmer, for which reason the name was bestowed upon him by the Senecas.

As a warrior, Cornplanter was daring and courageous, but not rash or impetuous. As a counsellor he was fearless and uncompromising in the advocacy of his views, yet his fearlessness and sternness were always tempered with discretion and prudence.

About the year 1810, Cornplanter, who was a firm believer in the Indian doctrines respecting the communication of men with the spirits of the other world, had a dream. His dream, as tradition preserves it, was, that he had had a sufficient time of service for the nation; that he was now grown too old to be of further use, either as a warrior or as a counsellor, and that he must therefore appoint a successor ; and, further, that in order to preserve the continued good will of the Great Spirit, he must remove from his house all vestiges or relics of the workmanship and invention of white men. In obedience to this dream, Cornplanter took the many presents which had been bestowed upon him by Presidents Washington and Adams, and burnt them up. His presents consisted of the full uniform of an American officer, including an elegant sword, a number of medals, together with some other evidences of friendship.

It is customary among the Iroquois, when any one has had a dream, to announce the fact, and to request that some one might guess it. When the dream is guessed, then an interpretation is requested. This custom of guessing dreams is usually practised at their annual or New-Year's festivals. This course was adopted by Cornplanter in relation to the dream above adverted to. He wandered naked for three days from house to house, to find some one competent to guess his dream. Upon the third day having entered a house and announced the fact that he had had a dream, he expressed a desire that some one might guess it. The man of the house (John Crouse, a Seneca,) said that he would relate his dream, which he did, the substance of which is given above. Crouse seeing him naked and shivering with cold, said, " You shall henceforth be called O-no-no," (meaning cold.) This signified that his name and title of chief as Gy-ant-wa-ka, had passed away. Cornplanter acknowledged that it was truly and correctly guessed.

In obedience to his dream, Cornplanter immediately designated his successor. He chose an old and intimate friend, O-ya-wah-teh, (small berry,) known under the English name of Canada.

At that time Canada was a resident of the Tonawanda reservation, and Cornplanter communicated to him his determination of making him his successor by sending, as an evidence of his

No. 30.]   101

selection and determination, the *tomahawk* now in the State collection, with a belt of wampum, as a token of his sincerity. By
the belt and wampum as evidences of his right, Cornplanter requested that he might be installed as a chief under the name and
title of Gy-ant-wa-ka. O-ya-weh-teh was, accordingly, raised up
and installed as the successor of Cornplanter. He received the
name of Gy-ant-wa-ka, and retained it until his death, which happened about the year 1835. Cornplanter, from his resignation
until his death in 1836, was known under the name of O-no-no.

Upon the death of Canada, his effects were distributed according to the Indian custom, and his widow retained this tomahawk
to keep as a family relic. She kept it until obtained from her
by me. At the time I purchased it, she informed me that the
wampum which was sent with the tomahawk by Cornplanter,
had all been used for other purposes, and no part of it could then
be had. The tomahawk, when received from Cornplanter, had
in it a different handle from the present. She described it as
being of better workmanship, with numerous silver ornaments
upon each side. Upon one side was engraved the name Gy-ant-
wa-ka ; and upon the reverse the name of John Andrus, who was
doubtless the manufacturer.

Although Cornplanter designated his successor, who was actually installed, and acted as a chief, Cornplanter was never in fact
deposed. He ever had the privilege of sitting with the chiefs in
council, and had a voice in their deliberations.

He continued to live upon his reserve, and died at an advanced age in 1836.   His reservation was known and is yet distinguished by the name of Deo-no-sä-da-geh, signifying the "Burnt House."

All which is respectfully submitted.

                                    Hä-sa-no-an-da.
                                    ELY S. PARKER.
Rochester, June 29th, 1850

NOTE.—It was contrary to the custom of the Iroquois for a chief
to resign his office and appoint his successor. But in this instance, out of reverence for his dream, a departure from their ancient customs was permitted.   E. S. P.

NOTES

Preface

1. Morgan, who customarily signed himself "Lewis H. Morgan" or "L. H. Morgan" was born "Lewis Morgan." He added the "H." as a young man. Later in life when he was asked what the "H." stood for, he replied, "Henry, if anything" (Hart 1883).

2. Morgan, *League,* p. 351.

1. Iroquois Material Culture in 1850

1. For an account of these meetings in the 1840s, see Tooker, "On the Development of the Handsome Lake Religion."

2. Morgan made no study of how the Tonawanda Senecas governed themselves. About all that can be known must be gleaned from these petitions.

3. Morgan, *League,* pp. 326–327.

4. Morgan, *Systems,* pp. 167–169, 279–376.

5. In *Death and Rebirth of the Seneca,* Wallace argues that this change was facilitated by Quaker technical aid. He bases this conclusion on the Quaker reports of their activities among the Allegany Senecas. It is entirely possible, however, that the Quakers—as missionaries are wont to do—overestimated their influence. The Quakers did not supply such aid on the Buffalo Creek and Tonawanda reservations, and so cannot be said to have been responsible for effecting the economic changes that took place there—essentially the same kind of changes that occurred on the Allegany reservation.

6. These figures were supplied to Schoolcraft by the Tonawanda Senecas in 1845 and published by him in his *Notes on the Iroquois* (1846), pp. 191–200.

7. See Graymont, *The Iroquois in the American Revolution*, p. 213.

8. Morgan (*League*, pp. 383–384) reports that the Iroquois made bowls, pitchers, and other vessels of wooden knot. These are not represented in the artifacts he collected for the state, perhaps because none of the Parkers were woodcarvers.

9. Reporting on his visit to Buffalo Creek in 1834, Maximilian, Prince of Wied, noted:

> Their dress is nearly the same as that of the Whites. Both the men and women frequently wear round felt hats: the men have, in general, a red girdle under their large blue upper coat, and the women wrap themselves in blankets. (Thwaites, *Early Western Travels*, vol. 24, p. 162)

Morgan (*League*, pp. 383–384) also reported that Iroquois women wore hats.

2. Lewis H. Morgan and the Study of Material Culture

1. Letter of James C. Pilling to Erminnie A. Smith, December 17, 1881, in Bureau of American Ethnology Letterbook, National Anthropological Archives, Smithsonian Institution; Hart, "Memoir of Lewis H. Morgan," p. 28.

2. Trautmann, *Lewis Henry Morgan and the Invention of Kinship*, p. 118.

3. Morgan, *Houses and House-Life*, p. v.

4. White, "Lewis H. Morgan's Journal of a Trip to Southwestern Colorado and New Mexico"; Hollcroft, "The Diary of William Fellowes Morgan."

5. Murphy, *Biographical Sketches*, pp. 238–239.

6. Trautmann, *Lewis Henry Morgan and the Invention of Kinship*.

7. Morgan, *Ancient Society*, p. 6.

8. Morgan, *The American Beaver and His Works*.

9. White, "Extracts from the European Travel Journal of Lewis H. Morgan," p. 370.

10. Morgan to White, October 27, 1868, Andrew D. White Papers, Cornell University Library.

3. Morgan's Early Iroquois Work

1. Second Regents report, p. 10.

2. Second Regents report (see chapter 8).

3. Morgan, "An Address by Schenandoah Delivered on the Second Anniversary," manuscript in Morgan Papers.

4. Hollcroft, "A Brief History of Aurora: XXX. Jedediah Morgan."

5. The date of 1841 is given on Morgan's plan of the site published in the Second Regents report (see fig. 19 this volume). Fort Hill became a cemetery in 1852 and remains so today.

6. Morgan, "Vision of Kar-is-ta-gi-a," pp. 241–242.

7. Copies of this constitution are in the Henry Rowe Schoolcraft Papers, Library of Congress, Washington, D.C., and the Morgan Papers, Dewitt Historical Society, Ithaca, N.Y. This preamble was retained in the constitution adopted on August 14, 1845 (Record Book of the Wolf Tribe of the Cayuga Nation, Morgan Papers), and in the constitution revised in August 1846 (manuscript in Morgan Papers).

8. Henry H. Haight to Morgan, January 30, 1869, Morgan Papers.

9. A portion of this correspondence is preserved in Morgan Papers.

10. Morgan's account of this meeting is contained in "An Address Read by Schenandoah Before the Gue-u-gweh-o-noh, April 17, 1844," manuscript in Morgan Papers.

11. Record Book of the Wolf Tribe of the Cayuga Nation, Morgan Papers. Clark's history, *Onondaga; or Reminiscences of Earlier and Later Times* was published in 1849.

12. Although Jemmy Johnson is usually referred to as a grandson of Handsome Lake (see, for example, Morgan, *League*, p. 230), the following statements indicate that Johnson was Handsome Lake's mother's sister's daughter's daughter's son (in Seneca kinship terminology this relationship is that of "grandson"): the statement in the *Manuscript Journals*, vol. 2, p. 158, that Jemmy Johnson was the son of Red Jacket's sister; the statement in the Lyman C. Draper Manuscripts (State Historical Society of Wisconsin) 4 S 56, p. 56, that Red Jacket's mother was a sister of Blacksnake's mother; and the oft-repeated statement that Blacksnake was Handsome Lake's "nephew."

13. This information is contained in Morgan, "Vision of Kar-is-ta-gi-a."

14. Schoolcraft's address and Hosmer's poem were published by the order in 1846.

15. Morgan, "Observations upon the Institutions of the Iroquois, August 1845," *Manuscript Journals*, vol. 1, no. 13.

16. *Manuscript Journals*, vol. 1, nos. 15, 18.

17. Morgan to Schoolcraft, October 7, 1845, Schoolcraft Papers, Library of Congress.

18. A copy of this address, "Notes on the Iroquois, Their Government, and Institutions," is preserved in *Manuscript Journals*, vol. 1, no. 17. The version of this paper that Morgan delivered to the New York Historical Society in April 1845 was published in 1928 by Arthur C. Parker under the title *Government and Institutions of the Iroquois by Lewis Henry Morgan;* although this manuscript version was once in the Morgan Papers at the University of Rochester, it is not now.

19. Johnson, *Papers of Sir William Johnson*, vol. 1, p. 765; vol. 2, p. 641; vol. 9, pp. 457–458; O'Callaghan, *Documentary History of the State of New-York*, vol. 2, p. 726.

Thirty years after Morgan's visit, almost all traces of the fort had been obliterated (see Conover, *Early History of Geneva*, p. 18).

20. *Manuscript Journals*, vol. 1, no. 20. An almost identical account is contained in a letter also dated November 22, 1845, now in Ashbel and George Riley Papers, William L. Clements Library, University of Michigan. This letter, which Morgan sent to Henry H. Haight and George S. Riley, is addressed to the Rochester chapter of the Grand Order of the Iroquois. In writing it, Morgan apparently merely copied his notes, including the sketch plan of the site.

21. The name of this village is variously spelled.

22. Hough (*Proceedings of the Commissioners of Indian Affairs*, p. 148 n.) also mentions this agreement and the once-annual visits of Indians at plowing time to see that its stipulation—that the white man's plow should not pass over the bones of their fathers—should not be broken.

Conover in his *Early History of Geneva* (pp. 18–19) reported that these annual visits became less frequent around 1835, and when they subsequently ceased, all the land except the burial mound was plowed and cultivated; a portion of the site was also destroyed by a railroad grading. (See also Conover, *Reasons Why the State Should Acquire the Famous Burial Mound of the Seneca Indians*, p. 3).

23. In place of the remainder of this sentence, Morgan's letter to Haight and Riley has: "We can also easily discover the size and shape. We can follow this trench as easily and distinctly as the rule on paper. The mound also, on which can be seen many graves, is still as they left it. We have the same features as at Tonawanda: the castle on the bank of a creek, and the burial ground in the rear." (The reference to the "castle" at Tonawanda is a reference to the village there.)

24. In place of the remainder of this sentence, Morgan's letter to Haight and Riley has: "for we understand that the Indians never built what might be called even a village of wigwams, as they are not arranged on streets, but erected as irregularly as the trees themselves grow up."

The letter does not include the remainder of this paragraph.

25. Kappler, *Indian Affairs: Laws and Treaties*, pp. 502–542.

26. Ibid., pp. 537–542.

27. Extracts from Thomas Love and Ira Cook Report, April 1, 1844, National Archives Microcopy 234, Roll 585, Frames 460–466.

28. Batavia [N.Y.] *Spirit of the Times*, March 10, 1846.

29. Ibid., March 17, 1846.

30. "Record of a Council Held upon the Tonawanda Reservation, January 1 and 2, 1846," *Manuscript Journals*, vol. 1, no. 3; Charles T. Porter to Henry R. Schoolcraft, Schoolcraft Papers, Library of Congress.

31. *Manuscript Journals*, vol. 1, no. 6.

32. Captain Frost was a noted Onondaga chief and religious leader. The inter-

view Morgan refers to had taken place the previous month (*Manuscript Journals,* vol. 1, no. 6).

33. *Manuscript Journals,* vol. 1, no. 5. This site in the town of Shelby is mentioned by Squier in his *Aboriginal Monuments of the State of New York,* p. 50, in a brief description of the site written by S. M. Burroughs. Of some historical interest is a longer description of this same site, titled "Antiquities of Orleans County, New York," by the youthful Frank H. Cushing. It was the first publication of this famous and controversial nineteenth-century anthropologist.

34. *Manuscript Journals,* vol. 1, no. 7.

35. The mass meeting held at the Batavia courthouse on March 21, 1846, was called to order by Samuel Richmond, who also read the recommendations of the grand jury for holding the meeting (Batavia [N.Y.] *Spirit of the Times,* March 31, 1846).

Nehemiah Woodworth's 1845 account of first coming to the region in 1788 is published in Carol Kammen, ed., *What They Wrote: 19th Century Documents from Tompkins County, New York,* pp. 3–5.

36. *Manuscript Journals,* vol. 1, no. 7.

37. Perhaps this is the Spanish Hill site, South Waverly, Bradford County, Pennsylvania. For descriptions of this site, see Louise Welles Murray, ed., *Selected Manuscripts of General John S. Clark,* pp. 18–23, 32–33; and Elsie Murray, "Spanish Hill: Its Present, Past and Future," pp. 13–14.

38. Perhaps this is one of the several sites near Waterburg in Ulysses township, Tompkins County. For descriptions, see David Trowbridge, "Ancient Fort and Burial Ground"; F. E. Herrick, "An Ancient Fortification in Tompkins County, N.Y."; and David M. Jones and Anne Jones, "The Defenses at Indian Fort Road, Tompkins County, New York."

39. Perhaps a heavy earthwork, slightly elliptical in shape, embracing about an acre in Portland township, that Cyrus Thomas had been told once existed. See Thomas, "Report on the Mound Explorations of the Bureau of Ethnology," p. 512.

40. "3-1/2" is added in manuscript over line.

41. That is, King Ferry, Genoa township, Cayuga county.

42. White birch, whose bark is superior to that of other trees for making canoes, did not grow in Iroquois territory.

43. Probably about 1792. The treaty mentioned is undoubtedly the Phelps and Gorham's purchase of 1788. Although the council initially was to be held in Geneva, it was actually held at Buffalo Creek (see Orasmus Turner, *History of the Pioneer Settlement of Phelps and Gorham's Purchase,* pp. 135–140).

44. "Major" added in manuscript by caret.

45. Armstrong, *Warrior in Two Camps,* p. 21.

46. Batavia [N.Y.] *Spirit of the Times,* March 17 and 31, 1846.

47. *Proceedings of the New York Historical Society for 1846,* p. 23; see also note 18 this chapter.

48. *Manuscript Journals,* vol. 1, no. 8.

49. Newspaper clipping in Parker Papers, American Philosophical Society Library; Ithaca [N.Y.] *Daily Chronicle,* August 17, 1846, also August 19, 1846; "An Address on the Indian Trails of N.Y. with Some Observations on the Joint Occupation of the County by the White Race and the Red by Skenandoah Read August 12, 1846 Before the Council of Delegates of the Iroquois Confederacy," *Manuscript Journals,* vol. 1, no. 14; "Address by Skenandoah on the Geography and Trails of the Hodenosaunee Delivered August 13, 1846 Before the Council of Delegates of the New Confederacy of the Iroquois at Aurora, Cayuga County, N.Y.," manuscript in Morgan Papers.

50. Morgan's field notes of this trip are in *Manuscript Journals,* vol. 2, no. 1.

51. The manuscript of this paper is in the New-York Historical Society.

4. Archaeology of the State

1. For a history of these discoveries see Robert Silverberg, *Mound Builders of Ancient America.*

2. Yates and Moulton, *History of the State of New York,* pp. 15–18; Lothrop, *Life of Samuel Kirkland,* pp. 282–285; Pilkington, *The Journals of Samuel Kirkland,* pp. 140–141.

3. "Newly Discovered Indian Fortifications," *The New-York Magazine; or, Literary Repository* 4 (1793): 23–24. The magazine had earlier published an illustration of this noted site at Marietta, titled "View of the celebrated Indian fortifications near the Junction of the Ohio and Muskingum Rivers" [*The New-York Magazine* 2 (1791), facing p. 555].

4. Clinton, *Discourse Delivered Before the New-York Historical Society,* pp. 53–58, and Clinton, *A Memoir on the Antiquities of the Western Parts of the State of New-York,* pp. 5–14.

5. Yates and Moulton, *History of the State of New York,* pp. 14–31.

6. Macauley, *The Natural, Statistical, and Civil History of the State of New-York,* vol. 2, pp. 106–115.

7. Schoolcraft, *Notes on the Iroquois,* 1846, pp. 206–208.

8. At least I would so identify him.

9. Dewey was a charter member of Pundit Club, the organization of Rochester men of scholarly bent that Morgan was instrumental in founding in 1854. Given their similar interests, it seems likely that Morgan met him shortly after moving to Rochester late in 1844. Dewey became a member of the Rochester chapter on the order in September 1845 ("Record of the Warriors of the T[urtle] T[ribe] of the S[eneca] N[ation]," manuscript in the Morgan Papers). For a biography of Dewey

see Martin B. Anderson, "Sketch of the Life of Prof. Chester Dewey, D.D., LL.D."

10. E. G. Squier and E. H. Davis, *Ancient Monuments of the Mississippi Valley*.

11. Squier to Morgan, December 4, 1848, Morgan Papers.

12. Squier, *Aboriginal Monuments of the State of New York*. Squier's "Report upon the Aboriginal Monuments of Western New York," delivered at the January 2, 1849, meeting of the New York Historical Society, was published in its *Proceedings*.

13. Second Regents report (see chapter 8); Anna Mary Jones, *The New York State Museum*, pp. 6–7; Hartnagel, "General Administrative Chronology," pp. 86–87; and *Journal of Meetings of the Board of Regents of the University of the State of New York* (manuscript in New York State Archives, Albany, N.Y.), vol. 5, p. 207.

The initial appropriation for preserving and increasing the cabinet was $150 annually for the years 1847 and 1848. It was increased in 1848 to $500 a year, making the total amount for these two years $1,000 (first Regents report, p. 3; second Regents report, p. 7). The annual reports of the regents, the first of which—that for 1847—was published in 1848, were necessitated by these annual appropriations.

14. Letter in Morgan Papers.

15. Second Regents report, p. 81.

16. Morgan to Parker, September 26, 1848, Parker Papers (Freeman no. 1855), American Philosophical Society Library. Parker's letter to Morgan in October 1848 has not survived. Parker's notes on the 1848 council at Tonawanda are in Parker Papers (Freeman no. 3261), American Philosophical Society Library; they are published in Fenton, "Iroquois Studies at the Mid-Century," pp. 306–309.

17. Letter in Parker Papers (Freeman no. 3467), American Philosophical Society Library. Parker did not send Morgan his account of the 1848 council until 1850 (see note 26, chapter 5).

5. Collecting for the State

1. Second Regents report, pp. 76–79; third Regents report, pp. 53–56.

2. Squier to Morgan, December 11, 1848, Morgan Papers. The proposed new journal apparently was never published.

3. Morgan to Squier, December 22, 1848, Squier Papers, Library of Congress. Morgan apparently did not undertake this trip to Tonawanda and Cattaraugus (there is no record of such a trip), nor was the article apparently ever written.

4. Morgan to Squier, December 22, 1848, Squier Papers, Library of Congress.

5. Morgan to Squier, April 12, 1849, Squier Papers, Library of Congress.

6. Second Regents report (see chapter 8).

7. Third Regents report, p. 10.

8. Ibid., p. 15.

9. Armstrong, *Warrior in Two Camps*, p. 10.

10. Ibid., pp. 6–8. For information on the Parker family, see also Arthur C. Parker, *General Ely S. Parker, Last Grand Sachem of the Iroquois and General Grant's Secretary.*

Elizabeth has been said to have been the daughter (or granddaughter) of Jemmy Johnson, perhaps because he was Ely's "grandfather" (Morgan, *League*, p. 210 n.). Morgan, however, records that Elizabeth's mother was Jemmy Johnson's sister (*Manuscript Journals*, vol. 2, no. 11). In the Seneca system of kinship terminology, this would make Jemmy Johnson Ely's "grandfather" (see also chapter 2, note 12).

Elizabeth also has been said to have been older than her husband. Morgan, however, believed her to be "below 50" in 1846 (*Manuscript Journals*, vol. 1, no. 5), an age more in accord with the ages of her children (see following note).

11. The approximate birth dates of these children indicated by Armstrong (*Warrior in Two Camps*, pp. 8–10) are:

Spencer, 1815
Levi, 1820
Nicholson, 1826
Ely, 1828
Caroline, 1830
Newton, 1833

The youngest son, Solomon, died in 1845; it is possible that William and Elizabeth Parker had other children who died before 1845.

12. Letter in Parker Papers (Freeman no. 3516), American Philosophical Society Library.

13. *Manuscript Journals*, vol. 2, nos. 4–5.

14. Letter in Parker Papers (Freeman no. 3468), American Philosophical Society Library.

15. Draft letter, Morgan to Parker, January 29, 1850, Morgan Papers.

16. Letter in Parker Papers (Freeman no. 3272), American Philosophical Society Library.

17. Third Regents report (see chapter 8).

18. "Proclamation of the Tek-a-ri-ho-ge-a Instituting and Confirming the Wolf Tribe of the Oneida Nation at Utica," manuscript in Morgan Papers. Morgan also remarks on the importance of costumes to a chapter's success in his letter to William Allen, February 11, 1845, New-York Historical Society.

19. Morgan, *League*, pp. 268–290.

20. Photostatic copy of letter, T. Romeyn Beck to Governor Hamilton Fish, received January 5, 1850, Morgan Papers.

21. Ibid.; draft letter, Morgan to Parker, January 29, 1850, Morgan Papers; Batavia [N.Y.] *Spirit of the Times*, June 4, 1850.

22. Third Regents report, p. 15.

23. Ibid.

24. Colton to Morgan, September 14, 1846, Morgan Papers. This letter is published in Tooker, "The Structure of the Iroquois League," p. 149.

25. The latter engraving has been presumed to be of Nicholson Parker. However, the name on it (Dä-ah-de-a) belonged to Levi Parker, not Nicholson (*Manuscript Journals*, vol. 2, no. 4, p. 159).

26. Parker did not send Morgan his account of the 1848 council until 1850, and then only sent the description of the proceedings of the first two days. His account of the final two days was sent to Morgan sometime later that year. After Morgan had received the first part of Parker's account, he apparently copied it before returning it to Parker; the first part of the manuscript (*Manuscript Journals*, vol. 1, no. 1) is in Morgan's hand, the remainder in Parker's.

27. At the time, Morgan apparently intended that the Brant medal should eventually go to the state. In his will dated May 30, 1851 (Morgan Papers), he bequeathed it to the state to be placed in its historical and antiquarian collection. At his death in 1881, by the provisions of a subsequent will, the medal (without specific mention) was bequeathed to the University of Rochester along with his other Indian artifacts. These were later transferred from the University to the Rochester Museum, where the medal is now.

28. Morgan to Caroline Parker, Morgan Papers.

29. This overdress is most likely one preserved in the New York State Museum that has the number 36644.

30. It is possible that on this trip to Tonawanda or that of the previous year Morgan purchased from Jemmy Johnson the Red Jacket medal that Ely Parker is shown wearing in fig. 26. Jemmy Johnson had been given this medal after Red Jacket's death. It had been given to Red Jacket by President George Washington when Red Jacket was in Philadelphia in 1792 as a member of an Indian delegation. The medal itself is a typical example of the kind of peace medal the government was giving to various Indians as expressions of friendship in this period.

The evidence that Morgan purchased the Red Jacket medal and then gave it to Parker for what it had cost him comes from a statement in an item in the *New York Times* for October 29, 1865: "In 1851 . . . some parties prevailed upon **Johnson** to part with it for a small consideration, to the New-York State Museum at Albany. In its transit it was intercepted by Col. [Ely] Parker, then living at Rochester, New-York, who paid the consideration that **Johnson** expected of it."

"Parties" undoubtedly referred to Morgan, and the date 1851 may well be the date Parker bought it from Morgan, not the date collected, perhaps 1850. Parker had worn the medal on occasion while it was still in Johnson's possession, perhaps to symbolize that he was Johnson's delegate, and it may have taken little on Parker's part to convince Morgan to sell it to him.

When the other leader of the Tonawanda Senecas, John Blacksmith, the only League chief residing at Tonawanda, died later that year, Parker was elevated to his place, assuming the last name-title on the Roll Call of the Chiefs. At that time he also assumed the Red Jacket medal as a badge of office.

31. Fourth Regents report, p. 11.

32. *Journal of the Meetings of the Board of Regents of the University of the State of New York* (manuscript in New York State Archives, Albany, N.Y.), vol. 5, p. 446.

33. Fifth Regents report, p. 10.

34. White, "How Morgan Came to Write *Systems of Consanguinity and Affinity*," p. 262.

35. Hartnagel, "General Administrative Chronology," pp. 87–88; and Clarke, "Chronological Sketch of the Archaeological Work of the State Museum," pp. 105–107.

36. Fenton, *Parker on the Iroquois*, Editor's Introduction, pp. 1–21; and Hertzberg, "Nationality, Anthropology and Pan-Indianism in the Life of Arthur C. Parker," pp. 47–58.

37. Parker, "Fate of the New York State Collections," pp. 169–71.

6. Classification of Articles in the Collection

1. An example of the kind of classification used by museums is to be found in Blackwood 1970.

2. I adopt here Conklin and Sturtevant's (1952) felicitous phrase for Seneca musical instruments, "singing tools" and by analogy extend the word "tools" to other kinds of objects not usually so characterized.

7. Morgan's Field Notes

1. For To-do-da-ho (Thadodaho) see *League*, pp. 67–68.

2. In the manuscript "white" is crossed out.

3. In the manuscript this sentence is written over the line.

4. Morgan is here describing the Bowl Game as it is played at the New Year's (Midwinter) and Green Corn ceremonies. On those occasions the two moieties play against each other, keeping score with 100 beans.

5. While at Fort Erie in 1796, Isaac Weld observed some Senecas, probably from Buffalo Creek, hunting with the blowgun and later published what may be the most detailed description of its use among the Iroquois:

> The blow-gun is a narrow tube, commonly about six feet in length, made of a cane reed, or of some pithy wood, through which they drive short slender

arrows by the force of the breath. The arrows are not much thicker than the lower string of a violin; they are headed generally with little triangular bits of tin, and round the opposite ends, for the length of two inches, a quantity of the down of thistles, or something very like it, is bound, so as to leave the arrows at this part of such a thickness that they may but barely pass into the tube. The arrows are put in at the end of the tube that is held next to the mouth, the down catches the breath, and with a smart puff they will fly the distance of fifty yards. I have followed young Seneka Indians, whilst shooting with blow-guns, for hours together, during which time I have never known them once to miss their aim, at the distance of ten or fifteen yards, although they shot at the little red squirrels, which are not half the size of a rat; and with such wonderful force used they to blow forth the arrows, that they frequently drove them up to the very thistle-down through the heads of the largest black squirrels. The effect of these guns appears at first like magic. The tube is put to the mouth, and in the twinkling of an eye you see the squirrel that is aimed at fall lifeless to the ground; no report, not the smallest noise even, is to be heard, nor is it possible to see the arrow, so quickly does it fly, until it appears in the body of the animal. [Weld, *Travels,* pp. 328–329]

6. That is, Feather dance (see *League,* p. 279).

7. Morgan first wrote "Gä-ga-dä-ayn-duk." He later changed this to "Gä-na-gä-o," apparently in order to have different names for the two different javelin games.

8. Morgan originally wrote "sumac generally," then crossed out "sumac" and wrote above the line "hickory, maple, alder, and any kind of hard wood. The shaft must be straight and slick" apparently forgetting to cross out the word "generally."

9. The word meaning 'two' apparently refers to the number of the basket.

10. A Cayuga sachem name (see *League,* p. 65).

11. This line is not in Morgan's hand.

12. This and the following lines through "Necklace Gă-teäs-hă Any necklace" are not in Morgan's hand.

13. In the manuscript, "Two sticks lying side by side" is written below "Tä-yen-dä-ná-ga." It is the translation of Brant's Indian name: Tä-yen-dä-ná-ga as Morgan has written it.

14. Iroquois tradition states that when the League was established the amount of the gift to be given by the murderer's clan to the murdered person's family to smooth relations between them and so prevent retaliation was fixed. The "value of a life" refers to the amount at which the gift was fixed. This amount has been given more recently as ten strings of wampum (Hewitt, "Some Esoteric Aspects of the League of the Iroquois," p. 323; "A Constitutional League of Peace," p. 541).

15. By Iroquois custom wampum should accompany any important message; it attests to the validity of the message itself. Hence, Iroquois say that the message is "read into the wampum" and that wampum belts "contain their laws and usages."

16. This sheet of paper has not been preserved.

17. A reference to David Cusick, *Sketches of the Ancient History of the Six Nations.*

18. In the manuscript "to be well disposed or beneficent beings" has been crossed out and "to have the power of inflicting disease and pestilence" added.

19. In the manuscript "Finger snake mouth" has been crossed out. Finger catcher is neither described nor illustrated in the Regents reports.

20. This list of materials for making the table spread is not in Morgan's hand. The table spread itself is probably that one now in the Morgan collection in the Rochester Museum and Science Center.

21. See also Morgan, *Houses and House-Life,* p. 65.

22. Greenhalgh records the name of this village as Tiotohattan (O'Callaghan, *Documentary History of the State of New York,* vol. 1, p. 13). Morgan here (and in the fifth Regents report) has apparently changed the spelling on the basis of O. H. Marshall's identification of this village with that called Totiakto by Denonville and on information Marshall obtained from John Blacksmith on the Seneca name of the latter (Marshall, "Narrative of the Expedition of the Marquis De Nonville," pp. 161–162).

In *League* (p. 19) Morgan identifies Da-yo-de-hok-to [*tetyótiha:'ktǫ:h* 'a bended creek'] as a village at the bend of Honeoye Creek west of Mendon, the largest village of the Seneca according to Denonville.

23. Probably a reference to the colonists' use of wampum as small change among themselves.

24. Written over line in manuscript: called Ta-ken-e-o-quä-hos-tä.

25. Although Morgan describes Skä-no-wan-de as the wampum keeper of the League, this name-title is not that of the wampum keeper (the seventh Onondaga name on the Roll Call of the Chiefs), but the last Onondaga name. Thus, it is not without interest that Hale (*The Iroquois Book of Rites,* pp. 41, 158) reports that the holder of this last Onondaga name, John Buck also performed the duties of wampum keeper although his brother George Buck held the name-title of that position. It is possible that John Buck was also performing these duties at the time of Morgan's visit although the implication of Morgan's wording is that a man named Hill was (the name of John Buck's predecessor is not now known).

26. Ceremonies may begin with a rite of confession of sins in which individuals in turn confess their sins while holding a string of wampum.

8. Morgan's Reports

NOTE ON THIRD REGENTS REPORT

p. 183. "Basswood makes the most pliable rope." In *League,* p. 365, this has been changed to "Slippery-elm makes the most pliable rope."

NOTE ON FIFTH REGENTS REPORT

p. 215. The reference to Baylie is to Francis Baylies, *An Historical Memoir of the Colony of New Plymouth,* vol. 1, p. 37. The reference to Hutchinson is to Thomas Hutchinson, *The History of Massachusetts,* vol. 1, p. 406 n.

BIBLIOGRAPHY

Anderson, Martin B. "Sketch of the Life of Prof. Chester Dewey, D.D., LL.D." *Annual Report of the Board of Regents of the Smithsonian Institution for 1870* (1871): 231–240.

Armstrong, William H. *Warrior in Two Camps: Ely S. Parker, Union General and Seneca Chief.* Syracuse: Syracuse University Press, 1978.

Baylies, Francis. *An Historical Memoir of the Colony of New Plymouth.* 2 vols. Boston: Hilliard, Gray, Little and Wilkins, 1830.

Blackwood, Beatrice. *The Classification of Artefacts in the Pitt Rivers Museum, Oxford.* Occasional Papers on Technology 11. Oxford: Oxford University Press, 1970.

Chafe, Wallace L. *Handbook of the Seneca Language.* New York State Museum and Science Service Bulletin 388 (1963).

———. *Seneca Morphology and Dictionary.* Smithsonian Contributions to Anthropology 4. Washington, D.C.: Smithsonian Press, 1967.

Clark, Joshua V. H. *Onondaga; or Reminiscences of Earlier and Later Times.* Syracuse: Stoddard and Babcock, 1849.

Clarke, Noah T. "Chronological Sketch of the Archaeological Work of the State Museum." *New York State Museum Bulletin* 313 (1937): 105–110.

Clinton, De Witt. *Discourse Delivered Before the New-York Historical Society.* New York: James Eastburn, 1812.

———. *A Memoir on the Antiquities of the Western Parts of the State of New-York.* Albany: I. W. Clark, 1818.

Conklin, Harold C., and William C. Sturtevant. "Seneca Indian Singing Tools at Coldspring Longhouse: Musical Instruments of the Modern Iroquois." *Proceedings of the American Philosophical Society* 97 (1952): 262–290.

Conover, George S. *Early History of Geneva (Formerly Called Kanadesaga)*. Geneva: Courier Steam Presses, 1879.

———. *Reasons Why the State Should Acquire the Famous Burial Mound of the Seneca Indians Adjacent to the State Agricultural Station*. n.p.: n.p., 1888.

Cushing, Frank H. Antiquities of Orleans County, New York. *Annual Report of the Board of Regents of the Smithsonian Institution for 1874* (1875): 375–377.

Cusick, David. *Sketches of the Ancient History of the Six Nations*. Lockport: Turner and McCollum, 1848.

Engels, Frederick. *The Origin of the Family, Private Property and the State in the Light of the Researches of Lewis H. Morgan*. New York: International, 1942.

Fenton, William N. "Iroquois Studies at the Mid-Century." *Proceedings of the American Philosophical Society* 95 (1951): 296–310.

———. *Parker on the Iroquois*. Syracuse: Syracuse University Press, 1968.

Graymont, Barbara. *The Iroquois in the American Revolution*. Syracuse: Syracuse University Press, 1972.

Hale, Horatio. *The Iroquois Book of Rites*. Philadelphia: D. G. Brinton, 1883.

Hart, Charles Henry. "Memoir of Lewis H. Morgan of Rochester, N.Y." *Proceedings of the Numismatic and Antiquarian Society of Philadelphia for the Year 1882* (1883): 20–29.

Hartnagel, Chris A. "General Administrative Chronology of the State Geological and Natural History Survey, State Cabinet of Natural History and the State Museum." *New York State Museum Bulletin* 313 (1937): 86–88.

Herrick, F. E. "An Ancient Fortification in Tompkins County, N.Y." *The Antiquarian* 1 (1897): 86–87.

Hertzberg, Hazel Whitman. "Nationality, Anthropology, and Pan-Indianism in the Life of Arthur C. Parker (Seneca)." *Proceedings of the American Philosophical Society* 123 (1979): 47–72.

Hewitt, J. N. B. "Some Esoteric Aspects of the League of the Iroquois." *Proceedings of the 19th International Congress of Americanists* (1917): 322–326.

———. "A Constitutional League of Peace in the Stone Age of America: The League of the Iroquois and its Constitution." *Annual Report of the Smithsonian Institution for 1918* (1920): 527–545.

Hollcroft, Temple R. "The Diary of William Fellowes Morgan." *Scientific Monthly* 77 (1953): 119–128.

———. "A Brief History of Aurora: XXX. Jedediah Morgan." *Wells College Alumnae News* (Spring 1958): 10–11.

Hough, Franklin B., ed. *Proceedings of the Commissioners of Indian Affairs, Appointed by Law for the Extinguishment of Indian Titles in the State of New York*. Albany: Joel Munsell, 1861.

Hutchinson, Thomas. *The History of Massachusetts*. 3d ed. 2 vols. Salem: Thomas C. Cushing, 1795.

Johnson, Sir William. *The Papers of Sir William Johnson.* 15 vols. Edited by James
  Sullivan et al. Albany: University of the State of New York, 1921–65.

[Jones, Anna Mary]. *The New York State Museum: A Short History.* Albany: The
  University of the State of New York, 1964.

Jones, David M., and Anne Jones. "The Defenses at Indian Fort Road, Tompkins
  County, New York." *Pennsylvania Archaeologist* 50 (1980): 61–71.

Kammen, Carol, ed. *What They Wrote: 19th Century Documents from Tompkins
  County, N.Y.* Ithaca: Department of Manuscripts and University Archives,
  Cornell University Libraries, 1978.

Kappler, Charles J., comp. *Indian Affairs: Laws and Treaties.* Vol. 2. Washington,
  D.C.: Government Printing Office, 1904.

Lothrop, Samuel K. *Life of Samuel Kirkland, Missionary to the Indians.* Boston:
  Charles C. Little and James Brown, 1852.

Macauley, James. *The Natural, Statistical, and Civil History of the State of New-York.*
  3 vols. New York: Gould and Banks, 1829.

Marshall, Orasmus H. *Narrative of the Expedition of Marquis De Nonville, Against
  the Senecas, in 1687.* Collections of the New York Historical Society, 2d ser.,
  2 (1848): 149–192.

Morgan, Lewis H. "Mind or Instinct: An Inquiry Concerning the Manifestation
  of Mind by the Lower Order of Animals." *The Knickerbocker* 22 (1843): 414–420,
  507–513.

———. "Vision of Kar-is-ta-gi-a, A Sachem of the Cayuga." *The Knickerbocker* 24
  (1844): 238–245.

———. "Letters on the Iroquois." *The American Review* 5 (1847): 177–190, 242–257,
  447–461; 6 (1847): 477–490, 626–633.

———. *League of the Ho-dé-no-sau-nee, or Iroquois.* Rochester: Sage and Brother,
  1851.

———. *The American Beaver and His Works.* Philadelphia: J. B. Lippincott, 1868.

———. "Indian Migrations." *North American Review* 109 (1869): 391–442; 110
  (1870): 32–82.

———. *Systems of Consanguinity and Affinity of the Human Family.* Smithsonian
  Contributions to Knowledge 17. Washington, D.C.: Smithsonian Institution,
  1871.

———. "Architecture of the American Aborigines." In *Johnson's New Universal
  Cyclopaedia,* Vol. 1, 217–229. New York: A. J. Johnson and Son, 1875.

———. "Houses of the Mound Builders." *North American Review* 123 (1876):
  60–64.

———. "Montezuma's Dinner." *North American Review* 122 (1876): 265–308.

———. *Ancient Society.* New York: Henry Holt, 1877.

———. "On the Ruins of a Stone Pueblo on the Animas River in New Mexico; With a Ground Plan." Twelfth Annual Report in *Annual Reports of the Trustees of the Peabody Museum of American Archaeology and Ethnology* 2 (1880): 536–556.

———. "A Study of the Houses of the American Aborigines." *Annual Report of the Archaeological Institute of America* 1 (1880): 27–80.

———. *Houses and House-Life of the American Aborigines.* Contributions to North American Ethnology 4. Washington, D.C.: Government Printing Office, 1881.

Murphy, William D. *Biographical Sketches of the State Officers and Members of the Legislature of the State of New York in 1861.* New York: Printed for the author, 1861.

Murray, Elsie. "Spanish Hill: Its Present, Past and Future." *Pennsylvania Archaeologist* 6 (1936): 13–18.

Murray, Louise Welles, ed. *Selected Manuscripts of General John S. Clark Relating to the Aboriginal History of the Susquehanna.* Publications of the Society for Pennsylvania Archaeology 1. Athens: E. B. Yordy, 1931.

O'Callaghan, E. B., ed. *Documentary History of the State of New-York.* 4 vols. Albany: Weed, Parsons, 1849–51.

Parker, Arthur C. "Fate of the New York State Collections in Archaeology and Ethnology in the Capitol Fire." *American Anthropologist* 13 (1911): 169–171.

———. *The Life of General Ely S. Parker, Last Grand Sachem of the Iroquois and General Grant's Secretary.* Buffalo: Buffalo Historical Society, 1919.

———. *Government and Institutions of the Iroquois by Lewis Henry Morgan.* Researches and Transactions of the New York State Archaeological Association, Lewis H. Morgan Chapter 7 (1). Rochester: Lewis H. Morgan Chapter, 1928.

Pilkington, James, ed. *The Journals of Samuel Kirkland.* Clinton: Hamilton College, 1980.

Schoolcraft, Henry R. *Notes on the Iroquois.* New York: Bartlett and Welford, 1846.

———. *Notes on the Iroquois.* Albany: Erastus H. Pease, 1847.

Schoolcraft, Henry R., and W. H. C. Hosmer. *An Address, Delivered Before the Was-ah Ho-de-no-son-ne or New Confederacy, by Henry R. Schoolcraft . . . . Also Genundewah, A Poem, by W. H. C. Hosmer . . . .* Rochester: Jerome and Brother, 1846.

Silverberg, Robert. *Mound Builders of Ancient America: The Archaeology of a Myth.* Greenwich: New York Graphic Society, 1968.

Squier, E. G. *Aboriginal Monuments of the State of New York.* Smithsonian Institution Contributions to Knowledge 2 (9). Washington, D.C.: Smithsonian Institution, 1849. [Republished as *Antiquities of the State of New York.* Buffalo: George H. Derby, 1851.]

———. "Report upon the Aboriginal Monuments of Western New York." *Proceedings of the New York Historical Society for 1849* (1850): 41–61.

Squier, E. G., and E. H. Davis. *Aboriginal Monuments of the Mississippi Valley.* Smithsonian Contributions to Knowledge 1. Washington, D.C.: Smithsonian Institution, 1848.

Thomas, Cyrus. "Report on the Mound Explorations of the Bureau of Ethnology." *Annual Report of the Bureau of Ethnology* 12 (1894).

Thwaites, Reuben Gold, ed. *Early Western Travels, 1748–1846.* 38 vols. Cleveland: Arthur C. Clark, 1904–07.

Tooker, Elisabeth. "The Structure of the Iroquois League: Lewis H. Morgan's Research and Observations." *Ethnohistory* 30 (1983): 131–154.

———. "On the Development of the Handsome Lake Religion." *Proceedings of the American Philosophical Society* 133 (1989): 35–50.

Trautmann, Thomas R. *Lewis Henry Morgan and the Invention of Kinship.* Berkeley and Los Angeles: University of California Press, 1987.

Trowbridge, David. "Ancient Fort and Burial Ground." *Annual Report of the Smithsonian Institution for 1863* (1864): 381–382.

Turner, Orasmus H. *History of the Pioneer Settlement of Phelps and Gorham's Purchase.* Rochester: William Alling, 1851.

Wallace, Anthony F. C. *Death and Rebirth of the Seneca.* New York: Alfred A. Knopf, 1970.

Weld, Isaac, Jr. *Travels Through the States of North America, and the Provinces of Upper and Lower Canada.* London: John Stockdale, 1799.

White, Leslie A., ed. "How Morgan Came to Write *Systems of Consanguinity and Affinity.*" *Papers of the Michigan Academy of Science, Arts, and Letters* 42 (1957): 257–268.

———. "Extracts from the European Travel Journal of Lewis H. Morgan. *Rochester Historical Society Publication* 16 (1937): 219–389.

———. "Lewis H. Morgan's Journal of a Trip to Southwestern Colorado and New Mexico, June 21 to August 7, 1878." *American Antiquity* 8 (1942): 1–26.

Yates, John V. N., and James W. Moulton. *History of the State of New York.* New York: A. T. Goodrich, 1824.

INDEX

ABOUT THE AUTHOR

ELISABETH TOOKER is professor emerita of anthropology, Temple University. An acknowledged authority on both the Iroquois and Lewis H. Morgan, she is the author of *An Ethnography of the Huron Indians, 1615–1649*, and *The Iroquois Ceremonial of Midwinter*.